SOCIAL ORIGINS
OF THE NEW SOUTH

SOCIAL ORIGINS
OF THE NEW SOUTH
Alabama, 1860–1885

JONATHAN M. WIENER

LOUISIANA STATE UNIVERSITY PRESS
Baton Rouge and London

Copyright © 1978 by Louisiana State University Press
All rights reserved
Manufactured in the United States of America

Design: Albert Crochet
Type Face: VIP Caledonia
Composition: G & S Typesetters, Inc., Austin, Texas
Printer and Binder: Thomson-Shore, Inc.
Louisiana Paperback Edition, 1981

LIBRARY OF CONGRESS CATALOGING IN PUBLICATION DATA

Wiener, Jonathan M
    Social origins of the new South.

    Includes index.
    1. Alabama—Social conditions.   2. Alabama—Rural conditions.   3. Social
classes—Alabama—History—19th century.   4.   Southern States—Social conditions.
I. Title.
HN79.A4W53   309.1'761'06   78–6596
ISBN 0–8071–0397–7
ISBN 0-8071-0888-X pbk.

For Temma

Contents

Tables

Acknowledgments

I began this work as one of Barrington Moore's students. He sought to develop our ability to ask important questions and offered us the opportunity to work hard. In return, he gave us his penetrating criticism. The theoretical framework of his *Social Origins of Dictatorship and Democracy* lies at the root of much of my own work.

Eugene D. Genovese agreed to send comments on my project, and he kept it up with amazing good will, draft after draft, year in and year out. He provided essential advice about the strategy of research and writing, and about the larger theoretical problems as well. His criticism has been indispensable—always strong and always generous. He insisted that I do it right. To the extent that I have, he deserves much of the credit.

Stephan Thernstrom, after reading a first chapter, wrote, "There is some further evidence you could, in principle at least, probably lay your hands on." This simple sentence sent me into the genealogical library deep below the Mormon Temple in Los Angeles, to pour over microfilm of the manuscript census. Thernstrom's own work provided a splendid example of "making the significant quantitative," rather than the other way around; in addition, he has shown that it is possible to write about numbers with clarity and grace.

It is not necessary for me to remind readers that C. Vann Woodward's *Origins of the New South* set a standard as a work of both historical interpretation and literature that will prevail for some time. Published in the heyday of consensus history, it argued that social conflict has lain at the root of southern politics. Woodward's subtle and masterly defense of that unfashionable position has put me greatly in his debt.

For seven of my undergraduate and graduate years I was a student of Michael Walzer. He never said much about Alabama, but he did teach me a great deal about politics and about intellectual commitment. This study only hints at my debt to him.

I owe special thanks to Theodore Rosengarten for the example of his own beautiful book about the South.

In my freshman year I began working with Arno Mayer and with Maurice Zeitlin. Each in his own way showed me how deep convictions can form the basis of scholarly craftsmanship in the study of politics and society.

I first studied the postwar South as a student in James McPherson's course, with Sheldon Hackney as preceptor. They gave me the grade "Flagrant Neglect," which accurately described my efforts. Since then, I have made this second try, and both have been admirably generous with their suggestions.

Stanley Engerman provided especially helpful suggestions about the quantitative sections, which I did not always accept. Jack P. Maddex, Jr. read the entire manuscript with scrupulous care and provided a great deal of help, even more than he gave me on my first freshman paper. Harold D. Woodman offered a blend of encouragement and constructive criticism which forced me to clarify my position.

Eric Foner, Lutz Berkner, Frank Brodhead, and Dale Rosen provided crucial encouragement and advice when I was getting started on this project. For their valuable comments and criticisms of parts of the manuscript, I am indebted to Robert Brenner, Pete Daniel, Ronald L. Davis, Robert W. Fogel, Robert Gilmour, James Henretta, Peter Kolchin, Jay Mandle, Michael Perman, Roger Ransom, Armstead Robinson, William W. Rogers, and Joel Williamson.

I owe thanks also to my colleagues who provided a community while I was revising this manuscript: John P. Diggins, Mark Poster, Spencer Olin, Jr., Karl Hufbauer, and especially Michael P. Johnson, who shared the traumas and triumphs of the life of the mind.

At the Alabama Department of Archives and History, Milo B.

Howard, director, and Mimi Jones were extremely helpful. I am also indebted to Nancy Fitch and Bill Smith for their excellent computer work

Financial support for travel and research expenses was provided by the Rabinowitz Foundation and the University of California. *Past & Present, The Journal of Interdisciplinary History,* and *The Alabama Review* graciously permitted me to include work here parts of which first appeared in their publications.

Looking for a dissertation topic on lords and peasants, I first considered not the southern United States, but southern Spain. Then I learned that someone else was working on such a project, someone named Temma Kaplan. Eventually we got married, and I switched my topic to the American South. The credit goes to Linda Gordon and Meredith Tax. Temma Kaplan contributed not only her expert editorial skills but, even more important, the example of her own book.

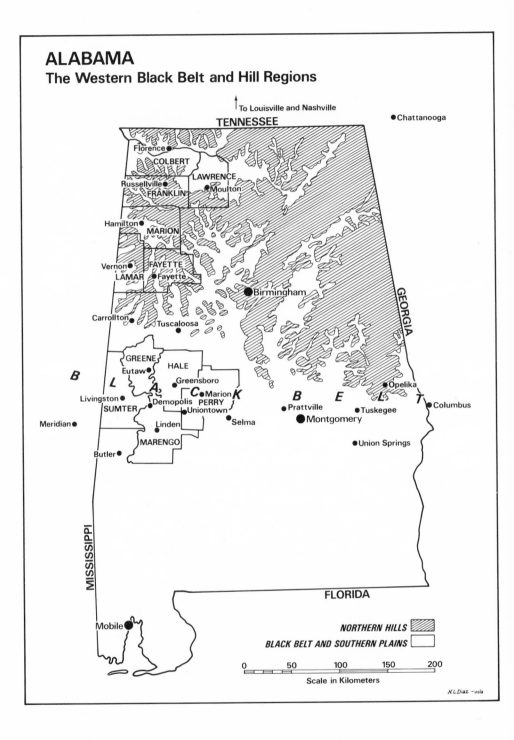

ALABAMA
The Western Black Belt and Hill Regions

To Louisville and Nashville

TENNESSEE

● Chattanooga

Florence ●

COLBERT

LAWRENCE

Russellville ●

FRANKLIN

● Moulton

Hamilton ●

MARION

Vernon ●

FAYETTE

LAMAR

● Fayette

● Birmingham

Carrollton ●

GEORGIA

Tuscaloosa ●

GREENE

HALE

Eutaw ●

● Greensboro

B

L

A

C

Marion

K

Livingston ●

Demopolis ●

PERRY

B

E

L

T

● Opelika

SUMTER

Uniontown ●

● Prattville

● Tuskegee

● Columbus

Meridian ●

Linden ●

● Selma

● Montgomery

MARENGO

Butler ●

● Union Springs

MISSISSIPPI

FLORIDA

Mobile ●

NORTHERN HILLS

BLACK BELT AND SOUTHERN PLAINS

0   50   100   150   200

Scale in Kilometers

N.L.Diaz —ucla

Part I

LAND AND LABOR

1

Postwar Planters: Persistence and Metamorphosis

Reconstruction was the culmination of a bourgeois revolution, a life-or-death struggle over the nature and extent of the nation's transition to modern society. In this conflict, northeastern businessmen formed an alliance with urban workers and small farmers in the Northwest, against southern planters; the victory of this bourgeois coalition destroyed the national power of the planter class and thereby abolished the principal obstacle to democratic capitalist development. In so doing, they ruled out the possibility that the nation would take what Barrington Moore has called the "Prussian Road" to modern society, based on a coalition of northern industrialists with southern planters, against small farmers, urban workers, and slaves, in a society which developed by preserving and intensifying the authoritarian and repressive elements of traditional social relations.[1]

Emancipation was the event that confirmed the revolutionary nature of this conflict, the assertion of the bourgeois ideal of free labor against those who resisted it. That emancipation was on a scale unique in modern history: eight times as many slaves were liberated in the American Civil War as by the Brazilian emancipation of 1888, five times as many as in the British West Indies in 1834. And the violence that was the midwife of emancipation testified to its revolutionary quality. Nowhere else was the resistance to emancipation so strong; in this period only the Napoleonic Wars and World War I exceeded the American Civil War in ferocity.[2]

1. Barrington Moore, Jr., *Social Origins of Dictatorship and Democracy: Lord and Peasant in the Making of the Modern World* (Boston: Beacon Press, 1966), 111–55.
2. C. Vann Woodward, "Emancipations and Reconstructions: A Comparative Study," XIII International Congress of Historical Studies, Moscow (August 16–23, 1970), 3–4.

The final revolutionary conflict of the Civil War era came after the fighting had stopped, when Radical Republicans mounted an offensive against the planters' remaining power within the South, in the name of popular democracy. This was defeated by a conservative coalition of northern industrialists and southern planters, similar to the classic Prussian reactionary coalition. But it formed only after the planters had been defeated and the nation set decisively on the democratic capitalist road. The postwar planters always remained the junior partner in this alliance.

From this perspective, the defeat of Radical Reconstruction poses a question: did the Civil War bring bourgeois revolution to the South? Did the war set the South on the same path of democratic capitalist development as the North? I want to argue that southern development following the defeat of Reconstruction was of a type different from that of the North, that the differences between postwar southern society and the rest of the nation were differences in kind, not just in degree, and that although the New South was undoubtedly new, its socioeconomic structure was nevertheless distinct from that of the North. This was a consequence of postwar planter domination, which weakened the genuinely bourgeois classes and moved the South closer to the Prussian Road than to the democratic capitalist one.

The social relation that gave the South its distinctive character was sharecropping, the relation between landlord and tenant. In the prevailing view, the antebellum planter class had been destroyed by the war and Reconstruction, and the postwar landlords were bourgeois merchants—a key element contributing to the northern-styled capitalism of the postwar South. But the destruction of slaveholding did not necessarily bring in its wake the abolition of the planter class, which some Radicals foresaw, and the freedmen were to discover all too soon. As the sun rose on a South without slaves, wealth and power continued to have the same basis they had before abolition: ownership of plantation land and control of the plantation labor force. Whoever held these controlled the surplus that was the lifeblood of the region.

The proper questions, then, concern the losses of particular classes, not the losses of the South as a whole. We must ask who lost what, which groups lost and which gained, and how these changes affected the region's characteristic patterns of power and economic relations. The planter elite, in whose interests the war was fought, is the proper starting point. All the planters lost their slaves, and some lost their land; what occurred, however, was not the "downfall" or "destruction" of the old planter class, but rather its persistence and metamorphosis. The national power of the planter class was broken; that was what the war had been about. But within the South, the new class that emerged from war and Reconstruction owning the land and controlling the labor force included a surprisingly large proportion of the antebellum planter families, while the structural basis of their wealth and power had been altered.

The postwar planters cannot be understood in isolation. Their metamorphosis was the consequence of conflicts with other social classes: tenants, small landowners, merchants, and industrialists. There are periods in history when fundamental issues of class relations do not arise, but the immediate postwar South was not such a "hegemonic" epoch. Social conflict was explicit and often intense. The postwar planters did not reach a position of dominance without first overcoming the resistance of the freedmen, restructuring plantation agriculture, defeating a challenge from the merchants, shaping the nature and extent of industrial development, and revising the cultural standards that justified their position in the postwar world they were making. Each of these "moments" requires analysis; the starting point, however, is the social composition of the postwar planter class itself, and its relationship to the land.

To understand the persistence and metamorphosis of the planter elite, it is necessary to look beyond the abolition of slavery, to focus on the politics of landholding. The traditional interpretation has exaggerated the consequences of the abolition of slavery for the planter elite. Woodward writes that the "downfall of the old planter class" occurred because it was "stripped of its economic foundations," but the foundation of the southern economy was plantation land, from which a surplus could be extracted by means other than slave labor. This was what U. B. Phillips was arguing when he wrote that "the plantation system . . . was less dependent upon slavery than slavery was upon it." Some Confederate leaders, including Jefferson Davis, argued that the planters could survive as a ruling class without slavery; in Alabama, both the Montgomery *Weekly Mail* and the prestigious Mobile *Register* made similar arguments during the war.[3]

The defeat of the Radicals' proposal to confiscate and redistribute the plantations of Confederate officers and officials was the crucial element shaping landholding in the postwar period. Thaddeus Stevens had the clearest understanding; he argued that the freedmen's political rights would be fragile as long as they did not have a secure economic foundation in the ownership of small farms. Charles Sumner agreed that "the great plantations . . . must be broken up, and the freedmen must have the pieces," and Congressman George Washington Julian argued, "Of what avail would be an act of Congress totally abolishing slavery, or an amendment of the Constitution forever prohibiting it, if the old agricultural basis of aristocratic power shall remain?" Freedmen and poorer southern whites understood the significance of the proposal; the Philadelphia *Press* reported that, in Alabama, if confiscation of the plantations were submitted to a vote, "a majority of both blacks and whites would vote for it."[4]

The manuscript schedules of the U.S. census of population are the kind of source Marc Bloch called "witnesses in spite of themselves." They provide a basis both for identifying the South's plant-

3. C. Vann Woodward, *Origins of the New South, 1877–1913* (Baton Rouge: Louisiana State University Press, 1951), 20–21; C. Vann Woodward, *Reunion and Reaction: The Compromise of 1877 and the End of Reconstruction* (Boston: Little, Brown, 1951), 52; Ulrich B. Phillips, "Decadence of the Plantation System," in Eugene D. Genovese (ed.), *The Slave Economy of the Old South* (Baton Rouge: Louisiana State University Press, 1968), 245; Robert F. Durden, *The Grey and the Black: The Confederate Debate on Emancipation* (Baton Rouge: Louisiana State University Press, 1972), 29–44; Mobile *Daily Register*, November 26, 1863. See also Jay R. Mandle, "The Plantation Economy: An Essay in Definition," *Science and Society*, XXXVI (1972), 49–62.

4. *Congressional Globe*, 39th Cong., 1st Sess., 2460, 2544; *ibid.*, 40th Cong., 1st Sess., 49, 203, 205; Eric Foner, "Thaddeus Stevens, Confiscation, and Reconstruction," in Stanley Elkins and Erik McKitrick (eds.), *The Hofstadter Aegis: A Memorial* (New York: Alfred A. Knopf, 1974), 154–83; E. L. Pierce, *Memoirs and Letters of Charles Sumner* (Boston: Roberts Brothers, 1893), IV, 198; *Congressional Globe*, 40th Cong., 1st Sess., 49, 203; *Congressional Globe*, 39th Cong., 1st Sess., 706; Patrick W. Riddleberger, "George W. Julian: Abolitionist Land Reformer," *Agricultural History*, V (1955), 108–15; Philadelphia *Press*, quoted in New York *Times*, May 30, 1867; James M. McPherson, *The Struggle for*

er elite, and for studying its transformation through the Civil War decade. In 1850, 1860, and 1870, the census asked each individual for the "value of real estate" he or she owned.[5] The responses can be used to identify the wealthiest landholders in each census year, to study persistence and change in the composition of this planter elite, and to compare antebellum patterns with the developments that accompanied war and Reconstruction.

The black belt of Alabama is the focus of this study. Along with Mississippi, it was the economic bastion of the planter class of the Deep South; its planters took the lead in the secession movement, and it provided the first capital for the Confederacy. It was a region where landholding was extremely unequal; in 1860, the top 5 percent of landowners held 24 percent of the improved acreage, 26 percent of the slaves, and 30 percent of the farm value. Five adjacent counties in the western half of the Alabama black belt were selected for the study; in 1860, they had a population of 114,000, of which 74 percent were slaves. (See map, p. xiv.) Politically, the five counties were a bedrock of planter support; their vote in favor of secession in December, 1860, was overwhelming, as was their opposition to Republican, Greenback, and Populist candidates for state office in the last quarter of the century.[6]

Equality: Abolitionists and the Negro in the Civil War and Reconstruction (Princeton: Princeton University Press, 1964), 246–59, 410–12. Du Bois and Frederick Douglass had the same interpretation: W. E. B. Du Bois, *Black Reconstruction in America, 1860–1880* (New York: Atheneum, 1969), 197–98; Douglass speech, August 1, 1880, quoted in McPherson, *Struggle for Equality*, 406. The issue was raised anew in Howard K. Beale, "On Rewriting Reconstruction History," *American Historical Review*, XLV (1940), 821; it has been criticized recently in Herman Belz, "The New Orthodoxy in Reconstruction Historiography," *Reviews in American History*, I (1973), 106–13.

5. Marc Bloch, *The Historian's Craft* (New York: Alfred A. Knopf, 1953), 61–62; for the instructions to census enumerators, see Appendix, herein.

6. Gavin Wright, " 'Economic Democracy' and the Concentration of Agricultural Wealth in the Cotton South, 1850–1860," *Agricultural History*, XLIV (1970), 63–93. Less than one-third of one percent of the white population of Alabama owned 28 percent of the state's total wealth in 1860, according to James B. Sellers, *Slavery in Alabama* (University, Ala.: University of Alabama Press, 1950), 42. William L. Barney, *The Secessionist Impulse: Alabama and Mississippi in 1860* (Princeton: Princeton University Press, 1974), 317–18; Allen Going, *Bourbon Democracy in Alabama, 1874–1890* (University, Ala.: University of Alabama Press, 1951), 220–31; William Warren Rogers, *The One-Gallused Rebellion: Agrarianism in Alabama, 1865–1896* (Baton Rouge: Louisiana State University Press, 1970), 223, 284, 315. The five counties are Greene, Hale, Marengo, Perry, and Sumter. Hale was created in 1866 out of parts of the other four; see Appendix, herein, for details. These five counties are part of Mandle's "plantation region" and Ransom and Sutch's "cotton South":

This study deals with the 236 planters who held the greatest wealth in real estate in each of the three censuses. The group included all planters with at least $10,000 in real estate in 1850, $32,000 in 1860, and $10,000 in 1870. These 236 constituted approximately the top 8 percent of the landholders in the western Alabama black belt and 3 percent of white adult males. Their mean real estate holding in 1860 (at $40 an acre) was roughly 1,600 acres; the smallest holding was around 800 acres, and the largest, close to 9,000 acres.[7] (In what follows, the top 10 percent of real estate holders in the five counties are referred to as the "local planter elite," but this statistically defined group by itself did not necessarily form a self-conscious social class, nor was membership in the actual planter class solely a matter of the value of individuals' real estate holdings.)

Since Roger Shugg's pathbreaking work in 1937, historians have accepted the view that the plantation survived the Civil War and Reconstruction, but they have argued that the antebellum planter

Jay R. Mandle, "The Plantation States as a Sub-Region of the Post-Bellum South," *Journal of Economic History*, XXXIV (1974), 732–38; Roger Ransom and Richard Sutch, *One Kind of Freedom: The Economic Consequences of Emancipation* (New York: Cambridge University Press, 1977), 273–75. For local histories, see W. Stuart Harris, *A Short History of Marion, Perry County, Alabama: Its Homes and Buildings* (Marion, Ala.: n.p., 1970); Nellie Jenkins, *Pioneer Families of Sumter County, Alabama* (Tuscaloosa: Willo Publishing Company, 1961); Winston Smith, "Early History of Demopolis," *Alabama Review*, XVIII (1965), 83–91; "History of the County of Sumter," Gainesville *News*, January 29, 1870; R. D. Spratt, "History of Livingston, Alabama" (n.p., n.d.), typescript in the Alabama Department of Archives and History. Photographs of the biggest plantations in these counties can be found in Ralph Hammond, *Ante-Bellum Mansions of Alabama* (New York: Architectural Book Company, 1951), Chap. 4. For local directories, see V. Gayle Snedecor, *A Directory of Greene County for 1855–1856* (Mobile: n.p., 1856); W. C. Tharin, *A Directory of Marengo County for 1860–1861* (Mobile: n.p., 1861). These directories list voters by occupation and residence as well as offering various statistics and some local history. J. Mills Thornton III, *Politics and Power in a Slave Society: Alabama, 1800–1860* (Baton Rouge: Louisiana State University Press, 1978), appeared too late to be included in this study.

7. The figure of $40 an acre for good plantations in the Alabama black belt is suggested by Lewis C. Gray, *History of Agriculture in the Southern United States to 1860* (Washington, D.C.: The Carnegie Institution, 1933), 2, 642–44. Actual acreage varied. Both Gaious Whitfield and E. A. Glover reported real estate valued at $200,000 in 1860, which would give an estimate of 5,000 acres. According to the manuscript reports of the 1860 census of agriculture, Whitfield claimed to have 7,500 acres, while Glover reported 3,500. See also Glenn Sisk, "Social Aspects of the Alabama Black Belt, 1875–1917," *Mid-America*, XXXVII (1955), 31–47; H. F. Cleland, "The Black Belt of Alabama," *Geographical Review*, X (1920), 375–87. For a discussion of the manuscript census as a source of evidence, see Appendix, herein.

class was destroyed. C. Vann Woodward writes that after the war a "revolution in land titles" signaled "the downfall of the old planter class," and virtually all subsequent studies have accepted this view.[8]

Evidence from the census manuscripts indicates that, of the 236 members of the planter elite in western Alabama in 1860, 101 remained in the elite in 1870; their persistence rate through the decade of war and Reconstruction was 43 percent.[9] (See Table 1.) The war thus appears to have destroyed more than half the planter elite of 1860, but the situation was more complex. The planters' persistence rate for the war decade was in fact similar to their antebellum persistence rate. Of the 236 wealthiest planter families of 1850, only 110 remained in the elite a decade later; the antebellum planter persistence rate was thus 47 percent. Less than half of the prewar planter elite maintained their status in the region for more than a decade.

Two aspects of these figures are noteworthy: first, the similarity of the antebellum and wartime persistence rates, which suggests

8. Roger W. Shugg, "Survival of the Plantation System in Louisiana," *Journal of Southern History*, III (1937), 311–25; Woodward, *Origins of the New South*, 179; Woodward, *Reunion and Reaction*, 52. Woodward's statement of his thesis was strongest in his first article: "The class that seized power . . . after the overthrow of the Reconstruction regime was neither the planter nor the small farmer. It was a rising class of industrial capitalists." C. Vann Woodward, "Tom Watson and the Negro in Agrarian Politics," *Journal of Southern History*, IV (1938), 14–15. Very little research had been done on the "revolution in land titles" when Woodward wrote *Origins of the New South*. He cites Shugg's statement that northern corporations bought up Louisiana sugar plantations after the war, but Shugg's discussion of cotton plantations has not received the same attention. "What evidence is available argues against any sudden or sweeping overturn in ownership," Shugg writes. "Scores of families who had once operated large plantations with handsome profit now managed simply to hang on to them for a comfortable livelihood." Roger W. Shugg, *Origins of Class Struggle in Louisiana* (Baton Rouge: Louisiana State University Press, 1968), 246.

9. I follow the usage of "persistence" established in Stephan Thernstrom, *Poverty and Progress: Social Mobility in a 19th Century City* (Cambridge: Harvard University Press, 1964), 96, except that I include both geographic and social persistence. Eighteen of the planters of 1870 came from families which had been present in the elite of 1850, but not 1860; thus 51 percent of the planter families of 1870 had persisted from at least one of the census years of the prewar period. Although this figure should not be compared with the decade persistence rate for antebellum persistence, it indicates that at least half of the postwar planters came from the antebellum planter elite. Similar figures for Clarke County, Georgia, can be found in Frank Jackson Huffman, Jr., "Old South, New South: Continuity and Change in a Georgia County, 1850–1880" (Ph.D. dissertation, Yale University, 1974), 39–45. See also Renwick C. Kennedy, "Black Belt Aristocrats: The Old South Lives on in Alabama's Black Belt," *Social Forces*, XIII (1934), 80–85.

Table 1. BLACK BELT POPULATION AND PLANTER PERSISTENCE[a]

	1850	1860	1870
Total population	103,807	113,765	115,426
White population	32,007	29,467	27,122
"Planter elite"	236	236	236
Number of planters remaining in area and in elite at end of decade	110	101	
Percent remaining: planter persistence rate[b]	47%	43%	

[a] For five Alabama counties: Greene, Marengo, Sumter, Perry, and Hale.
[b] Since these statistics refer to complete populations rather than samples, statistical tests of significance are not appropriate.

that war and Reconstruction did not significantly alter the ante-bellum pattern of elite persistence and social mobility; second, the relatively low persistence rate of the antebellum planter class, which is usually thought to have been as stable a social group as could be found in nineteenth-century America.

A social class, particularly a dominant one such as the planters, consists not of individuals but of families, as Maurice Zeitlin has recently argued. Individual planters die, but as long as their property remains in their family, the social composition of the planter class has not been transformed. Thus persistence has been defined here as family rather than individual persistence; if a planter did not appear in a subsequent list of the social elite, but his wife or son did, that was counted as a case of a persistent elite family.[10] Still, since not all elderly planters had heirs, and not all heirs kept the old plantation intact, dying was one source of nonpersistence. And death may have made a significant contribution to nonpersistence

10. Maurice Zeitlin and Richard Earl Ratcliff, "Research Methods for the Analysis of the Internal Structure of Dominant Classes," *Latin American Research Review*, X (1975), 5–61; see especially "Beyond individuals: The family as the basic unit of analysis," 21–28. See also Joseph Schumpeter, *Imperialism and Social Classes* (New York: The Macmillan Company, 1955), 113. "Death" and "inheritance" were inferred from the absence of a planter from a subsequent elite group, in which his son or wife had become a household head and a member of the landholding elite. See Appendix, herein.

between 1860 and 1870, when a quarter of a million southerners died in war. This is an issue that will be considered later.

Almost all of the wealthiest planters of 1870 had been members of the antebellum planter elite. Of the 25 planters with the largest landholdings in 1870, 18 (or 72 percent) had been in elite families in 1860; 16 had been in the 1850 elite group. (See Table 2.) Only 7 of the top 25 planters in 1870 had not been present in the 1860 elite group in the black belt of western Alabama, and they may well have come from elite families in other areas.

This phenomenon of planter persistence did not escape the notice of contemporaries. The Montgomery *Alabama State Journal* noted in 1871 that "the old oligarchies have come to the surface again." In 1866, the Montgomery *Advertiser* reported on "the disinclination of planters . . . to sell any portion of their lands." It added that a majority of planters were responding to the economic collapse by "curtailing their outlay of expenses, and contenting themselves with a smaller but surer income." Robert Somers's firsthand descriptions of widespread devastation of the plantations in 1870 should not overshadow his more telling observation that "generally the old homesteads and the old families continue to be the centres of reviving industry and cultivation."[11]

The planter families that did not persist were not necessarily "destroyed," nor were they necessarily "skidders" down the social scale. Few of those who remained in their county lost enough real estate (relatively) to move them below the top 236; the great majority simply moved out of the western Alabama black belt. Of the 1860 planter families who did not persist to 1870, only 9 percent could be identified as skidders, cases of downward social mobility within one county. The other 91 percent had left their county altogether; whether they maintained their high status is unknown. These figures suggest that, even during the war decade, geographic mobility was a much more frequent occurrence among the planter elite than downward social mobility in the locality. Skid-

11. Montgomery *Alabama State Journal*, April 4, 1871; Montgomery *Daily Advertiser*, June 20, April 21, 1866; Robert Somers, *The Southern States Since the War, 1870–1* (New York: Macmillan and Company, 1871), 114–15, 127. See also Mobile *Daily Register*, January 2, 1881.

Table 2. THE 25 WEALTHIEST PLANTERS IN 1870

Name	County	Real estate holdings[a]		
		1870	1860	1850
Minge, G.	Marengo	$85,000	——	30,000
Lyon, F.	Marengo	75,000	115,000	35,000
Paulling, William	Marengo	72,000	150,000	29,000
Hatch, Alfred	Hale	70,000	120,000	40,000
Alexander, J.	Marengo	69,000	38,000	10,000[b]
Whitfield, B.	Marengo	65,000	200,000[b]	100,000
Terrill, J.	Marengo	62,000	93,000	——
Taylor, E.	Marengo	61,000	——	——
Robertson, R.	Marengo	60,000	——	——
Dew, Duncan	Greene	52,000	200,000[b]	41,000
Walton, John	Marengo	50,000	250,000	25,000
Collins, Charles	Hale	50,000	201,000[b]	30,000
Hays, Charles	Greene	50,000	113,000	——
Brown, John	Sumter	50,000	69,000	13,000
Pickering, Richard	Marengo	50,000	42,000	15,000
Withers, Mary	Hale	50,000	40,000	75,000[b]
Jones, Madison	Hale	50,000	36,000[b]	27,000
Nelson, A.	Hale	48,000	——	10,000[b]
Taylor, J.	Hale	48,000	——	——
Pickens, Wm.	Hale	45,000	210,000[b]	51,000
Reese, Henry	Marengo	45,000	52,000	24,000
Walker, R.	Hale	42,000	55,000	——
Smaw, W.	Greene	42,000	32,000	——
Blanks, E.	Marengo	41,000	——	——
Walker, Morns	Marengo	41,000	——	——
Number of planters		25	18	16
Percent present in 1870			72%	64%

[a] Rounded off to nearest thousand; as reported in U.S. Census of Population, manuscript schedules. To convert to constant gold prices, see p. 14, note 13.
[b] Wealth of father or husband.

ding may have been a relatively infrequent phenomenon among elite planters, even between 1860 and 1870. The small number of planters who skidded out of the elite between 1860 and 1870 did not fall very far. Almost all of them ended up in 1870 in the top quarter of county landholders, and all were in the top half. To the extent that they could be identified, even those who were downwardly mobile during the sixties were not "destroyed"; they remained among the wealthier landholders of their counties.[12]

Although the planter elite persisted at approximately the same rate in the fifties and sixties, many have argued that the biggest landholdings in 1870 were considerably smaller than they had been in 1860—that the big planters, having the most to lose in war and Reconstruction, lost the most, and emerged from their ordeal relatively poorer in comparison with other groups in southern society. Between 1860 and 1870, the loss in land value in the western Alabama black belt was staggering. The total value of real estate owned by all 236 members of the planter elite fell from over $15 million in 1860 to not quite $5 million in 1870, a decline of two-thirds. The median holding dropped from $48,700 to $15,300. The reports of both contemporaries and modern historians correspond to these figures. Commissioner Horace Capron of the U.S. Department of Agriculture reported in 1868 that land values in Alabama had fallen 60 percent since 1860; the agricultural census shows that the average value per acre of Alabama farmland de-

---

12. Marengo County was selected for more intensive study of mobility patterns; it is the "one county" referred to throughout. There is no reason to believe it was atypical in any measurable way: see Jonathan M. Wiener, "Plantations, Politics, and Industry: Alabama, 1850–1890" (Ph.D. dissertation, Harvard University, 1972), especially pp. 61–62. Tracing geographically mobile people and ascertaining their social status has been the most serious obstacle to social mobility studies: see Appendix, herein. Of the 1860 planters who had risen to elite status in the preceding decade from within the county, almost all were relatively wealthy to begin with: 86 percent had been in the top quarter of landholders. This relatively low rate of upward social mobility in late antebellum Alabama is further evidence against the Owsleys' contention that there was a great deal of upward social movement in the South during the 1850s. Frank L. and Harriet C. Owsley, "The Economic Basis of Society in the Late Ante-bellum South," *Journal of Southern History*, VI (1940), 24–45; Frank L. Owsley, *Plain Folk of the Old South* (Baton Rouge: Louisiana State University Press, 1949); Warren I. Smith, "Land Patterns in Ante-Bellum Montgomery County, Alabama," *Alabama Review*, VIII (1955), 196–205. The authoritative critic is Fabian Linden, "Economic Democracy in the Slave South: An Appraisal of Some Recent Views," *Journal of Negro History*, XXXI (1946), 140–89.

clined by 67 percent, and that the value of all southern farms declined by 50 percent between 1860 and 1870.[13]

Earlier historians argued that this decline was the consequence of wartime destruction of plantation property. Roger Ransom and Richard Sutch, however, have recently shown that the destructive impact of the war on plantation agriculture has been greatly exaggerated. Emancipation was a fundamental cause of declining land values; the free black chose to work less than the slave had been forced to, and the resulting fall in tilled acreage "created a supply of 'redundant' land which acted to depress land prices." The high taxes imposed by Radical legislatures also depressed land prices.[14]

Although losses in land value were devastating to all southern landowners, the planter elite in 1870 was relatively wealthier than it had been in 1860. It held a greater share of the real estate value five years after the war than when it began. The elite increased its share of the land value held by county residents held by 8 percentage points between 1860 and 1870, from 55 to 63 percent.[15] (See Table 3.)

This relative expansion of the land value held by the planter elite came at the expense of the upper-middle group of county

13. Montgomery *Daily Advertiser*, March 31, 1868; Paul W. Gates, *Agriculture and the Civil War* (New York: Alfred A. Knopf, 1965), 373; Eugene M. Lerner, "Southern Agriculture and Agricultural Income, 1860–1880," *Journal of Political Economy*, LXII (1955), 20–40. The fall in value in gold prices was even greater: land worth $5 million in currency in 1870 was worth only $3,962,000 in 1860 gold prices, on the basis of the calculations outlined in Ransom and Sutch, *One Kind of Freedom*, Table 3.1.

14. Lerner, "Southern Agriculture"; James L. Sellers, "Economic Incidence of the Civil War in the South," *Mississippi Valley Historical Review*, XIV (1927), 179–91; John Townsend Trowbridge, *The South: A Tour of Its Battlefields and Ruined Cities* . . . (Hartford: L. Stebbins, 1866), 181; Walter L. Fleming, *Civil War and Reconstruction in Alabama* (Cleveland: A. H. Clark Company, 1911), 258; Matthew B. Hammond, *The Cotton Industry: An Essay in American Economic History* (New York: The MacMillan Company, 1897), 127; Ransom and Sutch, *One Kind of Freedom*, Chap. 3; Roger Ransom and Richard Sutch, "The Impact of the Civil War and of Emancipation on Southern Agriculture," *Explorations in Economic History*, XII (1975), 1–28; see also Joel Williamson, *After Slavery: The Negro in South Carolina During Reconstruction, 1861–1877* (Chapel Hill: University of North Carolina Press, 1965), 155.

15. Soltow found that the combined share of real and personal estate of the top 10 percent of white males in the South increased between 1860 and 1870 from 27 to 29 percent: Lee Soltow, *Men and Wealth in the United States, 1850–1870* (New Haven: Yale University Press, 1975), 99. Since slaves were reported as personal property in 1860 but not in 1870, the planters experienced a gigantic loss in the share of personal property they held over the decade; the only explanation for the increase in their total share is a significant increase in their share of the value of real estate, perhaps even greater than that reported here. Ransom

Table 3. SHARES OF WEALTH

	Share in Year[a] (percentage)			Change in share (percentage points)	
	1850	1860	1870	1850–1860	1860–1870
Top 10%	57	55	63	−2	+8
2nd 10%	18	19	17	+1	−2
3rd 10%	10	10	8	0	−2
4th 10%	4	6	4	+2	−2
5th 10%	4	4	3	0	−1
6th 10%	3	2	2	−1	0
7th 10%	2	2	1	0	−1
8th 10%	1	1	1	0	0
9th 10%	1	1	1	0	0
Bottom 10%	0	0	0	0	0
Number	811	989	828		

[a] Marengo County only. Share is share of value of real estate holdings.

landholders, the small planters and big farmers. While the planter elite of 1870 had increased its share of the real estate value by 8 percentage points over 1860, the upper-middle group—those below the top 10 percent but within the top 40 percent—lost a total of 6 percentage points. The top 10 percent was the only decile to improve its position as a result of the war; the nine lower deciles either lost part of their share of 1860, or did not change.[16]

and Sutch found a slight decrease in the share of wealth in real estate held by the top 10 percent in Dallas County, Alabama, between 1860 and 1870: *One Kind of Freedom*, Table 4.2. See also Robert Gallman, "Trends in the Size Distribution of Wealth in the Nineteenth Century: Some Speculations," in Lee Soltow (ed.), *Six Papers on the Size Distribution of Wealth and Income*, National Bureau of Economic Research Studies in Income and Wealth, XXXIII (New York: Columbia University Press, 1969), 1–25.

16. The increasing concentration of landed wealth during the 1860–1870 decade could be seen as a normal consequence of economic depression, since economic concentration tends to increase in periods of depression. The planters' ability to respond to the economic cataclysm of the Civil War and Reconstruction as a normal short-term cycle is evidence of their resilience and strength in the immediate postwar period.

The improvement in the relative position of the top planters becomes even more striking when it is compared with the trend for the antebellum decade 1850–1860. In that period, the top 10 percent were actually falling behind somewhat, their share dropping from 57 to 55 percent of the real estate value held by county residents, while the three upper-middle deciles were on the rise, increasing their share a total of 3 percentage points, from 32 percent to 35 percent.[17]

During the war and Reconstruction, then, the planter elite reversed the antebellum trend toward a relative increase in landholding by the upper-middle group. It not only regained ground that had been lost between 1850 and 1860, but increased its share considerably, all at the expense of the upper-middle groups. Between 1860 and 1870, the planter elite gained four times the share they had lost in the preceding decade. Although its losses were tremendous, the planter elite of 1870 was not only relatively persistent, it was also relatively wealthier in its share of real estate holdings than the 1860 elite.[18]

Factors in Persistence, 1860–1870

A surprisingly high proportion of the antebellum planters persisted through the sixties; nevertheless a majority did not. But death in the war does not seem to have been a significant cause of nonpersistence among planter families. In the conventional view, plant-

17. Wright, " 'Economic Democracy,' " reports similar trends in wealth distribution for 1850–1860. Bonner, however, reports that planters were buying up the land of small farmers and making it difficult for smaller landholders to enlarge their holdings between 1850 and 1860: James C. Bonner, "Profile of a Late Ante-Bellum Community," *American Historical Review*, XLIX (1944), 663–80. Barney notes that the census reports show the average number of acres per farm increasing in Alabama between 1850 and 1860, from 289 to 346. Barney, *Secessionist Impulse*, 14. For another measure of inequality in landholding, see Michael Schwartz, *Radical Protest and Social Structure: The Southern Farmers' Alliance and Cotton Tenancy, 1880–1890* (New York: Academic Press, 1976), 80–88.

18. The argument here is not aimed at a straw man. Randall and Donald describe as a typical postwar planter one who "peddles tea by the pound and molasses by the quart, on a corner of the old homestead, to the former slaves of the family, and thereby earns his livelihood": J. G. Randall and David Donald, *The Civil War and Reconstruction* (3rd ed., Boston: D. C. Heath, 1969), 545. After the war, "the planter aristocracy . . . was gone": John D. Hicks, *The Populist Revolt* (Minneapolis: University of Minnesota Press, 1931), 36. "The part of the Old South that passed away most quickly after the Civil War was its aristocracy": Clement Eaton, *The Waning of the Old South Civilization* (Athens, Ga.: University of Georgia Press, 1968), 139–40. "The antebellum planters lost ownership to a new landlord

ers' wartime deaths contributed significantly to the destruction of the planter elite. Estimates of Alabama war deaths range from 35,000 to 40,000. Walter L. Fleming reports as a typical black belt case "a company from Demopolis [which] . . . lost all except seven men . . . 125 lost by death in service."[19]

A great many planters gave their lives in defense of their world, but the death rate for planters does not seem to have been higher than that for nonelite groups, nor did planter war deaths reduce the persistence rate of their class: this is suggested by the relationship between age and persistence during the sixties. (See Table 4.) After a war one expects to find fewer young men, but the 1870 planter elite contained considerably more young men than the 1860 elite. Many more young planters persisted through the sixties than the fifties, and the new members of the 1870 elite tended to be younger than the new members of the 1860 elite.

The wartime death of planters would also result in the appearance of war widows among the 1870 planter elite. Governor Robert M. Patton reported that there were 20,000 war widows in Alabama in 1866, and a modern source gives the figure 80,000.[20] But there is little evidence that war widows made up a significant proportion of the 236 planters in the 1870 elite. The number of females in the planter elite did not increase after the war; nor did the proportion of persistent families in which the male planter of 1860 was succeeded in 1870 by his wife as the household head, which would have been the case if planters died on the battlefields and left the plantations to their wives.

---

class": Harold D. Woodman, *King Cotton and His Retainers* (Lexington, Ky.: University of Kentucky Press, 1967), 313. "The old wealthy planters were ruined . . . their names disappear from sight": Fleming, *Civil War and Reconstruction in Alabama*, 258. "The Southern plutocracy was destroyed by the Civil War": Soltow, *Men and Wealth*, 101. See also Jack P. Maddex, Jr., *The Virginia Conservatives, 1867–1879: A Study in Reconstruction Politics* (Chapel Hill: University of North Carolina Press, 1970), especially pp. xii–xiii, and William C. Harris, *Presidential Reconstruction in Mississippi* (Baton Rouge: Louisiana State University Press, 1967), 32. After a massive survey of the literature, Sheldon Hackney concluded that Woodward's interpretation "still stands": Hackney, *"Origins of the New South* in Retrospect," *Journal of Southern History*, XXXVIII (1972), 213.

19. New York *Times*, August 2, 1865; October 31, 1865; Fleming, *Civil War and Reconstruction in Alabama*, 252.

20. Fleming, *Civil War and Reconstruction in Alabama*, 252; Anne Firor Scott, *The Southern Lady: From Pedestal to Politics, 1830–1930* (Chicago: University of Chicago Press, 1970), 92.

Table 4. AGE, SEX, AND PLANTER PERSISTENCE

	Percentage of planter elite	
	1860	1870
Planters under 35 years old	14	29
New planters under 35 years old	33	37
Planters under 30 years old who had been present in elite a decade earlier	34	47
Female planters	9	10
Female planters who have succeeded male in persistent planter family	8	4
Number in planter elite	236	236

Thus data on the age and sex composition of the planter elite contain little evidence that death in war had significant effect on the persistence of planter families. This is not to say that no planters died on the battlefields; it is only to say that their wartime death rate was not great enough to affect the persistence rate, that death on the battlefield does not itself seem to have led to the "downfall of the old planter class."

The exemption from military service of one slaveholder (or overseer) for every 20 slaves may have been responsible for this apparently low wartime death rate. When the exemption was later increased to one for every 15 slaves, a plantation with 75 slaves was entitled to five exemptions, enough for a planter and four adult sons. Ownership of 30 slaves would exempt both father and one adult son—enough to make sure that death on the battlefield would not threaten the family's persistence in the landholding elite. (The slaveowners' exemption was vigorously opposed by representatives of the nonslaveholding districts, who argued that they should not be required to fight for the slaveholders' interests while the slaveholders themselves were excused.)

J. G. Randall and David Donald write that the exemption of slaveowners "freed only a few hundred men from military service" throughout the Confederacy during the entire war, but Fleming's figures contradict this. The total number of slaveholders exempted from military service in Alabama alone was 1,447; of nineteen categories of exemptions, slaveholding ranked second, after medical exemptions.[21] Since virtually every one of the 236 planter elite families had enough slaves to qualify for at least one exemption, since they made up the elite of half the black belt, and since almost 1,500 exemptions were issued to slaveholders, it seems likely that a great many of the 236 families claimed at least one exemption. This is not to argue that no planters or planters' sons died in the war— only that the planter elite may have had a disproportionately lower death rate than small slaveholders and nonslaveholders, and that exemptions were obtained frequently enough to reduce significantly the extent of nonpersistence resulting from death in war.

The war did affect planter persistence in other ways. The planters most likely to persist for the war decade were those whose plantations were out of the path of invading Union armies, those who owned a great deal of real estate, those who were younger, and those with big families.[22] Persistence depended first of all on where a planter had his plantation. In four of the five counties studied, between 43 and 49 percent of the 1860 planters were still present in the elite in 1870, but in the fifth—Perry County—only 29 percent were. In 1865, Perry was skirted by the federal cavalry forces of General James H. Wilson, known in Alabama history as "Wilson's Raiders," who were on their way to seize and destroy Selma's war plants. John Townsend Trowbridge visited the area several months later, and described the operation as "the most extensive and destructive raid of the war." Wilson's Raiders were

21. Randall and Donald, *Civil War and Reconstruction*, 251; Fleming, *Civil War and Reconstruction in Alabama*, 107.

22. The small number of cases of "double persistence"—an 1860 planter having two sons in the 1870 elite group—makes the persistence figures in this section slightly less than the overall persistence rate. For a wealthy family from Perry County which did not persist through the war, see Weymouth T. Jordan, *Ante-Bellum Alabama: Town and Country* (Tallahassee: Florida State University Press, 1957), 41–61; for another, see Weymouth T. Jordan, *Hugh Davis and His Alabama Plantation* (University, Ala.: University of Alabama Press, 1948). For a "nonpersistent" Alabama planter who moved to Georgia in 1866 and prospered, see Thomas A. Belser, Jr., "Alabama Plantation to Georgia Farm," *Alabama Historical Quarterly*, XXV (1973), 136–48.

Table 5. FACTORS IN PLANTER PERSISTENCE

	Persistence Rate[a] (percent)	
	1850–1860	1860–1870
County of residence:[b]		
Greene	38	48
Marengo	54	43
Perry	42	29
Sumter	52	43
Hale	—[c]	49
Value of real estate holdings:[d]		
Top 1/3	54	50
Middle 1/3	49	48
Bottom 1/3	38	46
Family structure:		
Spouse:		
Present	47	45
Not present	47	36
Sons:		
None present	39	33
At least one	50	47
Four or more	34	56
Age:		
30 and under	34	47
31–54	49	43
55 and over	46	33
Place of birth:		
South	47	43
Non-South	27	33

Sex:		
Male	47	43
Female	—[c]	30
Number persisting:	110	101

[a] Defined as the percent of the elite at the beginning of the decade in each category who were present in the elite at the end of the decade. Because of missing and illegible information, persistence rates on this table do not necessarily equal the overall persistence rates given in Table 1.

[b] Since Hale was created in 1866 out of parts of the other four counties, 1860–1870 persistence in the same county would classify as nonpersistent those who persisted in the elite but were made residents of the new county by changing county lines. Thus it has been necessary to calculate persistence on this variable only as the percent of the elite at the *end* of the decade in each county that were present in the elite at the *beginning* of the decade; on all other variables here and in the rest of the paper, "persistence" is defined as in note [a] above.

[c] No 1850 planters in this category.

[d] Real estate thirds: 1850: $10,000–13,000, $14,000–21,000, $22,000–117,000; 1860: $32,000–40,000, $41,000–60,000, $61,000–350,000. For 1860–1870, Perry County excluded on this variable (see p. 19).

notorious for the ruin they brought to plantation and town alike.[23] This may account for the fact that the wealthy planters of Perry County were hit particularly hard by the war.

If Perry County is set aside, planter persistence in wartime appears to be first of all dependent on the presence of sons in the household. (See Table 5.) Family men in 1860 were persistent men. Those who were married in 1860 were more likely to have families which persisted to 1870 than those who were unmarried; those with sons were more likely to persist than those without sons; and those with several sons were the most likely of all to have persistent families. Younger planters were more likely to persist than older ones. Wartime persistence was also a matter of wealth in land; the planters holding more real estate were more likely to persist, though not by much.[24] A few members of the 1860 planter

23. Trowbridge, *The South*, 425, 437–40; James P. Jones, *Yankee Blitzkrieg: Wilson's Raid Through Alabama and Georgia* (Athens, Ga.: University of Georgia Press, 1976), 187, 33.

24. Stephan Thernstrom and Peter Knights found a similar pattern in the urban North: "possession of property in the city discouraged migration from it." Thernstrom and Knights, "Men in Motion: Some Data and Speculations on Urban Population Mobility in Nineteenth Century America," *Journal of Interdisciplinary History*, I (1970), 7.

group had been born outside the South, and they were less likely to persist than their southern-born counterparts. There were 20 women among the 236 wealthiest landholders in 1860, and they did not persist as often as the men. (Nonpersistence of female planters may simply have been a consequence of marriage, which changed their names and makes them virtually impossible to trace in the census manuscripts.) In the antebellum period, family structure did not have as strong a relation to persistence as it did during the sixties, and the relationship between wealth in real estate and persistence was stronger.

The Persistent Core and the "New Men" of 1870

Forty-nine families were present in the planter elite in all three of the censuses studied—1850, 1860, and 1870. They were the "persistent core" of the elite, and made up 21 percent of the planters in 1850. This group can be compared with the "persistent fringe"—those who were present in 1850 and 1860, but not 1870—and to the nonpersistent, those who were present only in 1850. The core group persisted for two decades, the persistent fringe for one, and the nonpersistent for none. (See Table 6.)

The planter families of 1850 that were most likely to persist for two decades were those with sons in the household, those with the most valuable real estate holdings, and those with younger planters as household heads. The differences between persistent core, persistent fringe, and nonpersistent groups followed regular patterns. The planter in the persistent core was the most likely to have at least one son in his household; the persistent fringe was less likely, and the nonpersistent planters were the least likely. The more persistent groups were somewhat more likely to have a spouse present in the household, but the differences were considerably less for wives than for sons. This suggests that after the death of a planter, his son was much more likely to inherit the plantation than was his wife.

The persistent core contained the wealthiest planters in 1850, the persistent fringe had the next wealthiest, and the nonpersistent group had the smallest number of wealthy planters. The greater the landed wealth, the longer the planter family was likely to per-

Table 6. THE 1850 PLANTER ELITE: FACTORS
IN PERSISTENCE FOR TWO DECADES

	Persistent Core: Percent Present 1850–1870	Persistent Fringe: Percent Present 1850–1860	Non-persistent: Percent Present 1850 only
Value of real estate holdings:			
Top 1/3[a]	47	36	30
Middle 1/3	25	35	43
Bottom 1/3	29	29	27
Family structure:			
Spouse:			
Present	84	80	77
Not present	16	20	23
Sons:			
None present	12	28	41
At least one	88	72	59
Four or more	12	11	10
Age:			
21–40	39	32	27
41–52	39	33	29
53–70	22	34	44
Birthplace:			
South	98	96	96
Non-South	2	4	4
Number:	49	61	108[b]

[a] Real estate thirds: 1850: $10,000–13,000, $14,000–21,000, $22,000–117,000.
[b] Not included: 18 who were present in 1850 and 1870 but not 1860.

sist. The planters in the persistent core were considerably younger than those who did not persist, and were somewhat younger than those in the persistent fringe. The younger the planter in 1850, the more likely he was to persist as a member of the elite for two decades; this suggests that the death of elderly planters was a significant cause of nonpersistence among planter families.

Several families among the persistent core were prominent members of the South's political and social elite. The Whitfield family had two branches, each of which was at the top of the land-holding elite in western Alabama. The wealthiest landowner in Marengo County in 1850 was Gaious Whitfield, a forty-six-year-old planter with $100,000 in land and six sons. His older brother Nathan was fourth largest landowner in the county in 1850, with $55,000 in land, three sons, and two daughters. A decade later, in 1860, Gaious was still number one in his county, with real estate valued at $200,000, and Nathan, who now gave his name as "General N. B. Whitfield," was fifth largest planter, with $102,000 in land. After the war, Nathan's place in the elite was taken by his son, B. W., who ranked as the fourth wealthiest planter in his county; in 1870, Gaious's son C. B. was a thirty-one-year-old lawyer with $25,000 in land. Another member of his family, Newton L. Whitfield, was a member of the state legislature in 1860 and mayor of his town in 1870; he was called to testify before the congressional committee investigating the Ku Klux Klan. In 1880, a report on "Whitfield's convict farm in Marengo" indicated that the criminal "never goes there but once for he generally concludes it wisest and best to obey the law than incur its penalties duly enforced."[25]

The Poillnitz family was one of the most distinguished in all Alabama, and had two branches in the western Alabama planter elite.

25. U.S. Bureau of the Census, MS returns, 1850, 1860, 1870, Alabama Population. For 1860 only, additional information on Alabamians owning 50 or more slaves, from the censuses of slaves and agriculture, is available in Joseph K. Menn, "The Large Slaveholders of the Deep South" (Ph.D. dissertation, University of Texas, 1964), 261–542. The Whitfields are on 429–30. Thomas McAdory Owen, *History of Alabama and Dictionary of Alabama Biography* (Chicago: The S. J. Clarke Publishing Company, 1921), IV, 1759; Henry S. Marks, *Who Was Who in Alabama* (Huntsville, Ala.: Strode Publishers, 1972), 191; *House Reports*, 42nd Cong., 2nd Sess., No. 22, X, 1969–93; Mobile *Daily Register*, February 18, 1880. Portraits of B. Whitfield and B. W. Whitfield are reproduced in Historical Activities

The *Dictionary of Alabama Biography* reports that Baron Frederick Charles Hans Bruno Von Poellnitz came to Marengo County with a colony of Napoleon's adherents; he traced his lineage back to 1238. The baron's sons Julius and Charles were present in the planter elite in each census between 1850 and 1870. Charles referred to himself as "General C. A. Poillnitz" when the census enumerator visited him in 1860.[26]

The forty-nine families in the persistent core also included the Glover brothers. Their father had been a pioneer settler of Marengo County, arriving in 1819; his father had been a Scottish immigrant to South Carolina and a veteran of the Revolutionary War. In 1850, three Glover brothers—Edwin, Benjamin, and B. N.—were members of the planter elite of western Alabama, and Edwin, the oldest, was the third wealthiest landholder in his county, with $56,000 in land. In 1860, Edwin was second wealthiest, with 3,500 acres worth $200,000. B. N.'s son George had taken his father's place in the 1860 elite; the twenty-four-year-old had $100,000 in land, which made him sixth biggest landowner in the county. By 1870, the original three brothers were no longer present, but George F. and his cousin W. F. Glover represented the family in the local elite.[27]

The antebellum planters who did not persist were replaced by others in the postwar elite. Who were these "new men" in 1870, who had been able to acquire enough property during the turmoil of defeat and occupation to join the planter elite? Many contempo-

Committee, National Societies of the Colonial Dames of America in the State of Alabama (comp.), *Alabama Portraits Prior to 1870* (Mobile: National Societies of the Colonial Dames of America, 1969), 382, 383. "Gaineswood," the mansion near Demopolis built by N. B. Whitfield in 1842, was opened to the public in the mid-twentieth century: Workers of the Writers' Program of the Works Projects Administration, *Alabama: A Guide to the Deep South* (New York: Richard D. Smith, 1941), 294. The leading general history of Alabama devotes one of its six plates to the ballroom at Gaineswood: Albert Burton Moore, *History of Alabama* (Tuscaloosa: Alabama Book Store, 1934), plate facing 282. For a political attack on Governor Lindsay by N. L. Whitfield, see N. L. Whitfield to Robert McKee, October 19, 1871, in McKee Papers, Alabama Department of Archives and History.

26. Owen, *Alabama Biography*, IV, 1373. See also James Edmonds Saunders, *Early Settlers of Alabama* (New Orleans: L. Graham & Son, Ltd., 1899), 355–56. A portrait of B. B. Poellnitz is reproduced in *Alabama Portraits*, 281.

27. Owen, *Alabama Biography*, IV, 558–69; Marks, *Who Was Who*, 73. "Bluff Hall," the Glover mansion near Demopolis built in 1832, was opened to the public in the mid-twentieth century: Works Projects Administration, *Alabama: A Guide*, 294.

rary observers suggested that they were carpetbaggers—northern businessmen who were bringing their money South to take advantage of the economic prostration of the planter class and to buy up huge quantities of land. Others wrote of young, single northern men, released from the army in the South, who remained in the region to purchase land. Whitelaw Reid reported that there had been a "great rush of Northerners seeking plantations . . . who had made investments in the interior of Alabama." Trowbridge and Charles Nordhoff had similar reports from their visits.[28]

There were few if any carpetbaggers among the new planters of 1870; the new planters tended to be young, geographically mobile southern men. The war does not seem to have brought about an increase of upward social mobility into the planter elite. Only 8 percent of the new planters had been born outside the South, and a few of these had been born in foreign countries; the northern-born planters made up only 5 percent of the new group in 1870. (See Table 7.) And even that 5 percent were not necessarily carpetbaggers; the census asked only for the state of birth of residents, not for the length of time they had been in Alabama. The small number of northern-born new planters in 1870 might very well have come to the state before the Civil War. In fact there were slightly more planters who had been born outside the South in the persistent group than among the new planters; 10 percent of the 1870 planters who had persisted from 1860 had been born outside the South, and they couldn't have been carpetbaggers, but rather were antebellum migrants.

The new planters also do not seem to have been small landholders from the locality who had lifted themselves over their less fortunate neighbors to acquire plantations during the social dislocation that accompanied war and Reconstruction. Few of the new planters of 1870 could be identified as social climbers, local men

28. Whitelaw Reid, *After the War: A Tour of the Southern States* (Cincinnati: Moore, Wilstach & Baldwin, 1866), 454–55; Trowbridge, *The South*, 411; Charles Nordhoff, *The Cotton States in the Spring and Summer of 1875* (New York: D. Appleton and Company, 1876), 71. Allen Nevins holds that three out of four "failed ignominiously"; Nevins, *The Emergence of Modern America, 1865–1878* (New York: The Macmillan Company, 1927), 22.

Table 7. "New Men" in The Postwar Planter Elite

	1870 Planter Elite	
	Percent Persistent from 1860	Percent New in 1870
Value of real estate holdings:		
Top 1/3 [a]	41	27
Middle 1/3	37	33
Bottom 1/3	24	41
Family structure:		
Spouse:		
Present	63	47
Not present	37	53
Sons:		
None present	53	66
At least one	46	34
Four or more	4	4
Age:		
18–34	34	33
35–52	24	41
53–83	42	25
Birthplace:		
South	91	92
Non-South	10	8
Sex:		
Male	91	89
Female	9	11
Number:	101	135

[a] Real estate thirds: $10,000–12,000, $13,000–20,000, $21,000–85,000.

who had increased their real estate holdings enough (relatively) to join the elite. Most of them may have been high status planters from outside the western Alabama black belt who moved into it between 1860 and 1870. To separate cases of social from geographic mobility among the new planters of 1870, the 1860 census list of all property owners in one county was searched for the names of planters new to that county's elite in 1870. Only 15 percent of the new planters of 1870 were identified as climbers. The others had moved into the county from other areas, and it is impossible to determine their former social status. New planters in 1870 much more often represented cases of geographic mobility than of social climbing within the county.

The climbers among the new planters had not climbed very far; in 1860 their real estate holdings put them just below the elite, and by 1870 they had moved just across the line into the bottom quarter of the elite. The small number of such cases makes precise measurement foolhardy, but the pattern is that of climbers moving only a small distance up the social scale, from just below the elite to the bottom of the elite group. There seem to have been more climbers among the new planters of 1860 than there were in 1870. Thus the war does not seem to have brought about an increase of upward social mobility into the elite, although it may have increased their geographic mobility.

The new planters of 1870 differed from those who had persisted from 1860 in a number of ways. They were not as wealthy, they were likely to be middle-aged rather than elderly, and they were less likely to have wives or sons. This suggests that older men were not as likely to migrate, and that the new planters were poorer than the persistent ones because they were younger.

Female Planters and Planters' Wives

The end of the war left planter women in a novel position. During the war, many women had operated plantations while planter-husbands were fighting on the battlefields. Ann Firor Scott argues that war deaths created a "generation of women without men," and that the defeat of the planter regime undermined patriarchal ideology, which had defined the role of the "lady" in plantation society. As a result, Scott argues, many women became planters on their own account after the war.[29]

There may well have been a generation of southern women without men after 1865, but elite women do not seem to have been part of it. Evidence from the Alabama black belt indicates that, although 10 percent of the planter elite was female in 1870, there had been no increase in the proportion of females among the elite during the preceding decade of war and Reconstruction. Wartime deaths of planters did not increase the proportion of planter widows operating plantations, as was argued above. The women who were planters in 1870 appear to have been the elderly widows of elderly men who apparently died of natural causes, rather than young widows of young male war victims. (See Table 8.) While conclusive evidence is not available, this suggests that the females became planters relatively late in life as the result of the death of their husbands. Female planters in 1870 were considerably less wealthy than males. The biggest plantations were almost exclusively operated by males rather than females; although there were women in the elite, they tended to be at the bottom rather than the top in 1870.

Scott makes a telling point when she observes that, after the war, the census enumeration of occupations did not indicate the full extent to which women were effectively operating plantations by themselves; in many planter families with male household heads, the wives apparently were left in charge of the plantation because husbands were engaged in politics, law, or medicine.[30] Although the census manuscripts do not indicate whether wives were in fact operating plantations listed as the property of their husbands, the census did record the occupations of household heads, and some big landowners gave occupations other than "planter." The number of such nonplanter occupations among elite landowners in 1870 increased considerably since 1860. Twenty-one percent of the 1870 planters listed an occupation other than, or in addition to, that of planter, in comparison with only 4 percent of the 1860 elite, in one of the five black belt counties studied more intensively. If

29. Scott, *Southern Lady*, 81, 96, 106, 107.
30. *Ibid.*, 108.

Table 8. CHARACTERISTICS OF POSTWAR FEMALE AND
         MALE PLANTERS

	1870 Planter Elite	
	Percent Male	Percent Female
Real Estate:		
Top 1/3 [a]	35	17
Middle 1/3	34	26
Bottom 1/3	31	57
Number of sons:		
None	75	65
At least one	25	35
Four or more	2	4
Age:		
21–40	43	26
41–52	31	30
53–70	29	44
Birthplace:		
South	92	91
Non-South	8	9
Persisted from 1860	43	30
New in 1870	57	70
Number	213	23

[a] Real estate thirds: $10,000–12,000, $13,000–20,000, $21,000–85,000.

Scott is correct in arguing that wives were often operating the plantations of landowning males who had other occupations, there may indeed have been an increase in the number of females operating plantations after the war.

Of course females had held plantations in their own names before the war. Some southern women had been planters in their own right since the earliest settlement of the South. In the black belt of western Alabama, however, there were no females among the planter elite in 1850; it was not until 1860 that females appeared in the census lists as elite property owners. This may have been a consequence of the recent settlement of western Alabama in 1850. If the frontier had been settled by single men and men with wives, rather than by single women, that would account for the absence of women from the 1850 list of elite landowners. From this perspective, females became planters primarily through inheritance—as the widows of male property owners, or as daughters of planters without male heirs. Scott discusses a widow who ran an antebellum plantation "from the time her husband died until her son was old enough to assume responsibility." This way may well have been the typical pattern; females were landowners in their own right primarily as widows without adult sons. Scott cites one case of a daughter inheriting a plantation from her planter-father, and another case of a daughter following in the footsteps of her planter-mother. Single men regarded such unmarried female landowners as highly desirable spouses, and, given the stigma then attached to spinsterhood, it is extremely unlikely that daughters who inherited plantations remained single for long.[31]

The persistence rate of female planters was considerably lower than that for males during the war decade. Thirty percent of the female planters of 1860 were still members of the elite in 1870, in comparison with 43 percent of the males. This would be the expected finding if women became planters relatively late in life and only until their sons were old enough to become planters themselves. Many sons would be able to take over the plantation between the beginning and end of a decade; elderly female planters would be more likely to die during the decade than the younger male planters. Any female heirs would be likely to marry and change their names during the decade.

Some idea of how the war affected female planters can be gained by comparing the female planters of 1870 with their counterparts of 1860. The postwar female planters were relatively poorer. (See Table 9.) Before the war, there was little difference in the land-

31. *Ibid.*, 34, 23–25.

Table 9. CHARACTERISTICS OF FEMALE PLANTERS

	1860 (percent)	1870 (percent)
Real Estate:		
Top 1/3 [a]	35	17
Middle 1/3	35	26
Bottom 1/3	30	57
Number of sons:		
None	50	69
At least one	50	35
Four or more	15	4
Age:		
Youngest 1/3 [b]	50	26
Middle 1/3	30	30
Oldest 1/3	20	44
Birthplace:		
South	90	91
Non-South	10	9
Number	20	23

[a] Real estate thirds: 1860: $32,000–40,000, $41,000–60,000, $61,000–350,000; 1870: $10,000–12,000, $13,000–20,000, $21,000–85,000.
[b] Age thirds: 1860: 30 and under, 31–54, 55 and over; 1870: 34 and under, 35–52, 53 and over.

holdings of male and female planters; after the war, females were considerably less wealthy. Apparently the decade of war and Reconstruction had a more deleterious economic effect on female planters than on males, but without more detailed evidence it would be incorrect to conclude that female planters were less able to cope with war and Reconstruction than were males. The postwar female planters were considerably older than their prewar counterparts. If females became planters primarily as heirs of husbands or fathers, this suggests that postwar landowning females tended to be widows while the prewar female planters were more likely to be daughters who had inherited estates. The postwar female planters had families with fewer sons than their prewar counterparts, which appears to have been a consequence of a lower wartime birth rate, a higher wartime infant mortality rate, and also the greater age of the postwar female planters in comparison with the female planters of 1860.

Conclusion

From the antebellum period through 1870, the continuities in Alabama elite persistence patterns were greater than the changes. There was virtually no evidence that war and Reconstruction led to a "revolution in land titles," or to the "downfall of the old planter class." However persistence is measured, the rates for the fifties and sixties are similar; indeed on some measures the planters had a higher persistence rate in the sixties than before the war. Not only were the rates similar, but the factors associated with persistence also showed a remarkable degree of continuity, given the extent of social and economic dislocation during the sixties. The Alabama planter elite preserved its social position and its land through war and Reconstruction with remarkable tenacity.

Most planters who remained in the area maintained their status, in both prewar and wartime decades; if there was a substantial degree of downward social mobility, it occurred among planters who left the area, for whom there is no evidence one way or the other. Some might argue that they were more likely to have skidded than climbed; those who weren't making it would move and try again elsewhere, while those who were making it would stay. This is a plausible interpretation, but there is little evidence from either literary or statistical sources to support it. Indeed the data showing that the "new men" of 1870 were migrants suggests that there was a good deal of movement by the wealthy, that prosperous planters frequently moved into the black belt of western Alabama. The great tide of migration was moving steadily west during these years; already by 1860, 30 percent of the free population born in Alabama had settled outside the state, especially in Arkansas and

Louisiana. And they included big planters seeking to become bigger. As U. B. Phillips wrote, "the tide of small farmers advancing toward the frontier . . . was followed in many areas by a tide of planters who sought new openings where their capital might be employed more advantageously than in older areas where the competition was more stringent."[32]

Postwar planter spokesmen often waxed eloquent about the world they had lost. A reporter for the Mobile *Register*, anticipating Margaret Mitchell, wrote in 1871 that "not one of the colossal planters survives. . . . The old aristocracy, proud and exclusive, yet generous and chivalric, have disappeared. Their places are desolate, and in their ornamented grounds the owl and fox have their nests. . . . I pass through deserted halls, and seem to tread on dust and ashes—the dust of the loved and beautiful—the ashes of a once proud and noble people, upon whom the seven vials of wrath and vengeance have been poured." Henry Grady's perception was sharper. He wrote in 1881, "There is beyond question a sure though gradual . . . tendency toward the reestablishment of a landholding oligarchy. Here and there through all the cotton states . . . are reappearing the planter princes of the old time, still lords of acres though not of slaves."[33]

32. Gates, *Agriculture and the Civil War*, 281; Ulrich B. Phillips, "Origin and Growth of Southern Black Belts," in Genovese (ed.), *Slave Economy*, 97.

33. Mobile *Daily Register*, January 25, 1871; Henry W. Grady, "Cotton and Its Kingdom," *Harpers New Monthly Magazine*, LXIII (1881), 719–34. Du Bois came to a similar conclusion: "Men were seeking again to reestablish the domination of property in Southern politics. By getting rid of the black labor vote, they would take their first and substantial step. By raising the race issue, they would secure domination over the white labor vote, and thus the oligarchy that ruled the South before the war would be in part restored to power." Du Bois, *Black Reconstruction*, 428–29.

2

Freedmen and the Reorganization of Plantation Labor

The postwar planters were a new class because they were in new social relations of production. But they were a new class made up of families which to a significant extent had been part of the antebellum elite. The old families persisted in a quantitative sense; in a qualitative sense, their relationship to production had been transformed.[1] Yet they were not a fully modern bourgeoisie.

The development of the postwar southern economy can be understood first of all in terms of the relations between this planter class and the freedmen. After the war, the planters sought to preserve the plantation as a centralized productive unit, worked by laborers in gangs. The freedmen, however, wanted to own their own farms. These differences were resolved, not by the workings of the invisible hand of the free market, but rather by a process that can only be called class conflict. The planters used three tactics in particular: they sought informally to enlist the Freedmen's Bureau in preserving the gang labor plantation; they developed formal legal institutions to limit the free market in labor; and some turned from legalistic to illegal methods, from repressive law to terror, from the Black Codes to the Ku Klux Klan. The freedmen fought back in the only ways they could: they withdrew their labor,

---

1. In this regard see Barrington Moore, Jr., *Social Origins of Dictatorship and Democracy: Lord and Peasant in the Making of the Modern World* (Boston: Beacon Press, 1966), "A Note on Statistics," especially pp. 520–21, and Gareth Stedman Jones, "From Historical Sociology to Theoretical History," *British Journal of Sociology*, XXVII (1976), especially pp. 302–303. Thus I disagree with those who argue that Reconstruction accomplished no fundamental changes, especially Louis S. Gerteis, *From Contraband to Freedmen: Federal Policy Toward Southern Blacks, 1861–1865* (Westport: Greenwood Press, 1973), 4, 5, 50, and John S. Rosenberg, "Toward a New Civil War Revisionism," *American Scholar*, XXXVIII (1969), 271–72.

and they organized politically to demand the confiscation and distribution of plantations owned by rebels.

The outcome of this conflict gave the South its distinctive character, and indicates that the economic and political development of the South differed from that of the North not just in degree, but in kind. Postwar southern development was not following the same path as the North, in an evolutionary manner, because the landlord-tenant relation was of a different type than the capitalist-proletarian relation prevailing in the North. The key difference was the coercive mode of labor control the planters developed in their conflict with the freedmen.

The mood of the planters at the moment of their defeat is revealed in a message from Brigadier General C. C. Andrews to President Johnson, describing the planters of Selma. "The people are glad to have peace on almost any terms," Andrews reported, "but they prefer gradual emancipation." Michael Perman rightly comments that "submission on these terms was in fact hardly submission at all." Andrews, it might be noted, implicitly accepted the planters' assertion that "the people" excluded blacks. Colonel L. F. Hubbard in Demopolis came to the same conclusion, but stated it more directly: "The people hereabouts are fearfully rebellious, and indicate a purpose to remain so." James Yardley, Reconstruction registrar of voters in a black belt county, reported to his superior that "it is impossible to find loyal men to fill the offices necessary to carry on an election."[2]

The Gang Labor Plantation

At the direction of the occupying Union army, slave labor was replaced by the "contract system"; the freedmen were to sign contracts with planters specifying their duties and their pay. The

2. Michael Perman, *Reunion Without Compromise: The South and Reconstruction, 1865–1868* (New York: Cambridge University Press, 1973), 39, quoting Andrews to Johnson, May 11, 1865; Col. L. F. Hubbard to Capt. W. H. F. Randall, report on conditions in Demopolis, May 20, 1865, in U.S. War Department, *The War of the Rebellion: A Compilation of the Official Records of the Union and Confederate Army* (Washington, D.C.: Government Printing Office, 1897), Ser. 1, Vol. 49, Pt. 2, p. 855 (hereinafter cited as *Official Records*). James A. Yardley to Col. W. H. Smith, August 2, 1867, in Wager Swayne Papers, Alabama Department of Archives and History. Williamson reports that at the same time in South Carolina "there was a highly influential minority composed of former

contracts with planters for 1865 and 1866 provided for gang labor for wages rather than family tenancy. Because of the shortage of currency, wage laborers were usually paid with a share of the crop rather than in cash; this has led some to confuse the gang system of the immediate postwar period with its successor, sharecropping. But it is the organization of production, rather than the form of payment, that is crucial: wage laborers worked in a gang under an overseer, as they had under slavery; their hours and tasks were clearly specified in their contract, and carefully supervised; infractions, such as not showing up on time or taking extra days off, were punished. Ransom and Sutch have suggested that we refer to this system as "share-wages." It must be clearly distinguished from the system of family tenancy where the rent was paid with a share of the crop—"sharecropping."[3] Under sharecropping, the plantation was divided into small plots, each worked by a single family which largely determined its own hours and tasks. Although the planter or his agent often checked up on tenants, they did not use collective labor in work gangs, nor did they specify the division of labor among family members. The crucial difference was the greater power of the planters over the daily lives of gang laborers, and the sharecroppers' greater independence from supervision and control.

The Freedmen's Bureau reports on the reorganization of agriculture and labor in 1865 and 1866 described a system based on gang laborers receiving wages. The reports made few references to tenant farming. Travelers in the South during these immediate

---

slaveholders who believed the institution of slavery might, after all, be preserved," and made that an issue in the election for representatives to the state constitutional convention. Joel Williamson, *After Slavery: The Negro in South Carolina During Reconstruction, 1861–1877* (Chapel Hill: University of North Carolina Press, 1965), 72, 33. Roark argues that "the dominant theme in the planters' lives became the search for a substitute for slavery": James L. Roark, *Masters Without Slaves: Southern Planters in the Civil War and Reconstruction* (New York: W. W. Norton Co., 1977), 133; see also pp. 116, 118, 157–58, 201.

3. Roger Ransom and Richard Sutch, *One Kind of Freedom: The Economic Consequences of Emancipation* (New York: Cambridge University Press, 1977), Chap. 7. Williamson, also mindful of possible confusion, refers to sharecropping as "share-renting." Williamson, *After Slavery*, 128 n 9. See also Gunnar Myrdal, *An American Dilemma: The Negro Problem in Modern America* (New York: Harper & Row, 1944), I, Chap. 2, and [Jay] R. Mandle, "The Reestablishment of the Plantation Economy in the South, 1865–1910," *Review of Black Political Economy*, III (1973), 68–88.

postwar years similarly described the gang system as the prevailing one. Whitelaw Reid found one plantation on which sharecropping existed, and he described that in a chapter on "labor experiments." John Trowbridge listed only two "experiments" with sharecropping in his reports from 1865 and 1866.[4]

While wage labor was ostensibly the basis of plantation agriculture in 1865 and 1866, many planters avoided paying any wages at all to their former slaves. One Alabama Freedmen's Bureau agent reported incidents in which "the negro promises to work for an indefinite time for nothing but his board and clothes," and Peter Kolchin has concluded that, in numerous places in Alabama, blacks were "working without pay." The contracts were supposed to specify the tasks for which the freedmen were to be paid, but many planters apparently avoided this provision. Kolchin found typical labor contracts for the immediate postwar years which said only that "all orders . . . are to be promptly and implicitly obeyed under any and all circumstances"—a provision suggesting that, although the laborers would now receive wages, the planters wanted them to follow orders as they had as slaves. Indeed there is evidence that some planters went so far as to try to sell their laborers as if they were still slaves. An 1867 letter to General Wager Swayne, head of the Freedmen's Bureau in Alabama, reports of a "freedman who contracted to live with a man in this Neighborhood he has don a great deal of work for the man & He has now found fault of him & has Taken out a wornt for Him & the mgistrate has ordered Him to be sold next wednday at 10: o'clock to pay a fine they have entered against the said Negro I think that the order should be revoked for I dont think the contract is leagle for it is not approved by you nor non of your agents." Standard wage contracts prohibited laborers from leaving the plantation during working hours without the planters' consent, prohibited their bringing either guests or liquor to the quarters, and even prohibited conversing in

4. *Senate Executive Documents*, 39th Cong., 2nd Sess., No. 6, pp. 3–21; Whitelaw Reid, *After the War: A Tour of the Southern States* (Cincinnati: Moore, Wilstach & Baldwin, 1866), 572; John Townsend Trowbridge, *The South: A Tour of Its Battlefields* . . . (Hartford: L. Stebbins, 1866), 195, 204. On Reid, see Bingham Duncan, *Whitelaw Reid: Journalist, Politician, Diplomat* (Athens: University of Georgia Press, 1976).

the fields. To make sure the message was clear, contracts contained clauses requiring the freedmen to be "peaceable, orderly, and pleasant," and "kind and respectful."[5]

The planters not only tried to maintain many of the repressive aspects of slavery in the postwar wage system; they also tried to keep their own former slaves as laborers. Colonel George H. Hanks, superintendent of Negro labor in the army's Department of the Gulf, told the War Department's Freedmen's Inquiry Commission early in 1864 that the planters "make great endeavors to recover what they call their own negroes." An extreme case was that of one of the "richest and most extensive" planters, who refused to work his own plantation at all "unless he could have his own negroes returned to him." The planter was willing to accept the abolition of slavery and the creation of a wage system, but only on the condition that his former slaves serve as his wage laborers. The Montgomery *Advertiser*, consistently a leading voice of planter interests, reviewed the wage system early in 1867 and recommended that "faithful men, who have been former slaves of land owners, . . . would do well . . . and ought to be encouraged in their industry" by their former masters.[6]

The assumption behind this view could only have been that planters would have more control over wage laborers who had been their own slaves and then "stayed on." And the evidence is overwhelming that the freedmen were determined to avoid staying on for precisely this reason. Carl Schurz was one of the first to argue that leaving the old slave plantation was the most fundamental definition of "freedom" among the former slaves; "that they

5. Peter Kolchin, *First Freedom: The Response of Alabama's Blacks to Emancipation and Reconstruction* (Westport: Greenwood Publishing Company, 1972), 35, 36. Williamson similarly found contracts requiring that freedmen call a planter "master," and that they obey orders "strictly as my slaves." Williamson, *After Slavery*, 97, 131; Calvin C. Jones to Wager Swayne, April 20, 1867, in Wager Swayne Papers, Alabama Department of Archives and History; see also Leon Litwack, "Free at Last," in Tamara Hareven (ed.), *Anonymous Americans: Explorations in Nineteenth Century Social History* (Englewood Cliffs, N.J.: Prentice-Hall, 1971), 130–71.

6. James McKaye, *The Mastership and Its Fruits: The Emancipated Slave Face to Face with His Old Master: A Supplementary Report to Hon. Edwin M. Stanton, Secretary of War* (New York: Loyal Publication Society, 1864), reprinted in the *National Anti-Slavery Standard*, July 23, 1864; Montgomery *Daily Advertiser*, January 25, 1867.

could so leave their former masters was for them the first test of the reality of their freedom," he told a Senate committee. Kolchin documents massive geographical mobility among Alabama freedmen in the year after the war. Voluminous testimony by masters disappointed with their departing ex-slaves' "ingratitude" confirms the point.[7]

The planters in these immediate postwar years formed organizations to protect their interests, class conscious efforts to place plantation agriculture on a firmly repressive basis. In December, 1867, under the headline "The Regulation of Labor," the Montgomery *Advertiser* reported that a local "meeting of planters" resolved: "1. that when we hire freedmen they concede to us the right to control their labor as our time and convenience requires . . . 2. we require them to expressly stipulate to use their time and services for our own interest and advantage, and, if they . . . stop work and attend 'club meetings,' such hands shall be dismissed and wages forfeited."[8]

In Sumter County six weeks earlier, a "meeting of citizens" discussing the "labor system" unanimously resolved that "concert of action is indispensable among those hiring laborers." They agreed that all planters should offer the same terms: one-fourth of the crop for the laborer when the planter supplied the provisions, or one-half the crop when the tenants paid half the expenses as well as their own provisions. "Tenants who don't comply with terms will be discharged," the meeting declared, and concluded "we pledge ourselves not to employ any laborer discharged for violation of contracts." A similar "planters' meeting" was held in Greensboro in November, 1867, to discuss alternatives to wage labor, and in December a "state convention of planters at Selma" resolved that "the

7. *Senate Executive Documents*, 39th Cong., 1st Sess., No. 2, pp. 29–30; Kolchin, *First Freedom*, Chap. 1; Robert Manson Myers, *The Children of Pride* (New Haven: Yale University Press, 1972). The key passages have been selected in Eugene D. Genovese, *Roll, Jordan, Roll: The World the Slaves Made* (New York: Pantheon Books, 1975), 103–107; for an illuminating discussion of the implications of this experience for the paternalist ethos, see "The Moment of Truth," in *Roll, Jordan, Roll*, 98–112: "the immediate postwar trauma derived less from the sudden confrontation with the true attitudes of their slaves than from the enforced confrontation with themselves."

8. Montgomery *Daily Advertiser*, December 8, 1867. For similar reports from South Carolina, see Williamson, *After Slavery*, 99–100.

planters will not be able to pay the prices for labor they have been paying."[9]

An Alabamian told the Congressional Reconstruction Committee that "the planters formed a combination" in his county in 1865 to regulate wages. The organization's purpose was to "refuse to give the colored hands on the plantation more than one-eighth of the net proceeds of the crop," and to enforce those terms on planters paying more. General O. O. Howard, in the 1866 report of the Freedmen's Bureau, complained of the planters' efforts "to reduce wages by community of action." John Trowbridge reported in 1866 that "agricultural associations" had been formed in several Alabama counties, among whose self-declared "duties" was "to see that the freedmen shall comply with his contracts with his employer." The Greensboro *Alabama Beacon* argued in 1871 that "capital controls labor—provided there is concert of action." Blacks complained that "the landowners have formed combinations to have their large estates cultivated to their own advantage, at the expense of those who till the soil."[10]

A statewide "Planters Convention" met in the Alabama House of Representatives in February, 1871. Those who called for the convention announced that their purpose was for planters to "put their heads, and if need be, their means, together for mutual benefit and protection." The Montgomery *Advertiser* reported that "the attendance at this important meeting was large and extremely gratifying." The convention, widely reported in the planter press, seemed to echo the sentiments of an Alabama planter who summed up his view of the labor situation for John Trowbridge in 1866: "The nigger is going to be made a serf, sure as you live. It won't need any law for that. Planters will have an understanding among themselves: 'You won't hire my niggers, and I won't hire yours;' then what's left for them? They're attached to the soil, and we're as much their masters as ever."[11]

9. Montgomery *Daily Advertiser*, October 31, November 26, December 22, 1867.

10. *House Reports*, 39th Cong., 1st Sess., No. 30, Pt. 2, p. 9; *House Executive Documents*, 39th Cong., 2nd Sess., No. 1, p. 706; Trowbridge, *The South*, 431–32; Greensboro *Alabama Beacon*, February 21, 1871; Montgomery *Alabama State Journal*, January 5, 1871.

11. Montgomery *Alabama State Journal*, February 9, 10, 1871; Montgomery *Daily Advertiser*, January 14, February 10, 1871; Greensboro *Alabama Beacon*, February 25, 1871;

The planters' attempt to preserve the plantation as a centralized labor unit, using supervised gang labor, was a logical effort to preserve a mode of production that had evolved and developed over sixty years.[12] The planters' desire to incorporate wage labor into the organizational structure of the antebellum plantation was not only an effort to preserve planter domination of the freedmen, but also to continue production along the lines of established agricultural methods and procedures. This effort, comprehensible as it was in economic terms, confronted an insurmountable obstacle: the freedmen's refusal to agree to it. Their widespread resistance to working in gangs for wages appears in the historical record as a "shortage of labor," and it played a crucial role in the reorganization of plantation agriculture after the war.

The Labor Shortage

The planters complained that the departure of their former slaves was a sign of ingratitude. They complained that the freedmen were incapable of taking care of themselves, were lazy and ignorant and helpless, or lazy and ignorant and menacing. They complained that the freedmen were being manipulated by unscrupulous carpetbaggers and scalawags. They complained that drunkenness and theft were rampant among the freedmen. But most important, in 1865 and 1866, they complained of a "labor shortage."

Robert Somers's 1871 report on his visit to Marengo County was aptly entitled "Despair of the Planters for Labor." The Montgomery *Advertiser*, in a rare moment of candor, admitted the planters' concern over losing their black labor force altogether: "it is manifestly in our interest, as well as theirs, to keep the black laborers in the country. . . . we cannot spare the negro for the simple reason that there is none to supply the vacancy his absence would occasion." The tortured (but correct) syntax of this carefully worded statement does not fully conceal the planters' sense of desperation.

Livingston *Journal*, quoted in Tuscaloosa *Independent Monitor*, April 4, 1871; Tuscaloosa *Independent Monitor*, January 24, February 21, 1871; Trowbridge, *The South*, 427.

12. Ransom and Sutch, *One Kind of Freedom*, Chap. 4. They deny, however, that there were any genuine economies of scale associated with gang labor. For the opposite conclusion, see Stanley L. Engerman, "The Legacy of Slavery," Duke University Symposium on *One Kind of Freedom*, February 11, 1978, p. 14.

General Swayne, head of the Freedmen's Bureau in Alabama, concurred; in 1866 he reported that "a considerable portion . . . of the arable land in Alabama goes untilled this year, principally in consequence of the scarcity of labor." Loring and Atkinson, a Boston cotton firm, conducted a survey of the planters' problems in the early postwar period, and their reports from Alabama indicated that "the greatest drawback now is the want of labor," and that "generally, the planters have not labor enough."[13]

Why were Alabama planters and their counterparts across the South faced with this labor shortage in the immediate postwar years? The census shows that Alabama's black population increased by 10 percent between 1860 and 1870, and Ransom and Sutch have demonstrated that the death rate among blacks did not increase noticeably during and just after the war, nor did freedmen migrate out of the state. They conclude that the number of freedmen living in rural areas of the South in 1870 was at least no smaller than it had been in 1860. Kolchin's careful study of migration patterns of Alabama blacks in the immediate postwar years comes to the same conclusion, showing that the black population increased in three of twelve black belt counties, that it increased in one of those by 9 percent, and that in the other nine it stayed the same. The only Alabama counties to lose black population between 1866 and 1870 were outside the black belt.[14]

The most important cause of the labor shortage in 1865 and 1866 seems to have been the freedmen's refusal to work for wages, which was in turn based on their hope of becoming landowners. The Joint Congressional Committee on Reconstruction reported the freedmen had a "strong desire, amounting almost to a passion . . . to

13. Robert Somers, *The Southern States Since the War, 1870–1* (New York: Macmillan and Company, 1871), 165; Montgomery *Daily Advertiser*, August 25, 1865; *House Reports*, 39th Cong., 1st Sess., No. 30, Pt. 2, p. 140; F. W. Loring and C. F. Atkinson, *Cotton Culture and the South Considered with Reference to Emigration* (Boston: A. Williams & Co., 1869). See also Montgomery *Daily Advertiser*, January 5, 1871; Eutaw *Whig and Observor*, quoted in Greensboro *Alabama Beacon*, March 1, 1873. For reports of a "labor shortage" elsewhere in the South at the same time, see Joe Gray Taylor, *Louisiana Reconstructed, 1863–1877* (Baton Rouge: Louisiana State University Press, 1974), 324–37; Williamson, *After Slavery*, 110–11; Roark, *Masters Without Slaves*, 137.

14. U.S. Census Office, *Ninth Census, Population* (Washington, D.C.: Government Printing Office, 1872), 11–12; Ransom and Sutch, *One Kind of Freedom*, Chap. 5; Kolchin, *First Freedom*, 19.

obtain land." In the words of the Montgomery *Advertiser*, "the negro is ravenous for land." Genovese quotes a marvelously shocked plantation mistress who reported, "Our most trusted servant . . . claims the plantation as his own." Willard Warner, Alabama's radical senator, later recalled, "The negro, after he was emancipated, seemed to have an intuition that led him in the right direction. The first thing he wanted to do immediately after his emancipation was to get land." A Union officer wrote that "all concurred in the opposition to the contract system."[15]

A convention of black leaders met in Montgomery in May, 1867, and issued an "address . . . to the People of Alabama," which expressed the blacks' desire to own land. They explained that blacks supported the Republican party, among other reasons, because "it passed new homestead laws, enabling the poor to obtain land." The convention said of their planter-antagonists that "the property which they hold was nearly all earned by the sweat of our brows— not theirs. It has been forfeited to the government by the treason of its owners, and is liable to be confiscated whenever the Republican Party demands it."[16]

This expectation of land distribution was no idle fantasy in the

15. *House Reports*, 39th Cong., 1st Sess., No. 30, Pt. 3, p. 36; Montgomery *Daily Advertiser*, January 17, 1883; Genovese, *Roll, Jordan, Roll*, 108; *Senate Documents*, 48th Cong., 1st Sess., No. 1262, IV, 274; William S. McFeely, *Yankee Stepfather: General O. O. Howard and the Freedmen* (New Haven: Yale University Press, 1968), 159–61; Sidney Andrews, *The South Since the War* . . . (Boston: Ticknor and Fields, 1866), 97–98, 221–22. Genovese reminds us that the freedmen's "newly proclaimed aspirations . . . were not necessarily new aspirations," and elsewhere points to Du Bois' suggestion that the slaves' "experience with their gardens had generated that land hunger which became an important . . . demand during Reconstruction." Genovese, *Roll, Jordan, Roll*, 154, 538; W. E. B. Du Bois, *Black Reconstruction in America, 1860–1880* (New York: Atheneum, 1969), 123. Ransom and Sutch emphasize that the continuing "labor shortage" was a consequence of the freedmen's choice to work less than they had been forced to as slaves—Roger Ransom and Richard Sutch, "The Impact of the Civil War and of Emancipation on Southern Agriculture," *Explorations in Economic History*, XII (1975), 20–22—and that "the freedman was systematically denied the opportunity to become an independent farmer because of his race." Roger Ransom and Richard Sutch, "The Ex-Slave in the Post-Bellum South: A Study of the Economic Impact of Racism in a Market Environment," *Journal of Economic History*, XXXIII (1973), 144.

16. "Address of the Colored Convention to the People of Alabama," Montgomery *Daily State Sentinel*, May 21, 1867. "We wants land–dis bery land dat is rich wid de sweat ob we face and de blood ob we back," a former slave wrote in 1864: quoted in Herbert G. Gutman, *The Black Family in Slavery and Freedom, 1750–1925* (New York: Random House, 1976), 471. See also 166, 210.

black community, but one firmly based on political facts. General Nathaniel P. Banks, head of the military occupation of Louisiana, had provided small plots for freedmen in 1863 and 1864. John Eaton, who had jurisdiction over freedmen flocking to Grant's army, had 2,000 blacks on government-financed farms, and in January, 1865, Sherman provided for the establishment of homesteads for freedmen in the Sea Islands of South Carolina; this he did in direct response to requests from black leaders. The Freedmen's Bureau Bill, passed in March, 1865, provided that forty acres of abandoned and confiscated lands should be assigned to "every male citizen, whether refugee or freedman," to be rented for three years, and then purchased from the United States. Commissioner Howard of the Freedmen's Bureau had originally intended to turn over abandoned and confiscated land to freedmen, and it was only President Johnson's veto of this policy in the fall of 1865 that forced the bureau to begin returning confiscated land to its original owners. The following year, Congress passed the Southern Homestead Act, allowing blacks to file applications for homesteads in 1866, while most whites had to wait until 1867.[17]

The planters were as apprehensive as the freedmen were hopeful. One black belt newspaper summed up the prospects for the planter class if the land distribution should actually take place: "the negroes will become possessed of a small freehold, will raise their corn, squashes, pigs and chickens, and will work no more in the cotton. . . . Their labor will become unavailable for those products which the world especially needs. . . . The title of this law ought to have been 'A bill to get rid of the laboring class of the South.'"[18]

17. LaWanda Cox, "The Promise of Land for the Freedman," *Mississippi Valley Historical Review*, XLV (1958), 413–30; Martin Abbott, "Free Land, Free Labor, and the Freedmen's Bureau," *Agricultural History*, XXX (1956), 151–52; Paul W. Gates, "Federal Land Policy in the South, 1866–1888," *Journal of Southern History*, VI (1946), 307; Willie Lee Rose, *Rehearsal for Reconstruction: The Port Royal Story* (New York: The Bobbs-Merrill Company, 1964), 272–81; Williamson, *After Slavery*, 54–63, 89; Christie Farnham Pope, "Southern Homesteads for Negroes," *Agricultural History*, XLIV (1970), 201–12; Walter L. Fleming, " 'Forty Acres and a Mule,' " *North American Review*, CLXXXIII (1906), 721–37; Taylor, *Louisiana Reconstructed*, 335–36; Howard Ashley White, *The Freedmen's Bureau in Louisiana* (Baton Rouge: Louisiana State University Press, 1970), 107–109; McFeely, *Yankee Stepfather*, 213–20, 226–31.

18. *Clarke County Journal*, July 12, 1866, cited in Robert Gilmour, "The Other Emancipation: Studies in the Society and Economy of Alabama Whites during Reconstruction" (Ph.D. dissertation, Johns Hopkins University, 1972), 119–20.

The article correctly identified the implications of the forty-acre proposal: blacks might not provide the labor the planters needed to continue to exist as a class.

Even though the Freedmen's Bureau did not distribute free land to blacks, land confiscated for taxes during Reconstruction was often put up for sale in forty-acre units. Marengo planter F. S. Lyon complained to a congressional committee that the division of plantations into forty-acre units for tax sales was a plot by radical newspaper publishers to get more advertising, since the government placed a separate advertisement for each parcel. Lyon's real complaint was not that the newspaper publishers were making extra money off the tax sale announcements, but that the Radicals were deliberately dividing plantations confiscated for taxes in the hopes of bringing about land redistribution.[19] The freedmen's lack of cash blocked their becoming landowners by this route.

Freedmen hesitated to work for wages in the immediate postwar period for additional reasons. The increasing refusal to work for wages corresponded to a decrease in the wages planters offered. According to Department of Agricultural statistics, the annual wages offered black men in Alabama fell from $117 in 1867 to $87 in 1868, a decline of 26 percent in one year.[20]

The chief complaint of the freedmen working for wages, according to the Freedmen's Bureau, was "fraudulent division of the crops." Apparently planters were not only reducing wages, but also cheating on the shares paid to laborers—or at least the freedmen accused them of doing so. One authority reports that the number of such complaints rose "steadily." Undoubtedly the planters' organizations contributed to keeping wages low and restricting labor mobility. General Howard himself wrote that the planters' actions

19. *House Reports*, 42nd Cong., 2nd Sess., X, 1409, 1416. Lyon was attacking the Radical Demopolis *Southern Republican*, which indeed was filled with tax sale announcements. See also Williamson, *After Slavery*, 148–53.

20. U.S. Department of Agriculture, *Report of the Commissioner of Agriculture for the Year 1867* (Washington, D.C.: Government Printing Office, 1868), 416; Ransom and Sutch, *One Kind of Freedom*, Table 4.2. See also Montgomery *Daily Mail*, May 16, 1865; Matthew B. Hammond, *The Cotton Industry: An Essay in American Economic History* (New York: The Macmillan Company, 1897), 124; Walter L. Fleming, *Civil War and Reconstruction in Alabama* (Cleveland: A. H. Clark Company, 1911), 730.

"tended seriously to lessen the confidence of the freed people in them and increases suspicion."[21]

A final cause of the labor shortage was the withdrawal of women and children from the labor force. As slaveowners, the planters had commanded the labor of black women and children; as employers of free labor, they found black women and children unwilling to work as they had under slavery. *DeBow's Review* reported in 1866 that, in contrast to slave times, "most of the field labor is now performed by men, the women regarding it as the duty of their husbands to support them in idleness," and that "there is a settled opposition on the part of the women to go into the fields again."[22]

The Planters and the Freedmen's Bureau

The planters' bitter opposition to the presence first of the Union army and later of the Freedmen's Bureau in their own counties did not stop them from seeking to enlist the bureau in keeping the black labor force on the plantation. Their efforts tended to be successful; while the bureau opposed some of the more extreme proposals made on behalf of the planters, many bureau officials worked to perpetuate the planters' domination, and the bureau in some crucial respects became part of the repressive apparatus of the new agricultural system.

Walter Fleming recounted with barely concealed delight J. W. DuBose's experience with the Freedmen's Bureau in Demopolis.

21. Elizabeth Bethel, "The Freedmen's Bureau in Alabama," *Journal of Southern History*, XIV (1948), 76; *House Executive Documents*, 39th Cong., 2nd Sess., No. 1, p. 706; Montgomery *Daily Advertiser*, December 22, 1866. A "Colored Labor Convention" meeting in Montgomery in 1871 complained of "hardships imposed by the failure of their employers to make good their contracts." Montgomery *Alabama State Journal*, January 4, 1871; see also Montgomery *Daily Advertiser*, January 5, 1871. A similar complaint is in Calvin C. Jones to Wager Swayne, April 20, 1867, in Wager Swayne Papers, Alabama Department of Archives and History. The same situation was reported elsewhere in the South: James H. Croushore and David M. Potter (eds.), *John William DeForest, A Union Officer in the Reconstruction* (New Haven: Yale University Press, 1948), 29–30.

22. *DeBow's Review*, After the War Series, I (1866), 659, 305. DeBow repeated this argument in his testimony before the Joint Congressional Committee on Reconstruction: *House Reports*, 39th Cong., 1st Sess., No. 30, IV, 135. See also Gutman, *Black Family*, 167–68. Ransom and Sutch estimate that black laborers as a group did one-third less work after the war than they had under slavery, as the result of a combination of the withdrawal of the labor of women and children, the refusal to work Saturday afternoon, starting later in the morning, taking days off, and taking longer breaks for meals; this provides a measure of the compulsory element in slave labor. Ransom and Sutch, *One Kind of Freedom*, Chap. 5.

A group of freedmen from DuBose's plantation walked 12 miles to complain to the local bureau office about their treatment; DuBose himself came faster and met with the official before the freedmen arrived. Then "they told their tale, and the officer called for a sergeant and four mounted men. Sergeant, he said, take these people back to Mr. DuBose's on the *run!* You understand; on the *run!* They ran the negroes the whole twelve miles, even though they had already travelled twelve miles. Upon their arrival at home the sergeant tied them to trees with the hands above their heads, and left them with their tongues hanging out. . . . They never again had any complaints to pour into the ear of the 'office.'"[23]

Evidence from a variety of other sources tends to reinforce rather than contradict this picture of the way the bureau functioned in Alabama. In the spring of 1864, the Union army occupied Alabama with the task of supervising the new contract system of free labor; that summer the Freedmen's Bureau was officially established in Alabama. Thomas W. Conway, general superintendent of freedmen for the Department of the Gulf, arrived in Montgomery in April, but it was not until late summer that the bureau was established and functioning throughout the state.

Already by this time the repressive role played by Union officers toward the freedmen was gaining attention, and observers were reporting that the occupation army was doing the planters' bidding. In July of 1864, the War Department's Freedmen's Inquiry Commission investigated army activities, and James McKaye of the commission reported that subordinate army officials had become instruments of the planters in "perpetrating great injustice and ill-treatment on colored laborers." He reported that "provost marshalls did not interfere with the use of the whip on many plantations," and argued that the army's insistence that black laborers contract to work for a full year was "wrong in principle and liable to misuse." McKaye concluded with a warning that "the old planters desired to maintain control over laborers either directly or through military supervision" by the Union army.[24]

23. Fleming, *Civil War and Reconstruction in Alabama*, 450. For a similar story from South Carolina, see Williamson, *After Slavery*, 93–94.

24. McKaye, *Mastership*; Cox, "Promise of Land," 423–24. See also George Bentley, *A History of the Freedmen's Bureau* (Philadelphia: University of Pennsylvania Press, 1951),

McKaye's criticism was directed at the army's treatment of freedmen in Louisiana in 1863, but it was an ominously accurate forecast of the susceptability of Union officials in Alabama to planter pressure. Conway, on his arrival in Alabama, agreed with planters that the "perfect reign of idleness on the part of the negroes" had to be ended. "I issued a plan for the government of labor and freedmen," Conway reported to his superior in June of 1865, "which satisfied the planters. . . . I assured the planters on the one hand that the freedmen must work, but that on the other they must not be persecuted or murdered."[25] The bureau would oppose the persecution and murder of freedmen, but force them to work for the planters; this was not exactly an even-handed policy. The trade-off was just what the planters hoped to accomplish by threatening persecution and murder—to enlist the Union army in assuring the continued supply of black labor for the plantations. The system was described in the superintendent's report as one which would "promote the welfare and industry of the freedmen"; what he meant was that the army believed the freedmen's welfare lay in laboring industriously for the planters.

Brigadier General C. C. Andrews, commander of Union forces in Selma, observed that the freedmen were filled with "restlessness and disquiet" over the persistence of the plantation system; this led him to issue a proclamation to the freedmen of the west Alabama black belt in May, 1865, in which he supported the planters' claims. "Quite a number of freedmen have complained to me," he told the blacks, but "planters have represented to me that the loss they have suffered . . . and the depreciation of their currency . . . have cramped their means . . . so that they cannot promise you much compensation." Andrews found that what the

---

85–86; Gerteis, *From Contraband to Freedmen*; James E. Sefton, Jr., *The U.S. Army and Reconstruction, 1865–1877* (Baton Rouge: Louisiana State University Press, 1967), especially pp. 42–43, and J. Thomas May, "Continuity and Change in the Labor Program of the Union Army and the Freedmen's Bureau," *Civil War History*, XVII (1971), 245–51. William Faulkner noted the sympathetic treatment planters received from the occupying Union army. In *The Unvanquished* he describes a Union general returning blacks to a planter wife who claims them; Faulkner has an orderly say, "The general will be glad to give her twice the silver and mules [she claimed] just for taking that many niggers." William Faulkner, *The Unvanquished* (New York: New American Library, 1952), 88.

25. Conway to Christensen, June 3, 1865, *Official Records*, Vol. XLIX, Pt. 2, p. 954.

planters said was "true to a considerable extent," and told the dissatisfied freedmen, "you . . . appear misinformed of your real interests. [Therefore] I now offer you my advice: I do not believe you hazard your liberty by remaining where you are and working for such compensation as your employers are able to give."[26] This was not a confidential memo to a superior; it was a public proclamation by the commander of U.S. forces in the area. Andrews thus not only opposed efforts to obtain reasonable compensation for wage laborers, but also discouraged the movement of freedmen away from the old plantations. If emancipation in its most fundamental sense meant freedom to move off the old plantation, even that elemental freedom was publicly discouraged by the commanding Union general in western Alabama. It is difficult to imagine a clearer declaration of support for planter interests.

The army's regulations for blacks bore a striking resemblance to the resolutions concerning the labor system passed by the planters' own organizations. The freedmen of Mobile were instructed by the army to sign labor contracts "with their former masters," but signing with "anyone else" was also permissible. The regulations specified that laborers leaving the plantation "without cause or permission" were to forfeit all pay; "upon feigning sickness or refusing to work, a laborer was to be put at forced labor on the public works without pay," and after a "reasonable" period, "any negro found without employment" would be forced to work for the army. The Huntsville regulations were the same.[27]

Military authority over the freedmen gave way to the Freedmen's Bureau in Alabama officially in July, 1865. The assistant commissioner in charge of Alabama was Brigadier General Wager Swayne. Swayne's view of the labor situation in Alabama was classically laissez-faire capitalist: "The system of annual contracts was regarded as a make-shift," he wrote in his 1866 report, "which

26. C. C. Andrews, "To the Freedmen of Selma and Vicinity," proclamation of May 8, 1865, *Official Records*, Vol. XLIX, Pt. 2, p. 728. When Reconstruction officials said "blacks had to prove their worth by staying on the land and calling their old master, 'master,' " C. C. Jones observed that "the Nigs were quite disgusted." Myers, *Children of Pride*, 1279. See also Thomas Wagstaff, "Call Your Old Master—'Master,' " *Labor History*, X (1969), 323–45.

27. Montgomery *Weekly Mail*, May 12, 1865; Huntsville *Advocate*, July 19, 1865, quoted in Kolchin, *First Freedom*, 31.

it was hoped would disappear as confidence should grow out of experience on both sides, and leave to each the benefit of an appeal at any time to competition. The demand for labor promised a comfortable future for the freedmen on this basis." Swayne thought that legal regulation of labor was undesirable, that the free market in labor should be established, and that the high demand for black labor would assure the prosperity of the freedmen. In spite of these declarations of a laissez-faire policy, Swayne in practice intervened repeatedly on the side of the planters and against the freedmen. Fleming again provides the crucial clue; he found Swayne "a man of discretion and common sense" who was "afraid of negro insurrection" and "did not interfere with the attempts of the whites to control the blacks." Fleming characterized Swayne's policy toward Alabama planters as a "conciliatory" one. The equally reactionary Hilary Herbert praised Swayne for being "far more conservative . . . than his superior, General Pope."[28]

Upon his arrival in Alabama, Swayne took on the task of "removing" from the freedmen the "belief . . . that they could live without labor." He candidly identified his task as "compelling the able-bodied to labor." And he commented that he was pleased by the "reasonable temper of the planters," a temper which was not surprising, given the bureau's declared purpose of compelling the freedmen to labor for wages on the plantations. Swayne reported to Congress that, on his arrival in Alabama, both freedmen and planters were "at fault." The freedmen sought "confiscation . . . for their benefit" of plantation land, while the planters wanted "secure labor." The bureau resolved this dilemma, Swayne reported, in a manner "to meet the wants of both" by establishing and supervising a system of twelve-month labor contracts between freedmen

28. *Senate Executive Documents*, 39th Cong., 2nd Sess., No. 6, p. 6. Fleming interviewed Swayne, which gives his account particular authority; Fleming, *Civil War and Reconstruction in Alabama*, 279, 369, 427–29. For a similar conclusion regarding Swayne, see McFeely, *Yankee Stepfather*, 77–78. Hilary A. Herbert, *Why the Solid South? Or, Reconstruction and Its Results* (Baltimore: R. H. Woodward & Co., 1890); 43. On Herbert, see Hugh B. Hammett, *Hilary Abner Herbert: A Southerner Returns to the Union*, Memoirs of the American Philosophical Society, CX (Philadelphia: American Philosophical Society, 1976).

and planters.[29] But to put the bureau in the business of drafting and approving year-long labor contracts was to ally the bureau with the planters against the freedmen. The freedmen's "fault," in Swayne's analysis, was that they wanted land; in ordering them to sign twelve-month contracts, the bureau did not "meet the wants" they had expressed, but rather rejected them outright. The planters wanted "secure labor"; the bureau indeed met this "want" in ordering freedmen to contract for an entire year. Swayne's statement that the bureau worked to "meet the wants of both freedmen and planters" was a terrible falsehood, one which concealed the extent to which the bureau worked to achieve the planters' goals and oppose those of the freedmen.

The message was not lost on the planters. The Mobile *Register* wrote, "We are enabled to assure the planters that the liberal and enlightened chief of the Freedmen's Bureau, in this State, will co-operate with them and do all in his power to encourage and to press the negro population into the channels of laborious industry. He is engaged now in gathering up all negroes who have no visible means of support."[30]

The bureau did oppose "excesses" within the contract labor system. Swayne criticized the planters' "desire for unchecked control of labor," particularly the notorious Black Codes of 1865. He complained that the new stay law of 1865 was "so framed as to postpone the collection of wages, practically without limit," and he objected to the vagrancy statute of the Alabama Black Code.[31]

If Swayne criticized the Black Codes in principle, the bureau's practice regarding them left much to be desired, at least in the western Alabama black belt. Reporting with pride on how the Demopolis bureau saved freedmen from the Black Codes, the local

29. *Senate Executive Documents*, 39th Cong., 2nd Sess., No. 6, p. 4. A correspondent of McKee's wrote in 1866 that it was necessary to "induce industry" in the blacks: Lowell Morrisson to Robert McKee, April 9, 1866, Robert McKee Papers, Alabama Department of Archives and History. Williamson concludes that the Freedmen's Bureau "forced . . . a large majority of Negroes . . . to take employment on the lands of planters, the direct result of [the] failure to secure the sale of confiscated plantations exclusively to Negro laborers." Williamson, *After Slavery*, 68.

30. Mobile *Daily Register*, quoted in *Florida Times*, December 10, 1865; cited in Theodore Brantner Wilson, *The Black Codes of the South* (University, Ala.: University of Alabama Press, 1965), 58.

31. *Senate Executive Documents*, 39th Cong., 2nd Sess., No. 6, p. 7.

official reported that he arranged for the punishment of accused black vagrants "with a few days' confinement in the city calaboose or with working on the streets"; this was "successful [at keeping] vagrants out of the hands of civil authorities" who could impose a six-month sentence.[32] The bureau's response to the state vagrancy law was to accept the truth of planters' accusations of freedmen, jailing them without a trial on the accusation of their employers. The Freedmen's Bureau in west Alabama thus became a direct enforcer of a repressive labor system, taking the responsibility for punishing freedmen accused by their planter-employers, and then justifying their actions in terms of the freedmen's own best interests.

Such attempts to circumvent the Black Codes in fact went against official bureau policy. A circular order declared that, when freedmen were "absent" from the plantations "for a longer period than one day without just cause, or for an aggregate term of more than five days in one month, the authorities shall proceed against such person as a Vagrant." Thus while General Swayne denounced the vagrancy statutes before congressional committees, his bureau officials assisted in enforcing them. William McFeely rightly observes that "there was no equivalent punishment for planters who might violate the contracts."[33]

The bureau provided assistance to planters who had "problems" with particular black employees. Fleming reports that "when the negroes refused to work, the planters could sometimes hire the Bureau officials to use their influence." A Greene County planter complained to the Freedmen's Bureau about the work of "his" blacks, and brought a bureau agent from Greensboro to his plantation in June, 1865. According to Kolchin, the agent proposed a labor contract which granted the blacks one-eighth of the crop, and "made them sign it with their marks." The element of compulsion must have pleased the planter in question as much as the terms the bureau agent proposed. A planter from west Alabama told a northern reporter that the bureau "let you do pretty much as you liked. They had a mightly good man there—let you whip a nigger if you

32. Bethel, "Freedmen's Bureau in Alabama," 66.
33. McFeely, *Yankee Stepfather*, 154.

liked." The bureau sent federal troops to Sumter County to assist a Democratic sheriff with "some negroes who were reported to be turbulent."[34]

The justifications put forward by the bureau for its actions in such cases at times approached the ridiculous. In March, 1866, the bureau prohibited "the assembling of negroes at night for divine worship or at parties . . . on account of the prevalence of small-pox." To those who were not medical authorities, the bureau explained that "the disease is more easily contracted at night." The prohibition may have been a response to the fear that other, more political "diseases" were also contracted at night meetings. In October, 1866, the Montgomery *Advertiser* revealed to its planter-readers that "efforts are being made to induce the freedmen to move abroad, especially to Peru"; but the paper assured its readers that General Howard had ordered bureau agents to "disapprove of such proceedings."[35] No one would lure Alabama's blacks to Peru while the Freedmen's Bureau was on the job.

Of course not all bureau agents worked closely with local planters. One Alabama agent, shocked at the bureau's pro-planter policy, wrote that his predecessor "worked with a view to please the white citizens, at the expense of, and injustice to, the Freedmen." The previous officials "have invariably given permission to inflict punishment for insolence or idleness, and have detailed soldiers to tie up and otherwise punish the laborers who have, in the opinion of the employers, been 'refractory.'"[36] This evidence seems to confirm to the letter the occurrence of incidents of the type Fleming described. But there was a certain futility in directing such observations to Swayne, who was himself close to the leading planters of the state.

Why were the planters so successful in influencing the bureau? First of all, it was Swayne's policy to appoint "native whites" as

34. Fleming, *Civil War and Reconstruction in Alabama*, 437; Kolchin, *First Freedom*, 52; John Richard Dennett, *The South As It Is, 1865–1866* (New York: The Viking Press, 1965), 291–92; *House Reports*, 43rd Cong., 2nd Sess., No. 262, pp. 34, 1046–64.

35. Montgomery *Daily Advertiser*, March 11, October 19, 1866.

36. Kolchin, *First Freedom*, 33, quoting Geddis to Swayne, September 7, 1865. The Wager Swayne correspondence in the Alabama Department of Archives and History is filled with complaints that Freedmen's Bureau agents were too friendly with former Confeder-

bureau agents whenever possible, and to ignore the "tales of out-
rage" reported by agents who were northerners. Fleming suggests
that the appointment of agents from the locality contributed to
the closeness of the bureau to the local planter elite. The Montgomery *Advertiser* acknowledged the point in 1866, reporting that
Swayne "has made the sherriffs, mayors and civil officers of the
State his representatives. It has followed, as a matter of course,
that the existence of the Freedmen's Bureau has excited less preju-
dice and hostility among the citizens of Alabama than anywhere
else." The Montgomery *Weekly Mail* added, "virtually, the Bureau
for all offensive purposes is a 'dummy' in Alabama." Fleming goes
on to argue that bureau agents who were army officers "took the
side of the white" in conflicts between freedman and planter, particularly those officers who were "West Pointers." Hilary Herbert
explained that the Union officer "learned on the battlefield to respect his foe," which contributed to the "very kindly" relations
between them and the planter former officers.[37] Policy decisions
about the social origins of bureau agents thus appear to have played
a crucial role in shaping the bureau's activities in Alabama.

Those bureau agents in Alabama who were neither local whites
nor army officers met intense and calculated social pressure from
the planter-dominated communities to which they were assigned.
In his 1864 report to the War Department, McKaye warned that
officials in charge of the freedmen "are received into the houses of
the planters and treated with a certain consideration. It is hardly to
be expected that they should resist the influences that are brought
to bear on them or that often, without becoming fully conscious of
it, they should not become the employers' instrument of great injustice and ill-treatment toward . . . colored laborers." The Montgomery *Weekly Mail* explained in 1866, "Union officers . . . who
are gentlemen, are received into the best families in our city. It is

---

ates. See for instance F. S. Cramer et al. to Wager Swayne, April 20, 1867; R. Blair to
Superintendent of Registration, June 23, 1867; Joseph C. Bradley to Wager Swayne, April
26, 28, 1867; John Silsby to Wager Swayne, April 1, 1867, all in Wager Swayne Papers,
Alabama Department of Archives and History.

37. Fleming, *Civil War and Reconstruction in Alabama*, 427; Montgomery *Daily Advertiser*, June 29, 1866; Montgomery *Weekly Mail*, July 5, 1866; Herbert, *Why the Solid South*,
30. See also McFeely, *Yankee Stepfather*, 157.

true that they are taken in on probation. . . . Some [who] keep
company with Negroes . . . could not get into society. . . . But all
who are kind and considered gentlemen . . . will always be met by
kind and considerate southern people." Fleming reports that this
activity of the planters was a calculated and intentional effort to enlist bureau agents on their side. When the bureau opened an office
in Marengo County, Fleming writes, "the white people . . . determined to win their good will. There were 'stag' dinners and feasts,
and the eternal friendship of the officers, with a few exceptions,
was won."[38]

Fleming gives more credit to the persuasive power of stag dinners with the planters than they probably deserved. McFeely's
description of the process is more sensitive and more convincing:
he asks us to imagine the situation of a "young union officer, sent to
a remote town in an unfamiliar section of the country with the task
of mediating between the races." Initially the young officer is ostra-
cized by the white community; then one day the planters offer to
retract their ostracism. "With a nod or brief conversation about
discovered common cousins in Cincinnati, the white planters could
soon discuss the Negroes with the Bureau men. The advice was
expert; the planters had always known them, and, therefore, knew
them best."[39] As McKaye observed in 1864, agents in such a position, perhaps without being fully aware of it, gradually became
"the employers' instrument of great injustice" toward the freedmen.

As the months passed, the social ties between Freedmen's Bureau officials and local planter elite grew closer, particularly at the
top. General Swayne was on "cordial terms" with most members
of the Alabama Constitutional Convention of 1865, which refused
to ratify the Fourteenth Amendment. As Ryland Randolph wrote
to black belt planter spokesman Robert McKee in 1868, "you
either know, or may have friends who know . . . many of the U.S.
officers now in Selma." And an official investigation of the bureau

38. McKaye, *Mastership*; Montgomery *Weekly Mail*, April 26, 1866; Fleming, *Civil War and Reconstruction in Alabama*, 449–50. See also T. Harry Williams, "An Analysis of Some Reconstruction Attitudes," *Journal of Southern History*, XII (1946), 469–86.
39. McFeely, *Yankee Stepfather*, 158–59.

in Alabama reported that several agents were "engaged in operating plantations they had bought or leased." The Montgomery *Advertiser* understood the significance of such acts: "if the right sort of men, connected with the Bureau or any other Department, conclude to identify themselves with the South . . . , we perceive no substantial reason . . . why they may not do so."[40] As usual, the *Advertiser* confused "the South" with "the planter class." When Freedmen's Bureau officials not only socialized with the planter elite, but actually became planters themselves, was it any wonder that they would ally with the planter class against the freedmen?

A letter from Florence, Alabama, to the *New York Times*, in March, 1866, summed up the situation with startling brevity: "the negroes want the Bureau abolished so far as it relates to contracts." And a black man campaigning for adoption of the Radical constitution in Uniontown in February, 1868, told his black audience, "The Bureau never did anything but cheat you." This view received official endorsement in August, 1866, when Generals J. B. Steedman and J. S. Fullerton reported that the Alabama Freedmen's Bureau "considers a labor contract more sacred than a marriage contract. . . . What is the difference to the Negro whether he is sold . . . for 30 years to 30 masters, or for 30 years to 1 master? The system of contracts . . . enforced by the Bureau is simply slavery in a new form."[41]

Steedman and Fullerton exaggerated. The bureau's free labor ideology made it thoroughly antagonistic to slavery. Nevertheless it supported planter interests in some crucial respects. The profoundly bourgeois conception on which bureau policy was based regarded the lash of slavery to be both inhumane and inefficient as a form of labor discipline. The discipline of the market economy itself, however, was not only necessary, but a desirable way of shaping a free laboring class. Freedom the bureau understood to

40. Bethel, "Freedman's Bureau in Alabama," 57; *New York Times*, August 10, 1866; Ryland Randolph to Robert McKee, April 23, 1868, in Robert McKee Papers, Alabama Department of Archives and History; Montgomery *Daily Advertiser*, May 25, 1866. See also New York *Herald*, June 15, 1866; Montgomery *Weekly Mail*, May 24, 1866.

41. *New York Times*, March 12, 1866; Tuscaloosa *Independent Monitor*, February 19, 1868; Montgomery *Daily Advertiser*, August 14, 1866. On the Steedman-Fullerton report, see McFeely, *Yankee Stepfather*, 247–58.

be in large part freedom to enter into a wage contract with a planter; and the free man has an obligation to fulfill his terms of the contract. As for the planters, the bureau insisted that they too needed to fulfill their contracts, and to learn to use the market rather than the lash to discipline labor. The bureau and the planters, whatever their other differences, agreed that free labor was still labor, on the plantations and under the planter class.

Legal Represssion: The Black Codes

The passage of the Black Codes was the planters' attempt to end the "labor shortage" by legal means—parallel to their informal effort to enlist the aid of the Freedmen's Bureau in achieving the same goal. The Black Code of Alabama included two key laws intended to assure the planters a reliable supply of labor—a vagrancy law, and a law against the "enticement" of laborers. The "Vagrant Law" defined vagrants to include "stubborn servants . . . a laborer or servant who loiters away his time, or refuses to comply with any contract . . . without just cause." It provided as punishment for such hideous crimes a fine of $50 plus court costs, and allowed judges to "hire out" vagrants until their fines were paid, with a six-month limit.[42]

The House version of this bill provided for a bounty of five dollars to be paid to "any person making an arrest in pursuance of the provisions of this act," and included a clause which required that a laborer convicted of violating the law "shall forfeit his wages for the entire year." Thus a planter who turned in his laborers for vagrancy would get to keep their share of the crop and also receive a five dollar bounty from the state—at which point the judge could "hire out" the laborers to the same planter who turned them in. The House bill permitted the authorities to "cause to be inflicted on such vagrant 39 lashes upon his or her bare back." The legislature provided for the printing of ten thousand copies of the vagrancy bill "for the use of the country"—to be distributed to planters for them to read to their laborers.[43]

42. *Acts of Alabama 1865–1866*, 119–21.
43. *Alabama House Journal 1865–1866*, 99, 143–44, 601; New York *Times*, January 28, 1866.

W. E. B. Du Bois wrote that if a freedman were "caught wandering in search of work, and thus unemployed and without a home," under the vagrancy laws he could be "whipped and sold into slavery." The vagrancy acts gave local officials the power to arrest any freedman who did not have a labor contract. At harvest time, when planters needed more field hands, local authorities enforced the vagrancy laws with particular thoroughness, according to an authority. Even Swayne described the law as the expression of a "desire for unchecked control of labor."[44]

The second law, passed explicitly "for the purpose of regulating labor," made it a crime to "hire, entice away, or induce to leave the service of another" any laborer who had already contracted to work for another. The penalty for those who "induce laborers . . . to abandon their contracts, or employ such without the consent of their original employer," was a fine of $50 to $500. If a laborer was found working for "another," "that fact shall be *prima facie* evidence that such person is guilty of violating this act," unless the new employer "shall upon being notified of such antecedent contract, forthwith discharge said laborer."[45]

The Montgomery *Advertiser* explained, "We hear complaints that extensive operations were attempted with some success . . . to seduce hands away from their employers. . . . We warn our readers all that this will prove a destructive business, if persisted in, and that it is indespensable to the common welfare that everybody should unite in the creation of a strong public reprehension of the practice. . . . Let it go on and no planter . . . will be sure of a day's work ahead, and the whole community will be constantly engaged in the business of undermining and overbidding each other."

Once the anti-enticement bill was passed, the *Advertiser* printed a reproduction and urged its readers to "preserve it"—to clip and post it on the plantation. The state legislature provided that

44. Du Bois, *Black Reconstruction*, 130; William Cohen, "Negro Involuntary Servitude in the South, 1865–1940: A Preliminary Analysis," *Journal of Southern History*, XLII (1976), 47, 50; *Senate Executive Documents*, 39th Cong., 2nd Sess., No. 6, p. 7. See also Carl Schurz's testimony in *Senate Executive Documents*, 39th Cong., 1st Sess., No. 2, and *Congressional Globe*, 39th Cong., 1st Sess., Pt. 1, p. 94; and Huntsville *Advocate*, quoted in Montgomery *Alabama State Journal*, October 28, 1870.

45. *Acts of Alabama 1865–1866*, 111–12. The progress of the bill can be followed in *Alabama House Journal 1865–1866*, 139, 196, 295.

10,000 copies of this bill be printed. Fleming indicates that the purpose of the massive publicity surrounding the law was "to scare the negroes into work."[46] A planter wrote to Selma editor Robert McKee,

> I was gratified to see the sharp terms in which yr paper condemns the practice of unprincipled planters who entice, from other planters, the ignorant freedmen who are already under contract to those others. The practice of such men is to send negroes who live with them to persuade negroes to come over from other plantations to theirs and there they give them, whether by fair promises and every unfair means to induce the negroes to forfeit their contract and to come and live with them. . . . This villainous practice by unprincipled men, . . . this illegal course, if persisted in, will break up the industrial interests of the country by ruining the labor we now have.[47]

The law prohibiting enticement of labor was aimed not at the blacks, but at the planters; it was intended to reduce conflict within the planter class. It was also intended to stop agents from Mississippi seeking to recruit Alabama blacks. Mississippi planters during the late sixties were opening up new plantation areas in the western delta regions of the state, and had a severe shortage of black laborers there. They needed blacks not only to raise cotton, but also to drain swamps, build levees, clear cropland, and construct roads. Not only did private agents of Mississippi planters recruit in Alabama, but Mississippi established an official state bureau of immigration which sent agents into Alabama. Whitelaw Reid, traveling through the eastern part of the Alabama black belt in 1865, saw a Mississippian offering Alabama blacks fifteen dollars a month to come to a new Mississippi delta plantation; Reid reports that 55 were signed up, and that the agent could have hired as many more as he wanted.[48]

46. Montgomery *Daily Advertiser*, March 20, 22, 1866; *Acts of Alabama 1865–1866*, 601; Fleming, *Civil War and Reconstruction in Alabama*, 378.

47. Ben E. Grey to Robert McKee, September 4, 1870, in Robert McKee Papers, Alabama Department of Archives and History.

48. Reid, *After the War*, 563. A subsequent effort was the Emigrant-Agent Law, which levied prohibitively high license taxes on interstate labor brokers seeking black workers: *Acts of Alabama 1878–1879*, 205, amended in *Acts of Alabama 1880–1881*, 162; declared unconstitutional in *Joseph v. Randolph*, 71 Alabama 499 (1882), new statute written in

The planters' attempt to control black labor by legal means seems to have backfired. Even Fleming found the Black Code provisions for the regulation of labor to have been "carelessly drawn" and "technically unconstitutional." Whitelaw Reid described their effect with his usual insight and economy: the Black Code was "like the patent rat-trap. Nobody could make a safer contrivance. Rats couldn't possibly get out of it. The only difficulty was that they declined to go in."[49] The planters had proposed labor regulations whose repressive character was undeniable; the freedmen, however, refused to end the "labor shortage," and some planters, increasingly desperate to preserve the large-scale plantation organization based on wage labor, turned to terror, to the Ku Klux Klan.

The Social Base of the Klan

The extent to which the black belt Klan was an instrument of the planter class, rather than of poor whites, is often overlooked. The two white groups had conflicting interests, and the Klan in the black belt worked in pursuit of the goals of the planters. The congressional investigation of the Klan focused on its political use of terror against Republicans; subsequent interpretations have tended to emphasize this evidence. In so doing, they have underemphasized the role Klan terror played in creating and perpetuating the South's repressive plantation labor system.

The Ku Klux Klan was "more widespread and virulent" in the black belt of western Alabama in 1869 and 1870 than in any other part of the South, except perhaps for northern Alabama. Sumter and Greene counties alone accounted for 34 percent of Alabama murders attributed to the Klan by the congressional investigation.

Alabama General Laws 1903, 344–45: Cohen, "Involuntary Servitude," 39; see also Roark, *Masters Without Slaves*, 135–36. The enticement laws were also used in the immediate postwar period against blacks seeking to reunite families, especially parents seeking children held under abusive "apprenticeship" laws. Gutman, *Black Family*, 402–12.

49. Fleming, *Civil War and Reconstruction in Alabama*, 382, n 3; Reid, *After the War*, 291. The vagrancy act was repealed: *Acts of Alabama 1866–1867*, 504. See also William Warren Rogers, *The One-Gallused Rebellion: Agrarianism in Alabama, 1865–1896* (Baton Rouge: Louisiana State University Press, 1970), 8; Wilson, *Black Codes*, 76–77. The enticement act, however, was amended and "continued into the era of World War II and beyond"—Cohen, "Involuntary Servitude," 36, citing *Code of Alabama Recompiled 1958*, Titles 26-331 to 26-333.

Klan leader Ryland Randolph named Perry, Hale, and Marengo counties as targets for "Ku-Klux reformation" in 1871.[50]

Fleming, always an astute defender of the planter class, carefully distinguished between the hill country Klan and its black belt counterpart in his discussion of the Klan's social base in Alabama. Outside the black belt, he wrote, the Klan contained "a large element" of the "poorer whites. . . . this was generally true of all secret orders of regulators in the white counties from 1865 to 1875." The hill country whites used Klan terror to drive blacks off the land, opening it to white small farmers. But the social base and strategy of the Klan in the black belt was "exactly the opposite," Fleming wrote; there, "the planters preferred Negro labor, and never drove out the blacks."[51]

Planters used Klan terror to keep blacks from leaving the plantation regions, to get them to work, and keep them at work, in the cotton fields. Other sources support Fleming's interpretation that "the best men" were members of the black belt Klan. John L. Hunnicutt claims to have organized the Klan in the black belt of western Alabama; he wrote in his memoirs that he did so at the request of "some of the best citizens." Richard Busteed, a U.S. district judge for Alabama, told the congressional investigating committee that "gentlemen of education and intelligence . . . compose the class called Ku-Klux." Pearson J. Glover, another Marengo planter, denied knowledge of the Klan in the 1871 investigation, but admitted to a congressional committee in 1875 that the original organizer was a "prominent" resident of the black belt, whom he refused to name. When a black registrar of voters was murdered in Greensboro in 1867, and the murderer's accomplice was captured, his bond was "signed by 15 of the wealthiest citizens of Greensboro." Allen Trelease concludes from his own exhaustive study that the Klan in west Alabama "included some

50. Allen W. Trelease, *White Terror: The Ku Klux Klan Conspiracy and Southern Reconstruction* (New York: Harper & Row, 1971), 246; Tuscaloosa *Independent Monitor*, January 31, 1871. For a Klan raid on Demopolis, see Montgomery *Alabama State Journal*, June 23, 1871. See also Otto H. Olsen, "The Ku Klux Klan: A Study in Reconstruction Politics and Propaganda," *North Carolina Historical Review*, XXXIX (1962), especially pp. 358–59, which describes planter support for the Klan.

51. Fleming, *Civil War and Reconstruction in Alabama*, 660.

of the best citizens," and that "upper-class elements were apt to be involved."[52]

Although the Klan was used to intimidate Republican voters, to drive out black educators, to destroy black organizations, and to control black "crime," the extent to which Klan terror in the black belt contributed directly to the control of black labor has not been fully appreciated. One of the first tasks of the Klan was to use terror to prevent emigration of plantation laborers out of the black belt. Once this had been accomplished, its next task was to apply terror to blacks who refused to work, or whose work the planters found wanting. Of course the Klan was not the only weapon the planters used to discourage black emigration and force blacks to work. Terror was one means among many of achieving these goals; it stood as a last resort when more legitimate political methods, including the Freedmen's Bureau and the Black Codes, failed; and doubtlessly some planters had a greater taste for violence and terrorism than others.

William B. Jones, Marengo planter and mayor of Demopolis, reported in 1866 that "colored people from Sumter [county] . . . got together once to emigrate, and the disguised men went to them and told them if they undertook it they would be killed on their way." Jones explained that "that was to prevent them from leaving the county, and prevent the county from being deprived of their labor." A congressional committee was told that "the bulldozers killed off all the colored men that they knew intended going to Kansas. . . . more than a hundred men were killed" in one county. In spite of such terror, many blacks did flee from western Alabama, particularly to Mississippi, where Reconstruction was more radical and more long-lasting. Trelease reports that "predatory white gangs" from Alabama crossed the state line in pursuit of such emigrants, seeking to bring them back "on criminal charges, or, as in most cases, on charges of violating labor contracts by running away." Deputy sheriffs were apparently involved, but they "never

52. *Ibid.*, 667; John L. Hunnicutt, *Reconstruction in West Alabama: The Memoirs of John L. Hunnicutt* (Tuscaloosa: Confederate Publishing Co., 1959), 56–58; *House Reports*, 42nd Cong., 2nd Sess., No. 22, p. 323; *House Reports*, 43rd Cong., 2nd Sess., No. 262, pp. 882–83; J. C. Cadle to Wager Swayne, June 25, 1867, in Wager Swayne Papers, Alabama Department of Archives and History; Trelease, *White Terror*, 83, 307.

bothered with the formalities of the extradition; in effect they were kidnappers."[53]

Fleming, with typical directness, listed among the "causes of the ku klux movement" the fact that "people in the Black Belt felt that labor must be regulated in some way." The Klan was necessary, Marengo planter F. S. Lyon told the congressional committee, to counter the fact that blacks "are told by some . . . that planters do not pay sufficient wages for their labor." The *Rural Alabamian* agreed that, as long as labor was in short supply, blacks would continue to seek contracts providing "shelter and bread for the year, work or no work"—which made coercion necessary. The Klan was "intended principally for the negroes who failed to work," according to William H. Forney, a black belt lawyer. As early as 1866, masked bands in the black belt "punished Negroes whose landlords had complained of them."[54]

The close relationship between Klan activity and planter interests was traced in some detail by John H. Wager, the Freedmen's Bureau agent for Huntsville. "The Ku-Klux always remain quiet during what is called the planting season," he told the congressional committee. "They wanted to get the crop in the ground, and anything to punish these men they would reserve until after that was done. . . . they would reserve the punishment so as not to interfere with the labor of the negroes."[55]

The Klan terrorized a white teacher at a black belt school on Pearson J. Glover's Marengo County plantation, in one of many such incidents there. The congressional committee interpreted this as evidence of white opposition to educating blacks, but Glover himself had a different view. He told the committee he had hired the teacher himself in what proved to be a successful effort to attract black laborers to his plantation. Glover believed the Klan raid was the consequence of the "jealousy" of neighboring planters of his "obtaining labor by furnishing school facilities." In seeking to

53. *House Reports*, 42nd Cong., 2nd Sess., No. 22, p. 1466; *Senate Documents*, 46th Cong., 2nd Sess., No. 693, p. 413; Trelease, *White Terror*, 290.

54. Fleming, *Civil War and Reconstruction in Alabama*, 654; *House Reports*, 42nd Cong., 2nd Sess., No. 22, pp. 1411, 487; *Rural Alabamian*, II (1873), 453–54, quoted in Gilmour, "Other Emancipation," 146; Trelease, *White Terror*, 81.

55. *House Reports*, 42nd Cong., 2nd Sess., No. 22, p. 935.

"obtain and retain labor," Glover explained, he "offended those from whom this labor was taken," and they retaliated by kidnapping and whipping the white teacher.[56] The lesson of the incident was that the planters' primary concern was the "labor shortage" rather than black education.

The ideology which justified Klan terror was expressed most clearly in Alabama in the pages of the Tuscaloosa *Independent Monitor*, edited by the fanatical Ryland Randolph. Randolph declared he would "thank God for another war if it re-established slavery," arguing that "negroes, as bondsmen, were happier, more sleek and greasy-looking, and better-clothed, than they are now. We never hear the ringing horse-laughs . . . that formerly marked their *sans souci* existence." In another issue, Randolph examined the "cowardly, instinctive hatred, on the part of the tailless baboon race, for the whites, that can never be gotten rid of till the race itself shall be gotten rid of." He did not overlook the importance of the control of black labor as an element of terrorist ideology: "all negroes who . . . with docility, fall into traces, should be rewarded with plenty of work, porridge and kind treatment," he wrote. For the boldness and clarity of his justification of Klan terror, Randolph was elected to the state legislature.[57]

Needless to say, Randolph was not alone in dispensing his brand of invective. The ever-respectable Montgomery *Advertiser* often printed articles like the one which argued that "the negro's inherent sloth seems to communicate itself to domestic animals that live with him. His pigs are too lazy to root, his sneaking dogs won't bark, . . . his cabin looks more like a deserted dog kennel than a human dwelling." The Eutaw *Whig*, noting that northern white women were coming south to teach, wrote, "When they come the buck niggers will welcome them with ebony arms, to African couches, and then the next generation of Radicals in the South . . .

56. *Ibid.*, 1342.
57. Tuscaloosa *Independent Monitor*, Montgomery *Alabama State Journal*, quoted in Trelease, *White Terror*, 253–54, 259, xl-xli. Randolph was supported by, among others, the conservative Montgomery *Mail* and the black belt's *Wilcox News and Pacificator*; he also had a warm correspondence with Selma editor Robert McKee. See Montgomery *Mail, Wilcox News and Pacificator*, in Tuscaloosa *Independent Monitor*, March 28, 1871; Ryland Randolph to Robert McKee, April 23, 1868, May 7, 1873, in Robert McKee Papers, Alabama Department of Archives and History.

will smell only half as bad as the present generation."[58] It was cultured discourse of this kind, appearing in the most respected journals of the planter class, that was intended to justify Klan terror.

From Gang Labor to Sharecropping

In spite of the momentous political events taking place in 1867 and 1868—the attempted impeachment of the president and the beginning of Radical Reconstruction—Alabama planters were preoccupied first of all with their attempts to revive the plantation system. "The labor question is discussed on the stump, in the press, wherever two or three are gathered together," the Selma *Southern Argus* reported. On another occasion the *Argus* explained to those for whom it was not obvious that "in speaking of labor, we mean negro labor."[59] The discussions increasingly came to one conclusion: the attempt had failed to preserve the plantation as a single, large-scale unit, cultivated by labor gangs paid in wages. The planters in increasing numbers were dividing their plantations into small plots, and assigning each to a single family, which was paid with a share of the crop; the old slave quarters were broken up and replaced with cabins scattered across the plantation.

The planters' abandonment of gang labor was a major concession to the freedmen. The establishment of sharecropping as the prevailing organization of agricultural production was a consequence of the struggle of the freedmen against the gang system. The Selma *Southern Argus* admitted it explicitly: sharecropping was "an unwilling concession to the freedman's desire to become a proprietor. . . . It is not a voluntary association from similarity of aims and interests."[60]

The "labor shortage" was a leading cause of this momentous decision by the planters, but it was not the only one. A series of bad cotton crops in 1865, 1866, and 1867 contributed to the planters' doubts that the plantations could be reorganized profitably on

58. Montgomery *Daily Advertiser*, August 16, 1868; Eutaw *Whig*, quoted in Demopolis *Southern Republican*, June 6, 1870.

59. Selma *Southern Argus*, June 23, 1869, May 12, 1870.

60. Ransom and Sutch, *One Kind of Freedom*, Chap. 5; Selma *Southern Argus*, March 17, 1870. See also Richard W. Griffin, "Problems of the Southern Cotton Planters After the Civil War," *Georgia Historical Quarterly*, XXIX (1955), 103–17.

the basis of gang labor. The Radical constitutional convention met in December, 1867, and the Radical state constitution was ratified in February, 1868. The first Radical legislature gave agricultural laborers a lien on the crop in 1868.[61] This could only have discouraged the planters further; giving the laborer the first lien meant that, in case of a dispute over wages, the laborer's claim had precedence over that of the planter. And the freedmen's most common complaint, it should be recalled, was fraudulent division of the crop.

Once the planters accepted the breakup of the antebellum plantation into small units, why did they not simply rent them? The key issue was the planter's control over his tenants. The Montgomery *Advertiser* admitted that the crucial question was how "the employers can more efficiently control their operations." The Selma *Southern Argus* agreed, observing that if the black was permitted to rent, "the power to control him is gone."[62] The wage system gave the planters a maximum of control over the daily activities of the freedmen, and it was precisely to this extensive control that the freedmen objected. Once the hopes of a distribution of land to freedmen had faded, the freedmen apparently settled on renting as the next best alternative, the one involving the least supervision and control. But the planter who rented out his land had little power over the daily activities of his tenants; his principal means of control was to refuse to renew their leases, to evict—an all-or-nothing proposition. If renting was to become the basic form of agricultural tenancy, the blacks would be given an unprecedented amount of freedom and autonomy to organize their time and labor as they saw fit.

The planter press analyzed the perils of renting in precisely this way. For the blacks to "farm on a small scale for themselves" as renters would lead to a "great scarcity of hands," the Montgomery

61. U.S. Department of Agriculture, *Report of the Commissioner . . . For the Year 1867* (Washington, D.C.: Government Printing Office, 1868), 417; Kolchin, *First Freedom*, 45. For parallel political developments in South Carolina, see Thomas Holt, *Black Over White: Negro Political Leadership in South Carolina during Reconstruction* (Urbana: University of Illinois Press, 1977), 157.

62. Montgomery *Daily Advertiser*, February 6, 1869; Selma *Southern Argus*, February 17, 1870; see also Roark, *Masters Without Slaves*, 142.

Advertiser argued in early 1869; "any man of sense knows how this will result." "Some of the land-owners have rented lands to ne-groes," the *Advertiser* reported on another occasion. "This is cer-tainly ruinous to the general interest." The Selma *Southern Argus* argued early in 1870 that field labor was in short supply in part because "short-sighted landowners" were renting to blacks.[63]

The planters' argument was that black laborers required super-vision because they were lazy and incompetent workers. Share-cropping contracts gave the planter specified rights to supervise the labor of his tenants, since he was "investing" his own capital in the crop as well as renting his land. The planters' claim that blacks were incapable of labor without supervision was an ideologi-cal justification of their own existence as a class and of their right to the surplus they acquired.[64]

Not all the planters accepted the defeat represented by the aban-donment of the gang system of plantation organization. The Selma *Southern Argus* argued in 1870, "No railroad or factory or company of merchants shares with its employees, why should planters?" The *Advertiser* itself predicted initially that the planters would never accept sharecropping. "The farmers who are cropping on shares with freedmen . . . will, as a general rule, abandon the plan in another year," the paper wrote late in 1867. In 1871, a statewide planters' convention argued that "now is the time . . . to discard the ruinous policy of doing a partnership business in the way of planting." Abandoning sharecropping was desirable, because un-der it the black "is not so nearly under the control of the white man and feels his independence more." The Selma *Southern Ar-gus* and other planter newspapers argued that, rather than give in to the freedmen's demand for more autonomy, the planter class should give up cotton, diversify crops, introduce stock-raising and

63. Montgomery *Daily Advertiser*, February 11, 25, 1869; Selma *Southern Argus*, Feb-ruary 3, 1870. See also Chester McArthur Destler, "David Dickson's System of Farming and the Agrarian Revolution in the Deep South, 1850–1885," *Agricultural History*, XXXI (1957), 30–39.

64. This claim has recently been restated as an economic fact in Robert Higgs, *Competi-tion and Coercion: Blacks in the American Economy, 1865–1914*, Hoover Institution Publi-cation P 163 (Cambridge: Cambridge University Press, 1977), 121, 72, and in Joseph D. Reid, Jr., "Sharecropping as an Understandable Market Response: The Post-Bellum South," *Journal of Economic History*, XXXIII (1973), 127.

labor-saving machinery—all of which would reduce the demand
for labor, the blacks' source of strength in their conflicts with the
planters.[65]

Although the move to sharecropping represented a substantial
defeat for the planters, it was not without benefit for them. The
Advertiser pointed to the benefits of the labor repressive aspects
of the system, in which there was "no inducement to change homes
at the close of each year. As a consequence of localized labor, the
Conservative sentiment of each neighborhood would be strengthened and stimulated . . . securing a more peaceable and well-
ordered system of labor." Sharecropping offered the additional advantage of increasing the labor force considerably in comparison
with the gang system; by making the family the unit of labor rather
than the wage hand, it brought women and children back into the
fields. Somers was among the first to record this advantage for the
planters.[66]

Sharecropping and Economic Development

Thus the origins of sharecropping, the basis of postwar southern
agriculture, lie in class conflict, not in the abstract logic of the free
market system. To the extent that sharecropping gave the laborers
more freedom from the close supervision reminiscent of slavery, it
was a concession wrung out of the planters. But sharecropping was
established as a repressive system of labor allocation and control,
based as it was on informal agreements among the planters to limit
competition for labor, on state laws which established legal obstacles to the free market in labor, and on the intermittent use of terror against laborers.[67]

65. Selma *Southern Argus*, February 3, 10, May 12, 1870; Montgomery *Daily Advertiser*, September 13, 1867, January 24, 1871. As late as 1875 the *Southern Argus* continued
to argue that wages should be substituted for sharecropping and that diversification would
make this possible.

66. Montgomery *Daily Advertiser*, October 14, 25, 1867; Somers, *Southern States*,
146–47, 397.

67. The opposite interpretation, that sharecropping arose out of the rational functioning
of the free market system, is argued in Higgs, *Competition and Coercion*; Reid, "Sharecropping as an Understandable Market Response"; Joseph D. Reid, Jr., "Sharecropping in
History and Theory," *Agricultural History*, XLIX (1975), 426–40; and Stephen DeCanio,
Agriculture in the Postbellum South (New Haven: Yale University Press, 1975). For a powerful critique, see Harold D. Woodman, "Sequel to Slavery: The New History Views the

This coercive mode of labor control gave southern agriculture its distinctive character. Sharecropping was a form of "bound" labor, with restrictions on the free market in labor that did not prevail in fully developed capitalist societies such as that of the North. There, the market mechanism allocated "free" labor; capitalists competed freely for labor, and laborers were free to move in response to better offers. The sharecropper was not fully free in this sense, and thus was distinct from both the northern proletarian and the free capitalist farmer. Similarly, the planters' more directly coercive methods of labor allocation and control marked them off from a genuine bourgeoisie.[68]

In this respect the contrast between sharecropping and the gang system of the immediate postwar plantation is illuminating. In 1865 and 1866, those who provided only their labor were paid wages in the form of a share of the crop, but they labored in gangs, under overseers, on a plantation that was organized as a single centralized productive unit. The division of this centralized unit into small tenant farms, the substitution of family labor for gang labor, the end of constant supervision by overseers and the substitution of intermittent visits by the landlord himself, the loss of economies of scale and the end of centralized management— all these marked, not the creation of large-scale, thoroughly capitalist farms, but precisely a move away from a mature capitalist organization of agriculture.

Postbellum South," *Journal of Southern History*, XLIII (1977), 525–35; also Michael Schwartz, *Radical Protest and Social Structure: The Southern Farmers' Alliance and Cotton Tenancy, 1880–1890* (New York: Academic Press, 1976), 23–25; Jay R. Mandle, *The Roots of Black Poverty: The Southern Plantation Economy After the Civil War* (Durham: Duke University Press, 1978), Chap. 2; and Gavin Wright, "Comment on Papers by Reid, Ransom and Sutch, and Higgs," *Journal of Economic History*, XXXIII (1973), 170–76. For a particularly interesting interpretation of the irrationality of sharecropping in this period, see Gavin Wright and Howard C. Kunreuther, "Cotton, Corn and Risk in the Nineteenth Century," *Journal of Economic History*, XXXV (1975), 526–51, which has been challenged in Robert McGuire and Robert Higgs, "Cotton, Corn, and Risk in the Nineteenth Century: Another View," *Explorations in Economic History*, XIV (1977), 167–82; this in turn has been convincingly refuted in Wright and Kunreuther, "Cotton, Corn and Risk in the Nineteenth Century: A Reply," *Explorations in Economic History*, XIV (1977), 183–95.

68. Thaddeus Stevens at the end of his life denounced sharecropping as a new "system of peonage" which threatened to keep the freedmen permanently under the planters' control: *Congressional Globe*, 40th Cong., 2nd Sess., 108, 1966, 2214; Eric Foner, "Thaddeus

What resulted was distinct from genuinely capitalist agricultural development in that it was not based on growing mechanization, an increasing division of labor, and a substitution of capital-intensive for labor-intensive operations. Capitalist development consists of systematic increases in labor productivity, a qualitative transformation of production based on the investment of surplus in technological advances. Indeed, this is precisely the developmental path taken by the Northwest during this period: the family farm, owned by a small entrepreneur, steadily increasing his efficiency by investing in technological improvements; the region growing in prosperity and increasing its population in a way that provided a strong market for manufactured goods and created an expanding commercial network. This mutual development of productivity in agriculture and industry is the classic capitalist road to development that had been blazed by England in the seventeenth and eighteenth centuries, and followed by the northern United States. It was not the road the New South was taking.

For the dominant class in the immediate postwar South, there were two possible responses to a shortage of labor. One was to develop capital-intensive methods of production. The alternative to this classic capitalist road was to rely on the coercion of labor, to extract a larger surplus not by increasing productivity through improved technology, but by squeezing more out of the laborers. Because this intensification was likely to provoke resistance and flight, this second route required formal restrictions on labor mobility, laws that tied the workers to the land and restricted their access to alternative employment. This second route is not necessarily economically stagnant; it is capable of bringing economic development, but in a manner distinct from the classic capitalist method. Barrington Moore, mindful of European developments, has called it the "Prussian Road" to modern society: economic

Stevens, Confiscation, and Reconstruction," in Stanley Elkins and Eric McKitrick (eds.), *The Hofstadter Aegis: A Memorial* (New York: Alfred A. Knopf, 1974), 181. For discussions of the occupational structure of the black community, which demonstrate that not all blacks were sharecroppers, see especially Holt, *Black Over White*, 43–94; Gutman, *Black Family*, 442–43, 478–83, and also Williamson, *After Slavery*, 160–61, and Kolchin, *First Freedom*, 128–50.

development that preserves and intensifies the authoritarian and repressive elements of traditional social relations.[69]

The possibility that the South could take the classic capitalist road was not ignored in the immediate postwar period. Some of the most astute southerners pushed for precisely such a solution to the problems of postwar agricultural adjustment. The Selma *Southern Argus*, for one, argued tirelessly during the late 1860s that the planters should end their reliance on labor-intensive methods of producing cotton, and instead diversify crops, introduce stock raising, and substitute labor-saving machinery for black tenant labor.

The planter class, rooted as it was in the antebellum elite, chose the other solution, the Prussian Road. The Black Codes passed in 1865–1867 expressed that choice; temporarily abolished by the Radicals, many were resurrected by the planter regimes that regained power in the seventies.[70] And once the institutions of a labor-repressive system of agriculture had been established, the planters had little incentive to mechanize or introduce more rational techniques to increase efficiency and productivity. Thus while wheat-growing capitalist farmers in the North were transforming their productive techniques with a technological revolution, southern sharecroppers in 1900 relied on hand tools and mule power; the result was southern economic stagnation, as crop outputs, yields per acre, and agricultural technology changed little from year to year.[71]

Too much of the recent debate has treated southern economic and political development as separate questions. The South's characteristic poverty and political oppression arose out of the same social relations: the Prussian Road, with its dominant planter class

69. Moore, *Social Origins*, 459–67. See also Robert Brenner, "Agrarian Class Structure and Economic Development in Pre-Industrial Europe," *Past & Present*, No. 70 (1976), 30–74, and Brenner, "The Origins of Capitalist Development: A Critique of Neo-Smithian Marxism," *New Left Review*, No. 104 (1977), especially pp. 31–33, 67–82. For parallel developments in Latin America, see C. Vann Woodward, "Emancipations and Reconstructions: A Comparative Study," XIII International Congress of Historical Sciences, Moscow (August 16–23, 1970).

70. Cohen, "Negro Involuntary Servitude," 35.

71. Ransom and Sutch, *One Kind of Freedom*, 175–76.

and its labor-repressive system of agricultural production, which posed a major obstacle not only to economic development, but also to democracy, to the political freedoms present in the North and so glaringly absent from the South.

Part II

THE MERCHANT CHALLENGE

3

Merchants and the Politics of Agriculture

Although the postwar pattern of landholding reveals the persistence of the old elite families in the new planter class, the structural basis of their wealth and power had been altered. This metamorphosis was a consequence of the creation of new economic levers for plantation agriculture, above all the establishment of the crop lien for supplies as the basis of financing postwar cotton production on the tenant plantation. And, since the liens were held by merchants, the crop lien system gave the merchants an opportunity to challenge planter profits, planter control of the black labor force, and, eventually, planter land ownership itself—the structural basis of the planters' existence as a class.

With the collapse of southern banks and the decline of the cotton factors who had marketed the antebellum cotton crop, postwar planters had difficulty obtaining the credit necessary to finance the crop, to buy the seed, implements, and provisions necessary for their tenant farmers. The rural merchant, linked to northern wholesalers and cotton manufacturers, was the one most able to extend the necessary credit to the tenant. The legal provisions for financing the postwar cotton crop were established in crop lien laws, legislated in all southern states at the war's end. Alabama's, passed early in 1866, did not distinguish between planters who advanced supplies to tenants, and merchants; the law gave a lien on the crop to "any person" who advanced provisions, tools, or draft animals to a farmer or tenant. A subsequent amendment gave merchants the same "rights and remedies" landlords had to collect from tenants.[1]

1. *Acts of Alabama 1865–1866*, 44; *Acts of Alabama 1866–1867*, 211.

Thus the crop lien appeared as the universal basis of credit in the rural South: a tenant would pledge his crop as security against supplies advanced during the course of the year. The tenant signed a crop lien contract with a supply merchant at the beginning of the season, and did business only with that merchant; the merchant kept an account of the tenant's purchases, and, when the crop was harvested, the merchant took the portion he determined was due him. The tenant also owed rent to his landlord, for which cash tenants paid cash, and sharecroppers paid a share of the crop. Two-thirds of the crop went to the cropper if he provided his own tools, stock, seed, fertilizers, and other necessities, half if the landlord did.[2]

The alternative to merchants supplying the black tenantry was for each planter to supply his own tenants, at a plantation store. The planter could obtain store stock directly from wholesalers, and thus avoid dealing with local supply merchants. Planters with such stores usually required that their tenants make all of their purchases there; some planters paid their laborers in scrip good only at the plantation store. Other planters loaned cash to their tenants

2. Harold D. Woodman, *King Cotton and His Retainers* (Lexington, Ky.: University of Kentucky Press, 1967), Chap. 24. Some of the numerous descriptions and analyses of the crop lien system include Oscar Zeichner, "The Transition from Slave to Free Agricultural Labor in the Southern States," *Agricultural History*, XII (1939), 23; Chester McArthur Destler, "The Post-Bellum South: Some Letters and Documents," *Georgia Historical Quarterly*, XLVI (1962), 84; Jacqueline P. Bull, "The General Merchant in the Economic History of the New South," *Journal of Southern History*, XXVIII (1952), 37–59; Theodore Saloutos, "Southern Agriculture and the Problems of Readjustment, 1865–1877," *Agricultural History*, XXX (1956), 58–76; Thomas D. Clark, "Imperfect Competition in the Southern Retail Trade after 1865," *Journal of Economic History*, III (1943), Supplement, 40; George L. Anderson, "The South and the Problems of Post–Civil War Finance," *Journal of Southern History*, IX (1943), 181–95. On Alabama, see William Warren Rogers, *The One-Gallused Rebellion: Agrarianism in Alabama, 1865–1896* (Baton Rouge: Louisiana State University Press, 1970), 14–21; Peter Kolchin, *First Freedom: The Response of Alabama's Blacks to Emancipation and Reconstruction* (Westport, Conn.: Greenwood Publishing Company, 1972), 30–55; Robert Gilmour, "The Other Emancipation: Studies in the Society and Economy of Alabama Whites During Reconstruction" (Ph.D. dissertation, Johns Hopkins University, 1972), 137–41; Margaret Pace Farmer, "Furnishing Merchants and Sharecropping in Pike County, Alabama," *Alabama Review*, XXIII (1970), 143–51; and Glenn N. Sisk, "Rural Merchandising in the Alabama Black Belt, 1875–1917," *Journal of Farm Economics*, XXVII (1955), 705–15. The case against the lien system is presented in W. J. Cash, *The Mind of the South* (New York: Alfred A. Knopf, 1941), 151–52. Eighty to 90 percent of cotton growers in Alabama used the crop lien in 1890, according to Matthew B. Hammond, *The Cotton Industry: An Essay in American Economic History* (New York: The Macmillan Company, 1897), 149.

for them to spend on supplies bought from the local merchant; such loans were secured by crop liens.[3]

If it was not clear from the beginning, it rapidly became clear to both merchants and planters that the crop lien for supplies was a major new lever for the extraction of the surplus produced by the black tenantry, and that it was superior in many ways to the landlords' traditional lever, rent. The crop lien for supplies gave whomever held it much more flexibility in squeezing the tenantry. The amount the tenant owed for rent was fixed at the beginning of the season, but the amount he owed for supplies was never clear—to him, at least—until the crop had been harvested and the accounts figured. C. Vann Woodward has described the unusual flexibility of the crop lien for supplies: "the seeker of credit . . . [obtained] a loan of unstipulated amount, at a rate of interest to be determined by the creditor." The unscrupulous merchant could adjust the amount of the debt to match the value of the tenant's crop. And the accounts of travelers and contemporaries abound with descriptions of unscrupulous merchants.[4]

The newly freed slaves' inexperience with the workings of the system and, more telling, their powerlessness to challenge it were a second major reason for the superiority of the lien for supplies over rent as a method of squeezing the tenantry. These new consumers lacked the skills necessary to check over the year's account

3. Thomas D. Clark, "The Furnishing and Supply System in Southern Agriculture Since 1865," *Journal of Southern History*, XII (1946), 32; Vernon L. Wharton, *The Negro in Mississippi, 1865–1900* (Columbia, S.C.: University of South Carolina Press, 1952), 99–100; Woodman, *King Cotton*, 308–309. For travelers' descriptions of plantation stores, see John Townsend Trowbridge, *The South: A Tour of Its Battlefields and Ruined Cities* . . . (Hartford: L. Stebbins, 1866), 298; Charles Nordhoff, *The Cotton States in the Spring and Summer of 1875* (New York: D. Appleton and Company, 1876), 38, 70, 84, 106.

4. Robert Somers, *The Southern States Since the War, 1870–1* (New York: Macmillan and Company, 1871), 147; Trowbridge, *The South*, 366; Whitelaw Reid, *After the War: A Tour of the Southern States* (Cincinnati: Moore, Wilstach & Baldwin, 1866), 366; Charles H. Otken, *The Ills of the South* (New York: G. P. Putnam's Sons, 1894), 50; C. Vann Woodward, *Origins of the New South, 1877–1913* (Baton Rouge: Louisiana State University Press, 1952), 180. Ransom and Sutch conclude that the implicit interest charged by Georgia merchants in 1881 was 51.7 percent annually, and that the rate varied from 44 to 75 percent between 1881 and 1889: Roger Ransom and Richard Sutch, *One Kind of Freedom: The Economic Consequences of Emancipation* (New York: Cambridge University Press, 1977), Table 7.2. See also Michael Schwartz, *Radical Protest and Social Structure: The Southern Farmers' Alliance and Cotton Tenancy, 1880–1890* (New York: Academic Press, 1976), Chap. 6.

books, and often were denied the opportunity to do so. The lien contract often provided that the merchant's accounts were incontestable, and more than one contemporary reported that a tenant who challenged his account was murdered.[5]

The lack of distinction in the Alabama law between planters who advanced supplies and merchants meant that merchants were competing with planters as legal equals. The merchants' greater ability to extend credit gave them the opportunity to make substantial inroads on the planters' position. Thus, while the 1866 crop lien law ostensibly favored neither merchants nor planters, the merchants had a decisive economic advantage at the beginning of the ensuing six years of conflict, as the two groups competed for the profits from supplying black tenants.

The crop lien allowed the postwar merchants a source of additional profit that had previously been reserved for the planters. Under the antebellum system, the planter had been able to hold back his cotton, speculate on market fluctuations, and pay merchant suppliers in cash. Under the postwar system, the merchant lienholder got his share of the cotton as soon as it was baled; this allowed him to acquire any profit that could come from market speculation.

Of course the merchants themselves were not completely independent; they too needed credit. Before the war, the rural merchants' credit had come mainly from cotton factors in the port cities of the South who were social and political allies of the planter class. The postwar crop lien system gave the merchants considerable independence from these local powers, for which they traded greater dependence on northern manufacturers and wholesalers.[6]

The crop lien gave merchants the opportunity for great profits, but not all merchants prospered. The key to success for crop lien

5. Benjamin B. Kendrick, "Agrarian Discontent in the South, 1880–1910," *American Historical Association Annual Report 1920*, 271; Theodore Rosengarten, *All God's Dangers: The Life of Nate Shaw* (New York: Alfred A. Knopf, 1974), 29. On Nate Shaw, see Jonathan M. Wiener, Essay Review of *All God's Dangers*, *Journal of Social History*, X (1976), 170–78. For a similar incident, see Herbert G. Gutman, *The Black Family in Slavery and Freedom, 1750–1925* (New York: Random House, 1976), 438.

6. Mobile *Register*, quoted in Marengo *News-Journal*, April 28, 1881; see also Ralph H. Haskins, "Planter and Cotton Factor in the Old South: Some Areas of Friction," *Agricultural History*, XXIX (1955), 1–14.

merchants was constant surveillance of each tenant-customer's activity, personal knowledge and detailed information about each customer. Merchant enterprises as a result were small and localized, but established merchants enjoyed local monopoly power, as Ransom and Sutch have shown. Although it was difficult for one merchant to expand into another's territory, it was equally difficult for new competitors to enter a business which required detailed knowledge and experience in the locality.[7]

The merchant who held the tenants' liens for supplies not only obtained a large share of the profit from black tenants' labor; he also had the power to determine which tenants stayed on the plantation and which were forced off. If a merchant wanted a hardworking or compliant tenant to remain, the account books could show a debt to the store at the close of each year. And the books could be made to balance exactly for those who were to be asked to move on.[8]

Thus although the planter made a profit from the labor of the black tenants either in cash rent or a share of the crop, both of these amounts were fixed beforehand. However, the merchant, the holder of the lien for supplies, was able to squeeze the tenants with a wide variety of techniques: indeterminate but high interest rates, double pricing, and dishonest weighing and bookkeeping. The postwar merchant had gained considerable economic independence from the planter class and its local allies, had an opportunity for the first time to increase his profit by speculating in the cotton market, and even had the power to decide which tenants remained on the plantation. Thus merchants in such a position "divorced landownership from its age-old prerogatives," as Woodward says.[9] The crop lien for supplies had become a crucial means of acquiring the surplus produced by the freedmen, and, in years of low cotton

7. Ransom and Sutch, "Debt Peonage," 652–53.

8. Woodward, *Origins of the New South*, 184; Fred A. Shannon, *The Farmer's Last Frontier: Agriculture, 1860–1897* (New York: Farrar & Rinehart, Inc., 1945), 92. Neither of the two historians who used the surviving account books of the postwar southern merchants reported on the typical number of customers, the average size of accounts, the rates of change in the number of customers, or the merchants' own profits, losses, and sources of capital: Woodman, *King Cotton*; Thomas D. Clark, *Pills, Petticoats, and Plows: The Southern Country Store* (Indianapolis: The Bobbs-Merrill Company, 1944).

9. Woodward, *Origins of the New South*, 184.

prices or a poor crop, merchants often had a greater opportunity for making a profit off plantation agriculture than planters.

The crop lien law which offered Alabama merchants such opportunities was not passed during Radical Reconstruction, under the influence of northern capitalists. It was passed in February, 1866, before Radical Reconstruction began, by the same Alabama legislature that defied the Radical congress by refusing to ratify the Fourteenth Amendment. The original crop lien law was thus not a Radical antiplanter program for merchant power, but rather seems to have been accepted by the planters as a necessary concession to finance the cotton crop after the antebellum system had been destroyed. In the words of a black belt newspaper, it was "an act of wise, practical statesmanship."[10]

In the months between the end of the war and the passage of the first crop lien law, the Freedmen's Bureau and the planters searched for alternatives to permitting the merchants to supply the freedmen. General Swayne, head of the bureau in Alabama, proposed in 1865 that planters be required to pay their laborers partly in food, "lest the improvident . . . are obliged to purchase at unjust rates what they must immediately have." And Fleming writes that Alabama planters hoped that the government would advance supplies to black laborers in the months immediately following the war.[11] The bureau wanted the planters to do it and the planters wanted the bureau to do it, but both agreed that the merchants should not supply the freedmen.

The newspapers that spoke for the planters made explicit their dependence on merchant capital in this period of reorganization. A letter to the Montgomery *Advertiser* late in 1865 said that planters "wanted no animosity between the commission merchants . . . and the landowners." An 1867 article in the *Advertiser* was headlined "Merchants and planters: let them help one another." "Un-

10. *Acts of Alabama 1865–1866*, 44; Montgomery *Daily Advertiser*, March 8, 1866; Carrollton *West Alabamian*, January 1, 1879. The *West Alabamian* said the original crop lien law was necessary because the state supreme court ruled that a farmer could not mortgage something which did not exist—his next year's crop.

11. Swayne to Howard, September 4, 1865, quoted in Kolchin, *First Freedom*, 35; Walter L. Fleming, *Civil War and Reconstruction in Alabama* (Cleveland: A. H. Clark Company, 1911), 438.

less our planters receive help from the merchants," the article read, "and that right speedily, [the] beautiful prospect will go to naught. With all the rich promise that surrounds them [the planters] are absolutely helpless and dependent." A few months later, the newspaper expressed its fear that "merchants will withdraw their confidence and support" from the planter class. Open antagonism on the merchants' part would be a "disgrace"; it was necessary to avoid "the display of Shylock greed and illiberality on the part of the merchant."[12] The planter press's appeal to the merchants for help and support reveals that, although the planters had been weakened, they maintained their identity as a class and looked forward to preserving their social and economic position as well.

In addition to the black plantation tenants, there was another potential market for the merchant's consumer goods—the white yeomanry of the hill counties outside the black belt. But these small farmers tended to be self-sufficient, producing much of what they needed, and keeping on the fringes of the single-crop economy, operating instead a more diversified subsistence farm. The possibilities of making money by supplying this group would be greatly enhanced if they could be induced to plant more cotton and fewer crops for home consumption: cotton required seed, lots of fertilizer, and ginning, bagging, and marketing—all of which could be provided by a supply merchant. And all the time the yeoman was growing cotton, he would need to buy food. The spread of cotton cultivation to the hill counties was the prerequisite for successful merchant exploitation of the white yeomanry. In the late 1860s, this had not yet occurred.

Planter-Merchant Conflict during Reconstruction

Historians have argued that the crop lien law brought about the "merger" of landlord and merchant classes, that a new landholding elite, which combined the economic roles of planter and merchant, arose on the basis of the crop lien system.[13] But it makes a great

12. Montgomery *Daily Advertiser*, December 15, 1865, May 31, 1867, January 11, 1868.
13. Woodward, *Origins of the New South*, 21, 184; Woodman, *King Cotton*, 332–33; Rogers, *One-Gallused Rebellion*, 17. Similar arguments are made in John D. Hicks, *The Populist Revolt* (Minneapolis: University of Minnesota Press, 1931), 42; Horace Mann Bond, *Negro Education in Alabama: A Study in Cotton and Steel* (Washington, D.C.: Associated

deal of difference whether merchants became landlords, or planters became merchants. When merchants become landlords, they tie their customers to them more securely by taking over ownership of the land, and drive out the traditional landowners who have been competing for control of the surplus created by the tenants. Landownership for these "merchant-landlords" arises as a way of tying their crop-lien customers into the credit system more securely; it also permits the merchants to extract rent in addition to interest and profit from their store customers. But this is not a merger of merchant and planter social classes; it is instead the triumph of merchants over planters, the destruction of the old planter elite, and their replacement in the agrarian economy by the merchant class. If merchants became merchant-landlords, the crop lien law appears to have been the means by which this revolutionary transformation took place.

This is not what happened in postwar Alabama. There was no social revolution in which merchants displaced planters as the dominant class. Instead, the planters defeated a merchant thrust for power, in the process taking over the right to grant credit to tenants.

Since the planters obtained an additional lever for extracting the surplus, they were in a different class relation to their tenants; they were by definition a "new class" in terms of their means of surplus extraction. Thus it would be erroneous to conclude that

Publishers, 1939), 121; Shannon, *Farmer's Last Frontier*, 89–90; E. Merton Coulter, *The South During Reconstruction, 1865–1877* (Baton Rouge: Louisiana State University Press, 1947), 202; Sheldon Van Auken, "A Century of the Southern Plantation," *Virginia Magazine of History and Biography*, LVIII (1950), 372; Merle J. Prunty, Jr., "The Renaissance of the Southern Plantation," *Geographical Review*, XLV (1955), 459–91; Rupert B. Vance, *Human Factors in Cotton Culture* (Chapel Hill: University of North Carolina Press, 1929), 312; Edgar T. Thompson, "The Natural History of Labor in the South," in David Kelly Jackson (ed.), *American Studies in Honor of William Kenneth Boyd* (Durham: Duke University Press, 1940), 147; Benjamin Burks Kendrick and Alex Matthews Arnett, *The South Looks at its Past* (Chapel Hill: University of North Carolina Press, 1935), 109–10; Allen Conway, *The Reconstruction of Georgia* (Minneapolis: University of Minnesota Press, 1966), 227; Joe Gray Taylor, *Louisiana Reconstructed, 1863–1877* (Baton Rouge: Louisiana State University Press, 1963), 395, 402; F. B. Simkins, *The Everlasting South* (Baton Rouge: Louisiana State University Press, 1963), 69. Ransom and Sutch point out that "though generally accepted, the rise of a class of merchant-landlords has never been convincingly documented." Roger Ransom and Richard Sutch, "Debt Peonage in the Cotton South after the Civil War," *Journal of Economic History*, XXXII (1972), 654.

"nothing had changed" in the planters' defeat of the merchant challenge. The planters' relation to their tenants underwent a metamorphosis. But the planter class retained much the same social composition, the same history and traditions, and the same patterns of social relations. The most significant feature of postwar social developments was thus the persistence of many of the antebellum planter families in the new dominant class, while they had gained an additional lever for extracting an economic surplus from the underlying population.

For six years after the conclusion of the war, Alabama's merchants and planters competed as legal equals in the contest over control of the black tenants. During this period, both groups organized to protect their interests. A January, 1871, newspaper article headlined "Crisis in the Credit System" asked, "How shall merchants protect themselves? . . . A policy of self-preservation impels them to the adoption of some measure." A subsequent letter titled "Important to Merchants" proposed that they "adopt measures, similar to those other cities have adopted, for protecting themselves." It was signed "merchant." The Union Springs *Herald and Times* announced that country merchants, "following the example of the businessmen of Columbus and other places, have organized a Protective Society." The paper also noted that "the commercial interests of Union Springs" had formed a "Board of Trade."[14]

Although such organizations ostensibly had as their first task sharing information about credit risks, the planter press saw the potential for class-conscious political action in the merchant organizations. The Montgomery *Advertiser*, a consistent defender of planter interests, argued that "the merchants of the country have their 'chambers of commerce' and 'boards of trade,' for the purpose of fixing the value of their wares . . . , whilst the poor cotton growers plod along, every one on his own course . . . , sell for what they can get, and pay out of the proceeds for supplies at whatever price may be demanded of them. . . . Concert of action must be attained to protect the interest of the cotton grower." The news-

14. Montgomery *Daily Advertiser*, January 22, February 13, 1871; Union Springs *Herald and Times*, May 29, 1872. See also Schwartz, *Radical Protest*, 57–63.

paper called for the organization of "farmers' clubs," writing that
the planters "must now band together, or be immolated by the
cormorants, loan sharks, and skinflints, infesting every village,
town and city, throughout our land." Such planter organizations
would "stop speculation in all the necessaries of life on the farm,
such as fertilizers, implements, bacon, &c." The *Advertiser* regularly printed the resolutions of planter organizations. A typical
one declared that "we, a portion of the planters of Bullock county
. . . [seek] concert of action" against "middle men . . . our enemies . . . and their schemes."[15]

Throughout Reconstruction, the planter press argued that all
whites were united against the Radicals—planter and merchant
alike. Given the overwhelming developments in national politics
in 1867, 1868, and 1869, including the advent of Radical Reconstruction and the attempted impeachment of President Johnson,
it is surprising that merchant-planter conflict would receive any
attention at all in the southern press. Thus the relatively small
number of articles dealing with planter-merchant conflict which
appeared in southern newspapers in the late sixties and early seventies are particularly significant and made explicit what planter
spokesmen had good reasons to conceal.

The planters' antimerchant argument was summarized early in
1871 by the class-conscious Mobile *Register*, the most authoritative
voice of planter interests in the state. The paper reported, predict-
ably, that the freedman was rapidly "degenerating." What was less
predictable was the newspaper's analysis of the cause: it was not
the carpetbaggers who were responsible for the black's immorality,
lack of thrift, and poor health, but rather "a low, unprincipled class
of traders, keepers of small shops." These "cunning" merchants,
"by a little flattery and poisonous whiskey, easily cheat him out of
the little his bad management and indolence permit him to make."
The paper complained that the blacks were selling "their share of
the cotton crop . . . without prudence or proper calculation of the
supplies they may want at the little stores that have arisen everywhere, and they buy trash of all kinds at extravagant prices. . . .

15. Montgomery *Daily Advertiser*, July 11, 26, September 23, 1868.

Whether this evil can be reached by law or not remains to be seen."[16] The lesson was clear: the freedmen were being cheated by merchants; they were unable to act in their own best interests; therefore, control by the paternalistic planter class was necessary. Legislation, however, was required.

The argument that merchants' crop liens were responsible for the region's labor problems was also put forward by the Montgomery *Advertiser*. As early as 1866 the *Advertiser* wrote, under the headline "Cheating the Freedmen," that "traders are taking advantage of the ignorance of pecuniary matters existing among the freedmen." At the end of 1867, the *Advertiser*'s antimerchant tone became stronger: "Latterly the freedmen are more than ever addicted to the ridiculous practice of throwing their money away. . . . 'the freedman' comes to town, purchases a gallon of whiskey, a flask of powder, a shot gun, and a piece of cheese, and a few crackers. In this way, his money is soon gone, and he apparently forgets that his wife and children have no 'massa' to look to, as in the good old days gone by."[17]

The merchants were accused even more strongly in another article in the Mobile *Register* in early 1871, under the title "Now What?"

> The negroes were encouraged and invited by our local merchants to lease land and make crops on their own account. They readily advanced to the freedmen . . . , taking liens on the negroes' crop and stock. The negroes, true to nature, being clothed and fed without work, would not work to pay for it. . . . The merchants are seizing corn, cotton, and stock, and the negroes are stealing cotton and stock of every description. . . . And with all this, they now swear they will neither hire nor crop on shares with a white man. . . . Now what?[18]

On other occasions the planter press eliminated analysis and printed simple expressions of hostility to merchants. "The swarm of eastern drummers are overrunning the South—every city, village, and so to say, every crossroads where there is a store estab-

16. Mobile *Daily Register*, February 26, 1871.
17. Montgomery *Daily Advertiser*, March 9, 1866, December 22, 1867.
18. Mobile *Daily Register*, January 10, 1871.

lished," the Montgomery *Advertiser* reported late in 1866. As a result of the excessive numbers of crossroads merchants, "a great many failures of commercial houses will take place this spring," the newspaper predicted. A letter to the Montgomery *Advertiser* in 1867 complained about "money-mongers who make their living by charging usurious interest," and an editorial in the Tuscaloosa *Independent Monitor* argued the South's problem was that "the fate of the planters is sealed in bills of advances locked up in the empty safes of bankrupt merchants." The planters' objection to merchant competition was summed up simply by a Mobile planter testifying before a congressional committee: "these shark storekeepers . . . swallow up the whole thing."[19]

The planters' conception of the proper relationship between themselves, their tenants, and the local supply merchants was expressed by the Montgomery *Advertiser*. "The planter, as the representative class of the South . . . performs the office [for the black] of being his intermediary with the capitalist."[20] A whole theory of class relations is expressed in this sentence: the planters do not view themselves as capitalists; capitalists are part of the economic structure of the South, but they should not have direct economic relations with the black tenants; instead, the capitalists should do business with the planters, who act as the representatives of their tenants. Statements such as this one suggest that the slaveowners' paternalistic, antibourgeois ideology survived the destruction of slavery.

Another antimerchant theme in the planter press was opposition to young men's interest in joining the merchant class. "A large number of young men, instead of cultivating their land with their own hands, always an honorable calling . . . have taken to little country stores, where the temptation to cheat the ignorant negro is too strong for the virtue of many, and they become degraded by consciousness of making money in unjust and low ways, lose their self-respect and sense of honor, form a low standard of virtue

19. Montgomery *Daily Advertiser*, November 20, 1866, January 10, 1867; Tuscaloosa *Independent Monitor*, January 17, 1871; *Senate Documents*, 48th Cong., 1st Sess., No. 1262, IV, 74.
20. Montgomery *Daily Advertiser*, December 25, 1867. The Mobile *Daily Register* on January 19, 1883, denied "that there are any landed capitalists in Alabama."

and honesty, and will soon become an inferior class of citizens."
The Montgomery *Advertiser* agreed: "Probably three boys out of
four prefer to enter the counting-room, or find a place behind the
counter, under the delusive idea that they will in this way stand
higher in the social scale. . . . Merchants advertising for clerks or
salesmen will be overrun with applicants. Why one form of labor
should be considered so much more honorable than another we are
at a loss to understand." The 1871 statewide planters' convention
advised planters to "set your able-bodied sons to work instead of
learning all kinds of mischief in the village groceries."[21]

Another article described in vivid detail what awaited farm boys
foolish enough to seek employment with town merchants: "Merchandise [is] overcrowded now. Keep away from cities. When you
apply for employment, nine times out of ten you fail, have the cold
shoulder given you by busy and hurried men, get your feelings
mortified, lose your sense of independence, waste your money at
hotels, and depart, to still follow the *ignis fatuis* of getting into
business. Quit all this, and call upon mother earth for employment.
She will welcome you . . . and reward you."[22]

The Selma *Southern Argus*, another leading voice of planter
interests, joined the chorus in an 1870 article entitled "young men
choosing a profession." "Scores and hundreds of strong and hardy
young men are dragging out the best and most important years of
their lives . . . in our towns and cities, making barely enough to
live upon, groping along as slavish subordinates, and wearing out
their energies of body and mind in unmanly and unprofitable em-
ployments," the paper lamented. "[They] produce nothing, while
consuming the profits of the soil continually . . .[as farmers they
would be] free, independent, and prosperous, useful and long-
lived."[23]

What is noteworthy in these profoundly antibourgeois statements is the concern with "honor," "virtue," "manliness," and with
the danger of being "degraded," not by wealth itself but by "con-

---

21. Mobile *Daily Register*, February 26, 1871; Montgomery *Daily Advertiser*, November 1, 1866, February 5, 1871.
22. Montgomery *Daily Advertiser*, November 22, 1866.
23. Selma *Southern Argus*, May 19, 1870.

sciousness of making money," and finally, the explicitly class-conscious statement that merchants form an "inferior class" to planters. The planter press did not mince words when dealing with an antagonistic class.

This antimerchant refrain was nothing new in 1871; it had been a staple feature of the antebellum ruling ideology. That is precisely its significance: at a time when merchants were encroaching on the planters' position, the planters fought back by referring to traditional, antebellum ideals. The justification of their struggle in terms of an antibourgeois ideology suggests the extent to which the postwar planter class sought to preserve all they could of the prewar world they had made, the extent to which they refused to abandon their antebellum self-conception as a nonbourgeois landed class.

The merchants did not suffer the planters' attacks in silence. While they lacked the well-organized and skilled ideological organs the planters found in the Mobile and Montgomery press, merchant spokesmen did defend the interests of their class. The Mobile *Register* occasionally printed letters to the editor from such spokesmen. One, written in 1871, dealt with the planters' argument that merchants were responsible for the blacks' degeneracy.

> Some writers attribute the lethargy among them to . . . these cross-roads merchants, to be found everywhere. . . . This is not the cause. . . . The negro is fooled, the cross-roads merchant is fooled, the commission merchant is fooled, in fact everyone is fooled except the planter, who turns out to be the fooler, the sharpest of the lot. . . . The great and vital cause for dissatisfaction among the negroes lies in the planter . . . , who promises one thing and fails to comply with it.

The letter was signed "Cross-Roads Merchant."[24]

With the crippling of Reconstruction in Alabama by 1871, the planter class apparently had regained enough economic and political power to mount a political campaign to weaken the legal position of merchants holding crop liens. A new antimerchant law was proposed in Alabama in 1871 by an obviously class-conscious "planter convention." The convention met in the state House of Repre-

24. Mobile *Daily Register*, October 7, 1871.

sentatives; the Montgomery *Daily Advertiser* reported, "The attendance of this important meeting was large and extremely gratifying." One speaker complained that "the agricultural fraterni- ty . . . must continue to grope subserviently to a class who derive their support and business from products of their soil and their labor. . . . The commercial world is growing into affluence to the impoverishment of our agriculturalists. This would seem to be the reverse of legitimacy and an exaltation of the creature into superi- ority to the creator." Another complained that "the farmer pays exorbitant prices for supplies . . . . it takes *all* he makes to settle with his merchant at the end of the year; [this] is, perhaps, the primary cause of *imperceptible* profits. . . . there are too many merchants, and the supply is greater than the demand."[25]

Whereas the 1867 statute had given the landlord a lien for the year's rent, the new law would give the landlord a lien "superior to all other liens, for rent and *advances* made" to tenants. When a debtor was insolvent, this law required that after his rent had been paid, his crops go first to pay for the supplies his landlord had ad- vanced, and only after that to pay for supplies advanced by the local merchant. A letter to the editor of the *Advertiser* argued that the planters' convention bill "was demanded by the present condition of the planting interest—. . . . An Act, giving to the planter who undertakes in good faith to supply his hands, a *lien superior* to that of an interloping 'advancer.'"[26] The bill was voted into law by a sizable majority in the legislature.

From the viewpoint of the merchant, this legislation created two types of credit customers: tenants, those customers who had landlords, the great majority of whom were black in 1871; and yeomen who owned their own land, who didn't have landlords, virtually all of whom were white. If both a planter and a merchant

25. *Ibid.*, February 18, 1871; Montgomery *Daily Advertiser*, February 10, 1871; Montgomery *Alabama State Journal*, February 10, 1871.

26. *Acts of Alabama 1870–1871*, 19, emphasis mine; Montgomery *Daily Advertiser*, February 14, 1871. The controversy over revising Alabama's crop lien law is discussed in Rogers, *One-Gallused Rebellion*, 15–20, and Allen J. Going, *Bourbon Democracy in Alabama, 1874–1890* (University, Ala.: University of Alabama Press, 1951), 94–102. See also Montgomery *Daily Advertiser*, March 17, 1871; Tuscaloosa *Independent Monitor*, March 28, 1871.

advanced supplies to a tenant, the planter had the right to be re-paid first. In an economy where the profits of small producers were usually marginal, this was a serious blow to all merchants who were in competition with planters over supplying black tenants. The law's effect was to weaken the black belt merchants, and to pressure the merchant class to shift towards the white yeoman areas outside the black belt where they could continue to take crop liens without fear that the debtors' crops would go to planters instead of to themselves.

Thus the Alabama planters' success at making their lien for supplies legally superior to that of the merchants restricted future merchant gains primarily to the white yeoman areas. It divided those working the land by race, and reserved the profit from the blacks' labor on the great cotton plantations for the planters, giving the merchant class, as a sort of consolation prize, the right to appropriate by means of the crop lien the surplus created by the white yeomen.[27] The subsequent transformation of independent yeomen in the hills into tenants was accompanied by the transformation of hill merchants into merchant-landlords.

This was indeed a "merger" of landlord and merchant methods of appropriating the surplus, but there were two distinct versions of the merger in two different areas, with opposite social consequences for the merchant class. In the black belt, the planter appears to have obtained for himself the merchants' method of appropriating the surplus produced by the black tenantry; the planter became a "planter-merchant" by pushing the merchant class out of any position of substantial landed power in the black belt. This was a merger of economic levers for extracting the surplus, but they remained in the hands of a single class; it was not the merger of social classes. It marked not a transformation of the structure of power, but rather the return to the planters of their traditional

---

27. Fredrickson said it well: "one of the things that made 'the New South' new was the direct exploitation and dependent status of the kind of whites who had once been poor but independent landowning farmers under the old regime." George M. Fredrickson, *The Black Image in the White Mind: The Debate on Afro-American Character and Destiny, 1817–1914* (New York: Harper & Row, 1971), 203.

position of domination over the black plantation labor force—one which entailed a metamorphosis of the planters.

It was in the hills that a major transformation of the social structure took place. There, merchants became merchant-landlords, but again there was no merger of social classes, because there had been no planter class in the hills, a region of small farmers. The rise of a new class of merchant-landlords entailed the fall of the white yeoman farmers to tenant status. As the class structure of the hills came increasingly to resemble that of the black belt, as the white farmers in the hills were forced into tenancy by the merchant elite's monopoly on credit and increasing ownership of land, the position of the black belt planter-merchants and the hill country merchant-landlords appeared to converge; a single ruling class with two branches seemed to have arisen.

Two factors worked against this tendency: the different and antagonistic social origins of the two elite groups, and the distinct and similarly antagonistic cultural traditions of the two regions. Subsequent political developments revealed that this apparent structural convergence was more formal than real, and that the black belt planters remained a politically self-conscious class in the eighties. Not only did the identities of the two groups remain separate, but the rivalry between them continued to erupt into open political conflict.

"Redemption" and the New Planter Offensive

With the final collapse of Reconstruction in Alabama in 1874, planters launched a new attack on merchants. "Whenever Democracy has full swing," the Montgomery *Alabama State Journal* wrote, "it seems to realize intense delight in oppressing the mercantile class and relieving the landholders." Now the planters took new steps to weaken merchant ties with blacks and to strengthen the planters' authority over their tenants. The same planter organizations that had advocated restrictions on merchant crop liens in 1871 now proposed that merchants be prohibited from doing business with their black customers at night. They argued that merchants were purchasing farm produce which blacks had stolen from plantations, and that this trade was carried on under cover of darkness.

But when the "sunset law" was finally passed in 1875, it prohibited merchants from purchasing not just stolen produce, but any of the leading farm products between sunset and sunrise. Merchants convicted of buying produce after sunset faced up to twelve months' imprisonment at hard labor. The bill was introduced in the legislature by Democratic state senator W. G. Little, Jr., a conservative leader and planter from Sumter County. The final version contained a key amendment which unmistakably revealed the class nature of the law—it added that the bill would not apply to planters who traded with their own employees after sunset at plantation stores. Virtually all those who voted against the bill were Radicals; the bill was widely praised in the planter press. A subsequent session of the legislature expanded the sunset bill considerably, prohibiting anyone from purchasing seed cotton in the black belt except for planters seeking "payment of rent and advances."[28]

Planter representatives described the bills as anticrime measures, but merchant spokesmen had a different view. A United States Senate committee was told that the real purpose of the sunset law was "to keep the negroes from going to the stores." A black explained, "If I live three miles from a store, and I must work from sunup to sundown, I cannot go where I can do my trading to the best advantage. A man is prevented . . . from going and selling anything he has . . . as the landlord will not give him time between sunrise and sundown. . . . Every man ought to have a right to dispose of his own property." The effect of the bill banning purchase of seed cotton was to "place all the seed cotton into the hands of the

28. Montgomery *Alabama State Journal*, July 30, 1874 (I am indebted to Michael Perman for this quotation); Planters Convention Proceedings, Montgomery *Alabama State Journal*, February 10, 1871; Montgomery *Daily Advertiser*, February 14, 1871; *Acts of Alabama, 1874–1875*, 241–42. The bill's progress (Senate Bill 101 1/2) can be followed in *Alabama Senate Journal 1874–1875*, 36, 78, 120, 389, and *Alabama House Journal 1874–1875*, 397–400, 406. Senator Little was a member of the Constitutional Convention of 1875 and president of the state senate in 1878–79: Thomas McAdory Owen, *History of Alabama and Dictionary of Alabama Biography* (Chicago: The S. J. Clarke Publishing Company, 1921), 1054. Montgomery *Daily Advertiser*, February 18, 20, 1875; Greensboro *Alabama Beacon*, March 27, September 18, 1875; Mobile *Daily Register*, February 15, 1875; Selma *Southern Argus*, February 26, 1875. For a protest from Republicans, see Montgomery *Alabama State Journal*, March 9, 1875. The bill is discussed in Fleming, *Civil War and Reconstruction in Alabama*, 732; Going, *Bourbon Democracy*, 98; Rogers, *One-Gallused Rebellion*, 28–29. *Acts of Alabama 1878–1879*, 206.

landlord," to deprive the merchant of the right to trade this crucial commodity.[29]

That the sunset bill was a planter attack on merchants is suggested by the arguments of the bills' advocates. Representative Clements of Tuscaloosa said, "There has been inaugurated in almost every community in the State a regular system of robbery of which . . . every cross-road store [is] a place of deposit. . . . There are the captains of the band of robbers and thieves located to receive the booty. . . . Inducements too tempting to be resisted were held out to the poorer and more ignorant and less scrupulous." That the bill "imposes hardships upon the merchants, I will not deny," he added.[30]

"A bad man can establish a little grocery store," Senator Vance explained; "men would steal the seed cotton and sell it at night to mean merchants." The Montgomery *Advertiser* in a badly mixed metaphor described such a merchant as "this eating moth . . . that fastens and fattens upon the life blood of the hard fisted and trial worn tiller of the soiler [*sic*]." Representative Bierne, in the House debate, called on his fellow citizens to "raise the standard of morals to that sacred point which would suffer all things rather than that our neighbors should be injured by those who seek darkness rather than light because their deeds are evil." In the rush of rhetoric Bierne overlooked the fact that the legislature had permitted planters who "sought darkness rather than light" to trade with their tenants.[31]

The Greensboro *Alabama Beacon* emphasized that the sunset law was aimed not so much at the black as it was at the merchant, "the root of the evil," at whose hands "planters in Hale, and other counties in this state, have suffered seriously, for several years past." Fleming himself concludes that the merchants at whom the sunset bill was aimed "often became rich," and adds with a hint of resentment, "the prosperity of several large commercial houses in Alabama is said to date from the corner groceries of the sev-

29. *Senate Documents*, 46th Cong., 2nd Sess., No. 693, p. 466. See also Memorial to Legislature, *Acts of Alabama 1874–1875*, 4–5.

30. Montgomery *Daily Advertiser*, February 20, 1875.

31. *Senate Documents*, 46th Cong., 2nd Sess., No. 693, p. 473; Montgomery *Daily Advertiser*, February 19, 1875.

enties." Robert Somers's contemporary account is sympathetic to the planters' accusations of the merchants.[32]

Some planters believed the sunset bill did not go far enough. A meeting of planters in Hale County held to discuss the sunset law passed a resolution "requiring all traders in farm produce to keep a register of names, kind and quantity of produce purchased, and price paid for same. Vigilant committees were also appointed for each neighborhood," apparently to keep an eye on the "traders." Such "voluntary" agreements had also been made before the bill was passed. In 1871, "At a meeting of the citizens and merchants in Carthage today, all harmoniously, the merchants drew up an article of agreement binding themselves as good citizens not to purchase from negroes any product they may offer for sale at night, or any time, if the article of produce bears signs of dishonesty or being stolen," reported the Greensboro *Alabama Beacon*. "All the merchants, and many of the planters, have without hesitation, signed the restriction. . . . Now, if all other trading points will enter into the same agreement, the evil so much complained of will be removed."[33] The references to the merchants' "harmonious" attitude and lack of hesitation to do the planters' bidding suggests as much about their subservient position as it does about the merits of the planters' charges.

In South Carolina, according to Joel Williamson's study, the antagonism between planters and merchants was expressed in political terms by the merchants becoming Republicans. There is evidence that some Alabama merchants similarly became Republicans. The planter press on occasion urged Democrats not to patronize white Republican businesses, which clearly implies that there were Republican merchants. Wager Swayne was told that "the rebel element . . . exert their influence to the injury of every business man who takes an active part in behalf of the Govern-

32. Greensboro *Alabama Beacon*, September 18, 1875; Fleming, *Civil War and Reconstruction in Alabama*, 732; Somers, *Southern States*, 131.

33. Greensboro *Alabama Beacon*, September 18, 1875, December 23, 1871. This merchants' agreement was a response to charges made against them in the *Alabama Beacon* for December 9, 1871. No copy of this issue is in existence, according to Rhoda Coleman Elleson, *History and Bibliography of Alabama Newspapers in the Nineteenth Century* (University, Ala.: University of Alabama Press, 1954).

ment." The Republican *Alabama State Journal* in 1870 complained that the Democratic *Montgomery Mail* "had a long article yesterday which . . . means simply that Montgomery's proud and enterprising merchants must dishonor commerce and degrade themselves by making open and proscriptive war upon Republicans and Republicanism, or be themselves proscribed and hounded by the miserable small-brained crew who assume the leadership of the so-called Democracy."[34]

Two Republican merchants testified before an 1875 House committee investigating "Affairs in Alabama." F. M. Dunbar of Opelika said that since he had run for tax collector on the Republican ticket, "my patronage, so far as the white people are concerned, is almost entirely cut off." When asked "Who does patronize you, then?" Dunbar answered, "It is mostly colored men." Dallas B. Smith was another Republican merchant, also from Opelika; he reported that blacks came to him complaining that they had been "discharged since the election . . . on account of not voting the Democratic ticket." This is precisely the situation Williamson found in South Carolina: merchants and blacks forming a political alliance in the Republican party against the planter Democrats.[35]

In 1880 the Mobile *Register* reported that a reception and banquet for former president Grant had been given by "a comparatively small number of our merchants and not by the city generally." The paper noted that "the great bulk of our people did not approve of the invitation. . . . [The merchants] thought the invitation would aid in strenghtening friendly feelings between merchants of different sections. . . . Our people generally took a different view of the matter. They could not separate General Grant from the errors of his administration, the outrages of his party, the oppression heaped upon the South."[36]

On the other hand, a black belt planter told the 1875 House

34. Joel Williamson, *After Slavery: The Negro in South Carolina During Reconstruction, 1861–1877* (Chapel Hill: University of North Carolina Press, 1956), 174; *House Reports*, 43rd Cong., 2nd Sess., No. 262, p. 134; J. Silsby to Wager Swayne, April 1, 1867, in Wager Swayne Papers, Alabama Department of Archives and History; Montgomery *Alabama State Journal*, November 4, 1870.

35. *House Reports*, 43rd Cong., 2nd Sess., No. 262, pp. 209, 133.

36. Mobile *Daily Register*, April 10, 1880.

committee that "no man in town who calls himself a Republican is engaged in mercantile business," and the leading Republican newspaper in Alabama did not defend the merchants during the critical debate over the crop lien law, except to advocate building an ambiguous "community of feeling between the merchant and the farmer."[37] Some merchants were Republicans in Alabama, but there is little evidence that the merchants as a class supported the Republican party in their conflict with the planters.

Between 1875 and 1883 the debate over merchant crop liens continued, as planters' organizations proposed to abolish them altogether. The Mobile *Register* as usual argued the planters' case, identifying their opposition as the merchants rather than the agrarian radicals. The merchants' right to hold tenants' crop liens was "injurious in that it encourages profligate expenditure in advances of earnings, and produces a want of harmony and of mutual dependence between the landowner and farmer. . . . The tenant . . . can get advances from his landlord on just as good, if not better, terms."[38] "Mutual dependence" was a euphemism for the planters' monopoly on exploitation of tenants: the tenants were dependent on their landlord for supplies, and he was dependent on them for the surplus they created.

The Montgomery *Advertiser* agreed with the *Register*'s position in an editorial titled "The Crop Lien Full of Evil":

> Larceny and State convicts are the annual fruits of this system, and a certain class of merchants are sowing the seeds that produces the greatest amount of mischief. Not satisfied with their mercantile vocation and reasonable percentage, some are renting plantations to subrent, so as to control the colored labor and subordinate the planting business as far as they can to their high percentage. . . . This distribution forces [the laborer] to steal or suffer; the merchants' crop lien supplies a large percentage of colored convicts. . . . its object to aid the poor man has been thwarted by the cupidity of the merchants; the liens given on the crop secures the patronage of the tenant and binds him with mortgages to the discretionary percentage of the merchant until he chooses to close out the tenant and exchange him for a more profitable customer.

37. *House Reports*, 43rd Cong., 2nd Sess., No. 262, p. 228; Montgomery *Alabama State Journal*, June 1, 1871.
38. Mobile *Daily Register*, January 19, 1883.

. . . Is it not perfectly clear that the object of the law, to help the poor, is perverted to oppress them for the benefit of the extortionate merchant? . . . The repeal of this lien . . . would prove a blessing to the poor man . . . and add a great deal to the prosperity of the planting industry.[39]

The Livingston *Journal* agreed that "advancing merchants and crop liens are some of the maladies . . . that are affecting the patient." A planter wrote to the editor of the Montgomery *Advertiser* that "merchants feel no interest in common with the land owner."

A glance at the society and agriculture of the Black Belt, should suffice to settle this question [of the crop lien law] at once, in favor of its repeal. . . . It stands a ghostly spectre of demoralized labor, on half cultivated farms, run by the merchants. . . . This law opens wide the door for the covetous merchant to demoralize the labor, to undermine the agricultural interest of the county, and to sap the foundation of his own prosperity. Then, shall this class of merchants be licensed by law to set down in their *little retail shanties* and *manipulate* the great agricultural interest of our country to its ruin, with a little rotten calico, burst-head whiskey, sour flour and rotten tobacco.[40]

The Mobile *Register* made disparaging remarks about "oily-looking clerks . . . behind the counter" of small-town stores, and the Selma *Southern Argus* argued that merchants were not middlemen, but rather "enemies, vampires, and bloodsuckers." A special committee of the U. S. Senate took testimony on conditions in Alabama in 1880 and was quoted in the Mobile *Register* as reporting that "country merchants . . . who furnish supplies" were "frequently bad and dishonest men [who] would take advantage of the ignorance of necessity of the negroes, and exact exorbitant prices."[41]

Repeatedly the planter press argued that abolition of the merchants' crop lien would increase planter control over their tenants. "Repeal the law," the Carrollton *West Alabamian* wrote, "and let the colored laborer of Alabama be brought back under the manage-

39. Montgomery *Daily Advertiser*, January 24, 1883; see also January 17, 1883.

40. Livingston *Journal*, September 2, 1881; Montgomery *Daily Advertiser*, January 28, 1879.

41. Mobile *Daily Register*, March 14, 1880; Selma *Southern Argus*, August 13, 1875; Mobile *Daily Register*, June 4, 1880.

ment of white farmers" rather than merchants. The Marengo *News-Journal* wrote that repeal would "benefit the large planters by giving them exclusive control over the labor on their plantations." "The advancers have acted without regard to the interests of the land owners," the Mobile *Register* argued, "and have often threatened to remove tenants from one plantation to another unless their demands were complied with." It was now necessary to "break down the peculiar privileges afforded the outside advancers." A letter from a planter to the Montgomery *Advertiser* argued that the merchant's crop lien took "the management of the planting business largely [away] from the intelligent planter" and therefore should be repealed.[42]

Merchants defended themselves against these attacks as they had in the past. The Tuskegee *Weekly News*, in an article headlined "crop lien law," noted simply that "merchants are opposed to its repeal." "Many landlords exact a larger profit from their tenants than the merchant does," a merchant argued in the Montgomery *Advertiser*; "those tenants who trade on their own credit . . . are more prosperous than those supplied by the landlords. . . . If the 'black belt' desires the repeal, let it be made local, but speaking for the merchants of North Alabama, we do not desire the intervention of the landlord."[43]

Another merchant asked,

[W]hat would be the consequence of repeal? Repeal would benefit a few landlords of large means and not all the owners of the soil, for it would force many of them, unfitted to run plantations successfully, to injure themselves in the attempt; many . . . would be unable to obtain supplies to feed hired laborers; so that lands now yielding a good income from tenants obtaining supplies on lien notes . . . would fail to yield income to owners; would decrease in market value and fall into the hands of large capitalists. The merchant would not be injured by

42. Carrollton *West Alabamian*, January 8, 1879; Marengo *News-Journal*, January 9, 1879; Mobile *Daily Register*, December 9, 1882; Montgomery *Daily Advertiser*, January 28, 1879. See also Montgomery *Daily Advertiser*, January 24, 26, December 2, February 8, 1883; Marengo *News-Journal*, September 9, 1880; Carrollton *West Alabamian*, December 18, 1878; Butler *Choctaw Herald*, March 12, 1874; Marion *Commonwealth*, August 19, 1875; Mobile *Daily Register*, December 9, 1882, March 3, 30, May 28, 1883.
43. Tuskegee *Weekly News*, December 7, 1876; Montgomery *Daily Advertiser*, January 24, 1883.

repeal, as he would sell the same supplies to the rich landlord or plantation runner for cash, or on a credit cheaper because of the less risk to him, and he would furnish the same to his hirelings or workers at higher prices than they now pay to the merchant, as he would hire no competition as a creditor.[44]

A third asked, "Do you think the owners of the land would be less exacting than the merchant? I think not. Then we would have but two alternatives, either to get supplies from . . . landlords, or work for wages." An article in the Carrollton *West Alabamian* argued for merchants' crop liens in terms of property rights: "A lien note no more places one man in the power of another than a mortgage does, and to deprive a man of the right to mortgage his property, would deprive him of one of his most valuable property rights." Another merchant spokesman pointed out that it was not in the interest of smaller planters to abolish the merchants' crop lien. "Crop liens obtained by the county merchants have operated as a basis of credit for . . . the planter of small means," who otherwise might not be able to obtain the credit necessary to make his crops.[45]

"There is no way of improving a place so much as by encouraging good merchants," the decisive Birmingham *Iron Age* argued. "You may have sons growing up who will some day be the best merchants in town. Help lay the foundations of them now. It is a duty. . . . Your merchants . . . stand by you in sickness, are your associates." Another merchant spokesman wrote that "the lien granted outside parties . . . does not interfere with the landlord's rights. . . . The tenant ought not to be compelled to purchase from the landlord if he can get his supplies at less cost elsewhere."[46]

The first substantial change in the lien laws after the planter victory of 1871 came in 1883, in the form of a further expansion of landlord privileges in relation to tenants, a further loss of power for those merchants who were still competing with planters. Under the original lien law, the tenant pledged his crop as security for

44. Montgomery *Daily Advertiser*, January 17, 1883.
45. *Ibid.*, January 31, 1883; Carrollton *West Alabamian*, December 18, 1878, January 1, 1879.
46. Birmingham *Iron Age*, October 14, 1875; Mobile *Daily Register*, December 9, 1882. See also Marion *Commonwealth*, September 15, 1875.

credit. The 1883 law, establishing the "iron-clad" or "anaconda" mortgage, gave the landlord the right to take not only his tenant's crop in payment for advances, but also his furniture, household goods, and personal effects. Merchants were also given the right to take tenants' personal property, but only after the landlord had taken whatever he determined was necessary to repay his loan, and only if the landlord had given permission to his tenant to borrow from merchants.[47] The terms of the "anaconda" lien law in Alabama indicated that planter-merchant conflict remained a potent political fact in 1883, and that the planters were increasing their political strength in the state.

Agrarian Radicals Confront the Merchants

Nothing could have demonstrated more clearly the continuing antagonism between black belt planters and hill merchant-landlords than the political conflict over crop lien repeal in Alabama in 1884 and 1885. In 1884, agrarian radicals mobilized to demand repeal of all crop liens, those held by black belt planters as well as by hill merchant-landlords.[48]

The planters did not unite with the hill merchant-landlords against this attack on both of them; instead, a convention of 150 leading planters in the state passed a resolution in 1884 urging the legislature to repeal the merchants' crop lien. The Selma *Times* commented, "That so many and such intelligent and influential planters should be thus heartily in favor of a measure which is so pregnant with results to the agricultural interests, will go a long way toward influencing the action of the legislature."[49] Planter representatives formed an alliance with the radical element in the Alabama house and passed a bill repealing the merchants' right to hold crop liens. The bill preserved the landlords' right to advance supplies against future crops. It would permit the merchant-

47. In 1875, a new law subordinated the tenant's lien on crops to the merchant's as well as the landlord's. *Acts of Alabama 1875–1876*, 103–106; *Acts of Alabama 1882–1883*, 175–76; see also Mobile *Daily Register*, January 28, 1883.

48. Unsuccessful attempts to repeal the crop lien law were made in 1876–1877, and again in 1878–1879; in 1876, the proposed bill passed the state senate, but failed in the house. *Acts of Alabama 1876–1877*, 112–13; *Acts of Alabama 1878–1879*, 72, 167; Rogers, *One-Gallused Rebellion*, 15; Going, *Bourbon Democracy*, 99.

49. Selma *Times*, quoted in Eutaw *Mirror*, October 28, 1884.

landlords of the hill counties to continue to supply their tenant-customers, but it would eliminate black belt supply merchants who were not landlords but had remained in the black belt in spite of the inferior legal status of their crop liens.[50]

Although the merchant forces in the house had not attacked the planters, the state senate proved to have a class-conscious merchant bloc of twelve state senators (out of twenty-nine voting on this bill) who were firmly committed to defending their interests against the alliance of planters and agrarian radicals. The promerchant forces there called for the abolition of the landlords' liens for supplies, but not the merchants'. Such a move would have given merchants the exclusive right to advance supplies to tenants, and limited landlords to liens for rent. The proposal was defeated soundly in the planter-dominated state senate, but it dramatized the depth of the continuing conflict between merchants and planters.

Forced to accept the abolition of merchants' crop liens in the black belt, the merchant bloc's next tactic was to water down the bill to repeal such liens. They recognized that the real intent of the planter forces was to defend their own position in the plantation districts. Thus the merchant bloc proposed that merchants' crop liens be permitted outside the black belt. The agrarian radicals insisted that planters support their demand for repeal in the hills. The dominant planter forces worked out a compromise by which merchants' crop liens were abolished in two-thirds of the state's counties; they made sure that the counties where these liens remained legal were all outside the black belt.

The bill outlawed merchants' crop liens in all but one of the twelve counties where the population was more than 75 percent black, and in all but four of the twenty counties that were more than 50 percent black. Of the twenty-three counties in which merchants were permitted to hold crop liens, all except four lay in districts represented by members of the promerchant bloc; and of

50. *Alabama Senate Journal 1884–1885*, 556–58; *Alabama House Journal 1884–1885*, 814–15. The debate was over House Bill 182, repealing Sections 3286, 3287, and 3288 of the *Alabama Code*. The bill was also an effort by established merchants to protect themselves from newcomers.

the twelve promerchant senators, all but one got their districts excluded from repeal. Only two of the twelve black belt state senators
voted against the bill. A hard core of seven promerchant senators
opposed any restrictions on merchants' crop liens, wanting to deprive black belt planters of the right to supply their own tenants.
The bill became law in February, 1885.[51]

Thus the rise of the agrarian radical movement in the eighties
did not unite the two branches of the ruling class against a mutual
enemy. Instead, the planters used the agrarian radicals to further
weaken their merchant rivals in the black belt. The planters turned
their demand that all crop liens be abolished into a law which
pushed merchants out of the business of supplying black belt tenants. In exchange, the agrarian radicals won planter support for
abolition of merchant crop liens in a substantial number of hill
counties. The politics of the planters indicated that, while their
structural position may have converged with that of the hill merchant-landlords, the antagonism and rivalry between the two
groups was as potent as ever—even in the face of a threat from
below. The skill with which the planters defended their position
against the merchant threat suggests that the postwar planters
possessed a degree of class consciousness reminiscent of their antebellum counterparts.

Subsequent sessions of the legislature saw no changes in the
law abolishing merchants' crop liens, which remained outlawed in
twenty-nine of the state's sixty-five counties, including most of the
black belt. Merchants' liens remained legal in over half the state's
counties, but even there the merchants' position in relation to
planters remained one of subservience. The promerchant forces in
the legislature were never able to change the laws that made landlords' liens for supplies superior to those of merchants (passed in

51. Merchant crop liens remained legal in the Tennessee River Valley plantation district. *Alabama Senate Journal 1884–1885*, 563. In the next session of the legislature
(1886–1887), the promerchant forces succeeded in getting fourteen counties added to the
list of those where the merchants' crop lien was permitted. They closed in on the black belt
somewhat: in the twenty counties which were more than 50 percent black, merchants' crop
liens were legalized in six more, making a total of ten. The six counties in the heart of the
black belt, where merchants' liens continued to be outlawed, had the greatest population of
blacks in the state—two were 84 percent black, and one was 86 percent. *Acts of Alabama
1886–1887*, 164–65, 180–81.

1871), gave preference to landlords in the seizure of the personal property of insolvent debtors, and required landlord permission before tenants could pledge personal property to merchants (passed in 1883). These laws remained in effect to hamper merchants in the counties where their right to hold crop liens had not been abolished. In 1887, the state agricultural society's annual meeting discussed the compromise repeal of the merchants' crop lien in the preceding sessions of the legislature. The discussion focused on the question of whether the legislature had "accomplished its purpose of taking the Negro out of the merchant's hands and putting him in the hands of the farmers."[52]

The Alabama supreme court supported the planters in their attempts to weaken merchants' ability to do business with black belt tenants. One such case involved an attempt by merchants to hold landlords responsible for their tenants' debts to merchants. The case centered on one Green Cook, who had rented the Gilchrist plantation in Lowndes County from K. L. Haralson and E. L. James. The tenant had pledged his crop as security against the rent, and the landlords had given him permission to obtain advances of supplies from N. J. Bell & Co., merchants with whom tenant Cook signed a crop lien as security. At the end of the season, Cook had turned all his cotton over to his landlords, leaving N. J. Bell & Co. high and dry. The merchant sued the planters, arguing that they were responsible for their tenants' debts. The state supreme court sided with the planters.[53]

A few years later, the court considered a case in which two merchants each held crop liens for a tenant's cotton and both claimed the crop. The court ruled that even though one merchant clearly had signed a crop lien first, the other one should get the crop because the landlord had given him permission to supply the tenant. The court added, "The landlord may transfer his claim for advances, and clothe his transferee with his own paramount lien. But

52. *Code of Alabama, 1887*, Sections 3056–3075; *Code of Alabama 1897*, Sections 2703–2716; Alabama Agricultural Society, *Proceedings*, February 1887, cited in Going, *Bourbon Democracy*, 95.

53. *Bell v. Hurst*, 75 Alabama 237. See also Marjorie M. Applewhite, "Sharecropper and Tenant in the Courts of North Carolina," *North Carolina Historical Review*, XXXI (1954), 134–49.

the landlord can neither relinquish or transfer to another his *right* to make advances to the tenant."[54]

The most impressive court decision relating to planter-merchant conflict was an 1884 case in which the court distinguished between the landlord's lien for supplies and the merchant's, pointing out the comprehensiveness of the landlord's rights in comparison to the weakness and limitations which the law imposed on merchants. First the court examined the law dealing with "any person's" right to take liens as security for advances of supplies.

> Those sections, related to advances to make a crop, obtained from *outsiders*, from *persons other than the landlord*: to secure the statutory lien for such advances, many prerequisites must exist and must be conformed to. The articles are very restricted in number. . . . There must be a declaration in writing, with prescribed requisites, and it must be recorded; and such declared, recorded writing, does not preserve a statutory lien for advances made afterward.

The landlord's lien for supplies, in contrast, "is much more comprehensive. . . . It is not confined, . . . but embraces every thing of value . . . every thing useful or tending to the substantial comfort of the tenant and his family. . . . It requires neither writing nor registration."[55] The law would oversee the merchant's relations with tenant customers, imposing conditions and restrictions which did not exist for planters. On questions of the exploitation of tenant labor, state power in Alabama seems to have enforced planters' claims more than merchants'.

Conclusion

The crop lien was developed in the immediate postwar years as a new lever for extracting the surplus from the agricultural labor force. The surplus—the labor beyond that which is necessary for the subsistence of the actual producer—is in every society "the basis of all social, political and intellectual progress," according to Frederick Engels. Maurice Dobb has termed the surplus the "life-blood" of a ruling class; as a consequence, he writes, "any ruling class will of necessity treat its particular relationship to the labor

54. *Leslie* v. *Hinton*, 83 Alabama 266. Emphasis mine.
55. *Cockburn* v. *Watkins*, 76 Alabama 486. Emphasis mine.

process as crucial to its own survival."[56] Thus the merchants' challenge to the planters over control of this new lever for extracting the surplus was a life-and-death matter for the planter class. The merchants of the postwar South tried to use the crop lien to gain control of plantation agriculture, but the planter elite was able to use its political power to overcome this challenge. The planter-dominated Alabama legislature severely limited the activities of merchants in the black belt, but allowed the merchant class continued pursuit of wealth and power in the hills.

But the merchants were a challenge to the planter elite only in a limited sense. Although they sought to control southern agriculture, they did not represent a "revolutionary" threat to the prevailing mode of production. In this, they followed in the footsteps of European merchants two and three centuries earlier. Dobb, describing the merchant class in early modern Europe, came close to describing the southern merchant class of the late 1860s and 1870s: "Since its fortunes will tend to be bound up with the existing mode of production, it is more likely to be under an inducement to preserve that mode of production than to transform it. It is likely to struggle to 'muscle in' upon an existing form of appropriating surplus labor, but it is unlikely to try to change this form."[57]

The result was that planters became planter-merchants and continued their domination of the black belt, making use of a new lever for squeezing their tenants, while in the hills, the merchants became merchant-landlords at the expense of the white yeomen. Tenant farmers, black and white alike, tended to be driven into more or less permanent debt by the crop lien system.[58] Unable to

56. Frederick Engels, *Herr Eugen Dühring's Revolution in Science* (New York: International Publishers, n.d.), 221; Maurice Dobb, *Studies in the Development of Capitalism* (New York: International Publishers, 1947), 15. See also Robert Brenner, "The Civil War Politics of London's Merchant Community," *Past & Present*, No. 58 (1973), 53–107.

57. Dobb, *Studies*, 17–18. Whether the merchants of the small towns and villages of the postwar South formed a social class in the strict sense of the term is debatable. Excluded from consideration in this study are the big city merchants of Montgomery, Selma, and Mobile, the big cotton dealers and exporters, and the merchandise wholesalers, most of whom were outside Alabama. The most serious problem of definition involves the rural merchants' relationship to their urban counterparts.

58. On debt peonage, see Pete Daniel, *The Shadow of Slavery: Peonage in the South, 1901–1969* (Urbana: University of Illinois Press, 1972); William Cohen, "Negro Involuntary Servitude in the South, 1865–1940: A Preliminary Analysis," *Journal of Southern History*, XLII (1976), 31–60; Ransom and Sutch, "Debt Peonage," 641–69. This last article was

fully repay the lien holder at the end of a season, the tenant would be tied to the land, and to the landowner, for the next season, when the debt was to be repaid; the process was repeated annually. The crop lien thus reduced significantly the competition among planters for labor, sharply limited tenants' freedom to move in response to better offers, and came close to abolishing the free market in agricultural labor. Debt peonage arising out of the crop lien became a central element in the coercive apparatus of labor allocation and control that distinguished southern from northern capitalist development. By guaranteeing that laborers would remain tied to the land, it reduced incentives for the planters to mechanize agricultural production and modernize their techniques. Thus the South set off on the Prussian Road to modern society, under the domination of a reactionary agrarian elite.[59]

criticized in William W. Brown and Morgan O. Reynolds, "Debt Peonage Reexamined," *Journal of Economic History*, XXXIII (1973), 862–71, and Stephen DeCanio, "Cotton 'Overproduction' in late 19th Century Southern Agriculture," *Journal of Economic History*, XXXIII (1973), 608–33; Ransom and Sutch's convincing reply is in their little known paper "Economic Theory and Southern History," Southern Economic History Project, *Working Paper Series*, Number 13 (Berkeley: Institute for Business and Economic Research, University of California, 1974).

59. On the applicability of Barrington Moore's conception of the Prussian Road to American history, see Reinhard Bendix, Review of *Social Origins of Dictatorship and Democracy*, *Political Science Quarterly*, LXXXII (1967), 625–27; Eugene D. Genovese, "Marxian Interpretations of the Slave South," in *In Red and Black* (New York: Pantheon Books, 1972), 345–49; Michael Rogin, Review of *Social Origins*, *Book Week*, IV (January 1, 1967), 5; Stanley Rothman, "Barrington Moore and the Dialectics of Revolution," *American Political Science Review*, LXIV (1970), 61–85; Lawrence Stone, "News from Everywhere," *New York Review of Books*, IX (August 24, 1967), 31–35; C. Vann Woodward, "Comparative Political History," *Yale Review*, LVI (1967), 450–53. These discussions are examined in Jonathan M. Wiener, "Review of Reviews: *Social Origins of Dictatorship and Democracy*," *History and Theory*, XV (1976), especially pp. 166–67. For other comparative perspectives on southern development, see Eugene D. Genovese, *The World the Slaveholders Made* (New York: Pantheon Books, 1969), 228–30; David M. Potter, "The Civil War in the History of the Modern World: A Comparative View," in Potter, *The South and Sectional Conflict* (Baton Rouge: Louisiana State University Press, 1968), 287–300; and John Hope Franklin, *Reconstruction: After the Civil War* (Chicago: University of Chicago Press, 1969), 228–30.

4

The Rise and Fall
of the Merchants

Alabama's first crop lien law, passed in 1868, gave merchants an opportunity to challenge the planters' control of plantation agriculture. The most vivid picture we have of the successful southern merchant-landlord of this period is William Faulkner's Will Varner:

> He was the largest landholder and beat supervisor in one county and Justice of the Peace in the next and election commissioner in both, and hence the fountainhead if not of law at least of advice and suggestion. . . . He was a farmer, a usurer, a veterinarian; Judge Benbow of Jefferson once said of him that a milder-mannered man never bled a mule or stuffed a ballot box. He owned the store and the cotton gin and the combined grist mill and blacksmith shop in the village proper and it was considered, to put it mildly, bad luck for a man of the neighborhood to do his trading or gin his cotton or grind his meal or shoe his stock anywhere else.[1]

Alabama black belt merchants had an opportunity to make considerable gains in landownership, but in 1871 the planters succeeded in getting the legislature to pass restrictions on these merchants, which gave the planters a decisive advantage in the competition between the two groups. Since the planter-sponsored

1. William Faulkner, *The Hamlet* (New York: Vintage Books, 1956), 5. Faulkner gives the precise location of Varner's store on the map in *Absalom, Absalom!* (New York: The Modern Library, 1951), 382–83. Irving Howe correctly identifies *The Hamlet* as a "comic novel . . . second only to *Huckleberry Finn*" in American literature. But it is important not to exaggerate the relevance of Faulkner for historical studies of the South. Some critics, including Malcolm Cowley in his introduction to *The Portable Faulkner* (New York: The Viking Press, 1946), and in "William Faulkner's Human Comedy," *New York Times Book Review*, October 29, 1944, have described the Yoknapatawpha novels as a social history of

antimerchant legislation was effective primarily in the black belt, the consequence of the law was to focus the activity of the merchant class in the poorer hill counties, where merchants like Will Varner could still use the crop lien to exploit white yeoman farmers, while the planters exploited the labor of the black tenants who worked on the great plantations of the black belt.

The political record shows that the merchants had great opportunities. Evidence from the manuscript census suggests that the black belt merchant class took advantage of these opportunities and made significant economic gains, which could only have appeared to the planters as a threat to their own position. The political record shows that the planters blocked further merchant gains in the black belt; evidence from the manuscript census indicates that this antimerchant strategy was successful, that black belt merchants suffered considerable losses after 1870, while hill merchants continued to prosper.

The manuscript schedules of the United States census of population list individuals' occupations, making it possible to identify merchants and to follow their rising or declining fortunes from one census to the next between 1860 and 1880. In comparing merchants of five contiguous black belt counties with hill merchants from six contiguous counties in northwestern Alabama (see map, p. xiv), sharp social and political contrasts may be noted. In 1870 and 1880, blacks made up more than 75 percent of the black belt population, but only 25 percent of the population of the six hill counties. In 1860, the cotton production of these hill counties was only 20 percent of what the five black belt counties produced, and in 1870 it was only 25 percent. In the hill region, the average farm consisted of 82 improved acres, while the average farm in the black belt

---

the South comparable to Balzac. Against this view, Howe writes that "the *idea* of society does not entice [Faulkner] as it does Balzac; . . . no consistent or precise social point of view runs through his work. . . . A play of manners usually reflects nuances of individual character rather than the condition of social classes." Irving Howe, *William Faulkner: A Critical Study* (3rd ed., rev.; Chicago University Press, 1975), 7, 252. Woodward has essentially the same position on Faulkner: C. Vann Woodward, "The Historical Dimension," in *The Burden of Southern History* (Baton Rouge: Louisiana State University Press, 1960), especially pp. 34–37. On the discouraging state of Snopes scholarship, see Karen Paden Boyle, review of James Gray Watson's *Snopes Dilemma*, in *Mississippi Quarterly*, XXV (1972), 380–87.

region was 205 acres. Only 13 percent of hill farms had more than 500 improved acres, while 40 percent of the black belt farms did.[2]

The five black belt counties supported secession by overwhelming margins; the six hill counties all opposed secession. During the war, the hill counties were a center of disloyalty and desertion; after the war, they became the base of opposition to black belt Democratic candidates for state office. The black belt counties, on the other hand, consistently opposed Republican, Greenback, Independent, and Populist candidates for state office after Reconstruction—candidates who repeatedly received their largest majorities in the hill counties. In the 1894 election, for instance, the Populist candidate for governor carried four of the six hill counties and none of the black belt counties. Two of the hill counties elected Independents to the legislature in every single election between 1876 and 1886.[3]

As noted, merchants were identified from the occupation item on the manuscript census. Since the purpose in selecting the merchant group was to include all those who supplied farmers and tenants with general merchandise and offered credit based on the crop lien, specialized merchants such as "hardware dealer" and "boot and shoe merchant" do not appear. Those who gave their occupation as "clerk to merchant" or "works in store" were omitted from

2. The hill counties were Colbert, Fayette, Franklin, Lamar, Lawrence, and Marion; some were parts of others before 1870; see Appendix, herein. Walter L. Fleming, *Civil War and Reconstruction in Alabama* (Cleveland: A. H. Clark Company, 1911), 804–805; Gavin Wright, " 'Economic Democracy' and the Concentration of Agricultural Wealth in the Cotton South, 1850–1860," *Agricultural History*, XLIV (1970), 71, 73. For local histories, see Dorothy Gentry, *Life and Legend in Lawrence County, Alabama* (Tuscaloosa: n.p., 1962), and Glenn Sisk, "Town Business in the Alabama Black Belt, 1875–1917," *Mid-America*, XXVIII (1956), 47–55.

3. Stephen E. Ambrose, "Yeoman Discontent in the Confederacy," *Civil War History*, VIII (1962), 259–68; Hugh C. Bailey, "Disaffection in the Alabama Hill Country, 1861," *Civil War History*, IV (1958), 183–93; Bailey, "Disloyalty in Early Confederate Alabama," *Journal of Southern History*, XXIII (1957), 522–28; Bessie Martin, *Desertion of Alabama Troops from the Confederate Army: A Study in Sectionalism* (New York: Columbia University Press, 1932); Georgia Lee Tatum, *Disloyalty in the Confederacy* (Chapel Hill: University of North Carolina Press, 1934); Fleming, *Civil War and Reconstruction in Alabama*, 29; Allen Going, *Bourbon Democracy in Alabama, 1874–1890* (University, Ala.: University of Alabama Press, 1951), 220–31; William Warren Rogers, *The One-Gallused Rebellion: Agrarianism in Alabama, 1865–1896* (Baton Rouge: Louisiana State University Press, 1970), 223, 284, 315.

this study of the changing fortunes of the merchants themselves.[4] In the following pages these merchants will be compared to the planter class described in Chapter One to show the effect of crop lien legislation on merchant-planter competition in the black belt, the social characteristics of the black belt merchant group which distinguished it from the planters, and the social characteristics of the hill merchants which differentiated them from their black belt counterparts.

The Crop Lien Law and the Merchants

Both the wealth and the number of black belt merchants increased sharply between 1860 and 1870, the period in which the crop lien offered merchants an opportunity to expand their economic strength. And merchant wealth expanded most in precisely the area that posed the greatest threat to the planter elite—land. While the holdings of all other groups of landowners, rich and poor, were declining in value, the value of merchants' holdings was increasing. The total value of real estate owned by the planter elite fell from over $15 million in 1860 to not quite $5 million in 1870, a decline of 67 percent. In the same period, the total value of real estate owned by black belt merchants actually increased by 7 percent—from $538,000 to $579,000.

The merchants in 1870 still held only a fraction of the land owned by the planter elite, but the gap between them had been reduced considerably during the preceding decade. In 1860, the merchants as a group owned a total of 3.5 percent of the real estate owned by the planter elite in the black belt; by 1870, merchant holdings had risen to 12 percent. In one black belt county which was studied more intensively, the share of landed wealth owned by merchants almost tripled between 1860 and 1870, increasing from .9 percent of all land owned by county residents to 2.6 percent in

4. Curti, studying manuscript census records for a Wisconsin county in this same period, included among his "merchant" category the occupations "jeweler, saloon keeper, grocer, hardware dealer, lumber merchant, insurance agent, travelling salesman, clerk, dealer in miscellaneous items"; the definition herein is considerably narrower. Merle E. Curti, *The Making of an American County: A Case Study of Democracy in a Frontier County* (Stanford: Stanford University Press, 1959), 225. For a case study, see H. E. Sterkx, "Joel Dyer Murphee, Troy Merchant, 1843–1868," *Alabama Review*, X (1958), 117–24.

1870. (The county planter elite held 55 percent of the real estate value in 1860 and 63 percent in 1870.) Thus, while the merchants still held a small proportion of county real estate in 1870, their share of the total landholdings of black belt residents had increased considerably during the preceding decade.

The merchants increased in number as well as wealth. One hundred forty-six merchants were listed in the census manuscript for 1860 in five black belt counties. The number in 1870 had risen to 247, an increase of 41 percent. The number of merchants per 10,000 county residents increased from 13 in 1860 to 21 in 1870, an increase of more than 60 percent.[5]

Although both the total number and the total landholdings of black belt merchants increased between 1860 and 1870, not all merchants increased their landholdings. During the sixties, black belt merchants divided more sharply into two groups—the substantial landowners and the landless. The number of merchants in the middle, who were neither big landowners nor landless, declined sharply.

Several black belt merchants owned as much land as members of the planter elite. The number of such big landholders among merchants increased dramatically between 1860 and 1870. In 1860, only one black belt merchant owned as much real estate as the poorest member of the planter elite (the top 236 landowners in five counties); in 1870, fourteen merchants did.

In addition to those merchants who had become big landowners by 1870, nine of the 1860 merchants who no longer gave their occupation as "merchant" in 1870 had gained enough land during the sixties to join the planter elite. They had remained in the five-county black belt area, but, apparently on the basis of the crop lien law, left their stores behind and won elite status. A total of twenty-three merchants and former merchants in 1870 had landholdings equal to the planter elite—a number equivalent to 10 percent of the 1870 merchant group.

The expansion of merchant landholding attracted large numbers of merchants from other areas and occupations to the black belt be-

5. Because the 1870 census underenumerated blacks, the proportional increase of black belt merchants was somewhat less than this figure. See Appendix, note 6, herein.

tween 1860 and 1870. As a result, while the number of merchants
who were big landholders was increasing, the number of landless
merchants was increasing even more sharply. In 1860, 36 percent
of the merchants in the five black belt counties owned no land; in
1870 fully 65 percent of the merchants were landless. The number
of landless merchants increased between 1860 and 1870 from 52 to
161. The number of landless merchants was increasing at the expense of the merchants who had been small landholders. In 1860,
64 percent of the black belt merchants owned some real estate, but
less than the planter elite owned; virtually all the rest were landless. Ten years later, after the war, the proportion of landowning
merchants below the planter elite had dropped from 64 percent to
29 percent of the merchant group, while both the wealthier and
poorer groups had increased in size. The merchants with holdings
equal to the planter elite increased from less than one percent of all
black belt merchants to 6 percent, and the landless merchants increased from 36 to 65 percent.

Thus black belt merchants had made considerable gains in the
decade of Civil War and Reconstruction, during which the crop
lien system had been established. In 1870, in comparison with
1860, there were many more black belt merchants, the merchants
as a group owned considerably more black belt land, and the proportion of merchants who were big landowners had increased
sharply. These gains could only have been interpreted by the
planters as a threat to their own position.

As we have seen, the planters responded to this merchant threat
by using their political power in the state legislature to revise the
initial crop lien law in 1871, limiting merchant operations in the
black belt and leaving the hill region as the remaining focus for
the activity of the merchant class. The census indicates that merchants in the black belt declined between 1870 and 1880, while
merchants in the hills continued to prosper. Unfortunately, while
the census of 1880 recorded occupations, it did not record the value
of real estate owned by each county resident, as it had in 1860 and
1870. It is therefore impossible to find direct evidence in the census
of merchant gains and losses in real estate holdings for the seventies.

But other kinds of evidence are available. Changes in the total number of merchants provide a measure of the prosperity of the merchant class in the black belt and hills. In general, southern merchants were a geographically mobile group. Unlike farmers, their fortunes were not tied to a particular plot of ground; if they were not doing very well in one place, they moved. Rumors would sweep the merchant ranks of fortunes to be made in particular areas, and less prosperous merchants would pack their store stock and head for the latest promised land.

Merchant eagerness to move from county to county in pursuit of better business opportunities appears to have been a major factor in the large fluctuations in the number of black belt merchants. In 1852, J. H. Jelks, a store owner at Uchee, Alabama, urged his relatives in North Carolina to move with him to Texas, where he promised that store profits would exceed 100 percent. David Campbell, a storekeeper in Lebanon, Tennessee, was forced by the Panic of 1837 to move to Arkansas, where he estimated that he "could make a fortune in three years if other stores did not move in to compete." Robert Somers, writing in 1871, noted the tendency of merchants to pack up and leave: "In two or three years they ought to be very rich. Yet these local . . . traders often run away, leaving their city friends in the lurch. For, as Mr. Solomon truly says in extenuation of this offense . . . the large profits are often only in the books."[6]

Merchants flocked to the black belt in the sixties, and pulled out in the seventies. While the number of merchants in the black belt population increased by 70 percent between 1860 and 1870, from 136 to 247 merchants, the number fell to 148 in 1880, a decline of almost 40 percent. The ratio of merchants in the population decreased from 21 per 10,000 in 1870 to 14 in 1880, following the passage of the restrictions on black belt merchants' crop liens. One hundred ninety-three new merchants opened stores between 1860 and 1870; only 86 merchants opened stores between 1870 and 1880.

6. Lewis E. Atherton, *The Southern Country Store, 1800–1860* (Baton Rouge: Louisiana State University Press, 1949), 209; Robert Somers, *The Southern States Since the War, 1870–1* (New York: Macmillan and Company, 1871), 242. (I have cleaned up Somers's somewhat anti-semitic prose here.)

The private correspondence of several planters studied by James Roark suggests that, during the late 1860s, many were considering nonplantation careers, including storekeeping. Alabama planter Henry Watson wrote that he was looking for a position for his eldest son "where he will make a business man." John B. Grimball, a South Carolina planter, wrote of one son, "I don't know if John would like Mercantile life, but I think he will require some means of support." One of Grimball's sons opened a country store in 1866; according to Roark, his planter-father was upset, but wrote that to be a merchant was "better . . . than [to] be completely idle." Another South Carolina planter objected to his son entering the "business of drumming" because it was so "demoralizing," but permitted him to do it because "the business will be so remunerating to him."[7]

Almost twice as many planters became merchants between 1860 and 1870 as did so between 1870 and 1880. This difference between the decades in the number of downwardly mobile planters making the switch is further evidence for the argument that the merchant profession offered a route to landownership in the late sixties but not in the seventies. Fifteen planters who had fallen from the landholding elite after 1860 reported their occupation to the 1870 census enumerator as "merchant." The corresponding number for the subsequent decade was eight, two of whom were sons of 1870 planters who had become merchants in the locality. The proportion of 1860 planters who became merchants by 1870 was small—6 percent of the planter elite, 11 percent of the nonpersistent planters. Apparently these fifteen former planters opened stores during the later sixties, hoping to take advantage of the opportunities offered by the new crop lien law to regain their former status as elite landholders. (None of them succeeded.) While only 3 percent of the planters of 1870 appear in the 1880 merchant list, some of whom were planter sons, it is somewhat surprising that any former planters should turn toward merchant businesses after 1871, given the restrictions on black belt merchants. (None of these cases of planters becoming merchants re-

7. All quoted in James L. Roark, *Masters Without Slaves: Southern Planters in the Civil War and Reconstruction* (New York: W. W. Norton Company, 1977), 151.

sulted in the appearance of the hybrid planter-merchant; all had lost enough land so that they were no longer members of the landholding elite.)

The hill merchant class differed sharply in size and landhold-ings from their black belt counterparts, in ways that suggest that merchant opportunities in the seventies were greatest in the black belt, but in the eighties were restricted to the hills. The legisla-ture did not establish legal restrictions on merchant crop liens in any of the six hill counties studied, as it did in the black belt. And between 1870 and 1880, the number of merchants in the hill coun-ties increased by 17 percent, from 92 to 108. (See Table 10.) The number of merchants in the black belt during the same decade declined by 40 percent.[8] In 1870, there were proportionately more merchants in the black belt than the hills, while in 1880 there were more in the hills than the black belt. During the sixties, three times as many new merchants opened stores in the black belt than in the hills; during the seventies, more new merchants opened stores in the hills than the black belt.

Persistence provides another measure of the effect of crop lien restrictions on black belt and hill merchants. Persistence was de-fined in terms of "outflow," the percentage of merchants in one census who were still merchants in the same county a decade later. The same cautionary notes are necessary for the merchant persis-tence rates as for the planters', discussed in Chapter One; this defi-nition includes both geographic and social mobility as nonpersis-tence. If a merchant changed occupations, he was counted as not persisting; he was also counted as not persisting if he moved out of the counties being studied, to another area, where his occupation could not be ascertained.

Merchant persistence in the five black belt counties decreased between the decade of opportunity, 1860–1870, and the decade of restrictions, 1870–1880. Thirty-seven percent of the merchants of 1860 were still black belt merchants ten years later, while only 25

8. In terms of the proportion of merchants in the population, the black belt ratio de-clined from 21 to 11 per 10,000 between 1870 and 1880, while the hill ratio remained at approximately the same level; there were 16 merchants per 10,000 people in the hills in 1870, and 14 per 10,000 in 1880.

Table 10. MERCHANTS IN BLACK BELT[a] AND HILL[b] REGIONS

	1860		1870		1880	
	Black Belt	Hills	Black Belt	Hills	Black Belt	Hills
Total population	113,765	56,579	115,476	59,289	138,841	78,386
Percent black	74%	32%	76%	26%	79%	26%
Number of merchants	146	97	247	92	148	108
Merchants per 10,000 population	13	17	21	16	11	14

[a] Black Belt counties: Greene, Hale, Marengo, Perry, Sumter.
[b] Hill counties: Colbert, Fayette, Franklin, Lamar, Lawrence, Marion.

For 1860 county lines, see Walter L. Fleming, *Civil War and Reconstruction in Alabama* (Cleveland, 1911), 29; for 1870 county lines, see *Ibid.*, 750.

percent of the merchants of 1870 remained in the same five-county area in 1880. Of the 247 merchants in the black belt in 1870, only 62 remained in 1880. And few new merchants opened businesses in the black belt during the seventies; only 86 new merchants appear in the census lists of 1880, in comparison with 193 who appear for the first time in 1870. After 1870, the old merchants were less likely to stay in the black belt, and new merchants were less likely to come there to open stores. The changing crop lien legislation appears to have been responsible for much of this development.

Landless merchants in the black belt were more likely to remain merchants during the sixties than the seventies, but the pattern among hill merchants was exactly the opposite. The persistence rate of landless hill merchants increased by six percentage points between the decades 1860–1870 and 1870–1880 (from 19 to 24 percent), while the persistence rate of landless black belt merchants declined by six points in the same period (from 33 to 23 percent). One hundred twenty-four landless black belt merchants in 1870 do not appear in the census lists for 1880, in comparison with only 28 landless hill merchants in 1870 who do not appear in the 1880 lists.

Thus evidence about the persistence rates of black belt and hill merchants supports the argument that, as a result of changing crop lien laws, black belt merchants rose in the sixties but fell in the seventies, while hill merchants experienced no such fall. A larger proportion of black belt merchants left the area or went out of business in the seventies than the sixties; that is, the persistence rate of black belt merchants fell from the 1860–1870 decade to the 1870–1880 decade. Landless merchants were much more likely to remain in the black belt for the sixties than for the seventies, and landless merchants in the hills were more likely to remain for the seventies than they had been in the sixties.

The picture that emerges from the persistence data must be put together with the data on the changing numbers of merchants in black belt and hills. The number of merchants in the black belt decreased by more than 40 percent between 1870 and 1880, having risen by 70 percent in the preceding decade, while in the hills the number of merchants increased between 1870 and 1880 by a total of 17 percent. Few new merchants came to the black belt between 1870 and 1880. This suggests that the planter-sponsored legislation which restricted the activity of black belt merchants was effective in reducing the number of merchants in the black belt. Since the antimerchant legislation did not apply to merchants outside the black belt, the number of merchants in the hills increased sharply after the legislation was passed.

Black Belt Merchants and Planters

The events of the Civil War decade did little to alter the social composition of the merchant class. Compared to planters, black belt merchants in 1870 were less likely to have been born in the South, were younger, less likely to have sons, and less likely to have wives. The differences between 1860 merchants and planters were similar.

While 92 percent of the planters of 1870 were southern-born, only 68 percent of the merchants that year had been born in the

South. (See Table 11.) The merchants were not so much northern-ers as foreigners in 1870; 23 percent had been born outside the United States, while only 9 percent were northern-born. (The com-parable figures for the planters were 3 percent foreign-born and 5 percent northern-born.) But these merchants born outside the South were not necessarily carpetbaggers. Williamson reports that "northern-born merchants were particularly active" in some areas after the war, and indicates that, in general, a large number of post-war country stores "were begun by persons more or less alien to the community in which they were located."[9] The census gives the state of birth of all Alabama residents, but it does not indicate when individuals arrived in Alabama. Northern- and foreign-born merchants could well have migrated to Alabama before the war. In-deed, the birthplace of antebellum merchants suggests that this was the case. In 1860, 11 percent of the black belt merchants were northern-born and 16 percent were foreign-born; if there were carpetbaggers among the 1870 merchants, they were no more numerous than northern migrants had been in the antebellum merchant class. And the persistence data indicate that 20 percent of the nonsouthern 1870 black belt merchants had been merchants in the same area in 1860. The rest might well have been merchants in other parts of Alabama or the South.

Most of the foreign-born merchants had German names, and travelers reported that at least some of them were Jewish, recent migrants from the Northeast. Robert Somers, for instance, de-scribed an 1871 visit to the "local Jew traders" of Meridian, Missis-sippi, just across the state line from the Alabama black belt. "Much of the storekeeping business is conducted by sharply active young men of Jewish aspect, who talk German-English. . . . These peo-ple are sent down from New York and other large towns. . . . One firm in New York is said to make half a million dollars in this lucra-tive business per annum, after giving, it may be supposed, a fair share of the spoils to the Hebrew agents, who live on the spot and bear the heat and burden of the day." Edward King, traveling from

9. Joel Williamson, *After Slavery: The Negro in South Carolina During Reconstruction, 1861–1877* (Chapel Hill: University of North Carolina Press, 1965), 173.

Table 11. CHARACTERISTICS OF BLACK BELT MERCHANTS
AND PLANTERS

	1860		1870	
	Merchants (percentage)	Planters (percentage)	Merchants (percentage)	Planters (percentage)
Persistence Rate	37	42	25	NA
Family Structure:				
Spouse:				
Present	75	64	57	53
Not present	25	36	40	46
Sons present:				
None	63	39	71	60
At least one	37	61	29	40
Four or more	3	11	3	4
Age:				
30 and under	34	8	34	19
31–45	60	53	53	50
55 and over	6	39	13	31
Place of Birth:				
South	73	94	68	92
North	11	3	9	5
Foreign	16	1	23	3
Sex:				
Male	100	90	100	89
Female	0	10	0	11
Number	146	236	247	236

Opelika to Montgomery by rail in 1873, found "a sprinkling of commercial Hebrews" on the train, and a Chicago *Tribune* reporter the same year wrote about Alabama stores "whose fronts bear Hebrew names."[10]

Merchants tended to be younger than planters, but the proportion of older merchants was greater in 1870 than it had been in 1860. In the antebellum period, men became merchants when they were young, hoping to make money; their goal, however, was not to remain merchants all their lives, but to become farmers or small planters when they had accumulated enough money to buy land. A study of antebellum merchants in Perry County, Alabama, found that only 2 out of 144 were more than fifty years old. The typical crossroads merchant remained in business for a limited number of years, during which time he either went bankrupt or made enough money to leave the merchant profession. A few remained merchants their entire lives, but they were distinctly in the minority.[11] The doubling of the proportion of black belt merchants fifty-five or older between 1860 and 1870 suggests that this antebellum pattern was weakening; more of the older merchants remained in business when the crop lien law gave them the opportunity for unusually large profits. Perhaps because they were younger than planters, merchants tended to have fewer sons. About half the merchants had a wife present in the household, as did about the same proportion of planters. (The differences were greater in 1860.)

There were no female merchants listed in the census of five black belt counties in 1870. Eleven percent of the planters in 1870 were female. In fact, there were no females who gave the occupation "merchant" anywhere in the census lists of eleven Alabama counties between 1860 and 1880. It is noteworthy that the prevail-

10. Somers, *Southern States*, 151; Edward King, *The Great South* (Hartford: American Publishing Company, 1875), 331; Chicago *Tribune*, August 15, 1871, quoted in Mobile *Daily Register*, August 25, 1871; see also Thomas D. Clark, *Pills, Petticoats and Plows, the Southern Country Store* (Indianapolis: The Bobbs-Merrill Company, 1944), 23–24.

11. Atherton, *Southern Country Store*, 203, 206; another study found that antebellum merchants were considerably younger than planters in Hancock County, Georgia: James C. Bonner, "Profile of a Late Ante-Bellum Community," *American Historical Review*, XLIX (1944), 671.

ing standards permitted women to operate plantations but apparently not country stores in their own name. Without doubt the wives of male rural merchants worked in the stores, and may well have operated them, but such women were never described as merchants by the census enumerators.[12]

Finally, the merchants were less persistent than planters, though not by much. Thirty-seven percent of the black belt merchants of 1860 remained merchants in the black belt in 1870, in comparison to 42 percent of the 1860 planters who remained planters in 1870. The similarity in these rates is more remarkable than the difference.

The merchants most able to respond to the opportunities offered by the new crop lien law by moving into the black belt during the sixties were younger, less likely to be married, and less likely to have acquired real estate, in comparison to the antebellum merchants who remained in business in the black belt. (See Table 12.)

Merchants who left the area, or their class, between 1870 and 1880 were less likely to have wives, sons, or real estate than those who stayed. The differences in real estate holdings of persistent and nonpersistent merchants were not as great as the differences in family structure. There was very little difference between the persistent and nonpersistent groups in age or place of birth; similar proportions had been born in the North or in foreign countries, and the age distributions were virtually identical.

Nonpersistence of merchants could be interpreted as indicating either that their stores failed, forcing them out of business, or that their stores succeeded, permitting them to go into a different occupation. Some might find it surprising that only 40 percent of the merchants who persisted from 1870 to 1880 owned any real estate, especially since it has been argued here that the opportunities for merchants to acquire real estate were sharply reduced after 1871. Merchants who had acquired real estate by 1870 probably stayed

12. Frank Jackson Huffman, Jr., "Old South, New South: Continuity and Change in a Georgia County, 1850–1880" (Ph.D. dissertation, Yale University, 1974), 85, comes to a similar conclusion for Clarke County, Georgia; but see Anne Firor Scott, *The Southern Lady: From Pedestal to Politics, 1830–1930* (Chicago: University of Chicago Press, 1970), 81.

Table 12. FACTORS IN BLACK BELT MERCHANT PERSISTENCE

	1870 Merchants			
	New in 1870 (percentage)	Persist from 1860 (percentage)	Persist to 1880 (percentage)	Do not persist (percentage)
Real Estate Holdings:				
Some	33	41	40	33
None	67	59	60	67
Family Structure:				
Wife:				
Present	52	74	68	54
Not present	48	26	32	47
Sons Present:				
None	72	67	61	75
At least one	28	33	39	25
Four or more	3	6	5	3
Place of Birth:				
South	68	67	71	67
North	9	9	7	10
Foreign	23	24	21	24
Age:				
30 and under	39	15	34	34
31–54	48	69	52	53
55 and over	12	17	15	13
Number	193	54	62	185

through 1880, while those who had failed to acquire real estate before 1870 would have left. But it may well have been the case that many of the merchants who acquired real estate decided to give up their stores and become farmers or small planters. In some respects it is surprising that so many merchants who owned real estate in 1870 chose to remain merchants after 1871, given that they had an opportunity to earn a living as members of a more powerful and socially honored class. Those with real estate had the best opportunity of moving up out of the merchant class; those who had failed to acquire any real estate probably moved down and out.

Fourteen of the 247 black belt merchants in 1870 had real estate holdings as large as some members of the planter elite; these 14 differed from the remainder of the merchants in that they were older, and all were married. (See Table 13.) Indeed, these land-holding merchants were older than the planters, 19 percent of whom were thirty or under in 1870. The merchants who were big landholders differed from both planters and other merchants in that 100 percent of them had wives present in the household, in comparison with around 55 percent of both other merchants and planters who had spouses present. However, the landholding mer-chants were no more likely to have sons in the household than other merchants, and less likely than planters. Northern- and foreign-born merchants were represented among the big land-owners in about the same proportion as they were among other merchants.

Perhaps the most notable lack of difference between the mer-chants who were big landowners and the rest of the merchants was in their persistence rates. The big landholders among the 1870 merchants were no more likely to have been merchants in the re-gion in 1860, and were only slightly more likely to remain mer-chants until 1880. Virtually identical proportions of both groups— 22 percent—had been merchants in the black belt a decade earlier. The merchants who were big landholders in 1870 had either mi-grated into the five-county region during the sixties, or else had been local residents who were not merchants in 1860 but had gone into business during the decade. The big merchant landholders of 1870 came either from outside the county or outside the 1860 local merchant class.

One might think that big merchant landholders would be more persistent, that once a merchant acquired a lot of land, he would remain; but this was not the case for the seventies. Given the

Table 13. CHARACTERISTICS OF POSTWAR BLACK BELT
MERCHANT LANDHOLDERS AND PLANTERS

	Planters (percentage)	Merchants (percentage)	
		Big Landholders	Others
Family Structure:			
Spouse:			
Present	53	100	55
Not present	47	0	45
Sons present:			
None	60	71	71
At least one	40	29	29
Four or more	4	0	3
Age:			
30 and under	19	7	34
31–45	50	64	54
55 and over	31	29	12
Place of Birth:			
South	92	79	67
Non-South	8	21	33
Sex:			
Male	89	100	100
Female	11	0	0
Persistence Rate			
1870–1860	42	21	22
1870–1880	NA	29	25
Number	236	14	233

sizes of the two groups, the rate should be considered approximately the same. But it should be recalled that persistence was defined to include both social and geographic dimensions. If big merchant landowners gave up their stores during the seventies to become fulltime farmers or planters, they are counted here as cases of merchant nonpersistence. That indeed is their most likely fate; the merchant goal was not to remain the operator of a small crossroads store all his life, but rather to use the store to acquire enough land to be able to become a farmer. However, since the 1880 census did not record the value of individuals' real estate, the census offers no way of confirming this supposition.

Black Belt and Hill Merchants

More hill merchants than black belt merchants owned real estate, and the difference between the two groups was greater in 1870 than it had been in 1860. In 1860, 44 percent of hill merchants owned some real estate, as did 37 percent of black belt merchants; by 1870, fully 60 percent of hill merchants owned some real estate, while the black belt proportion remained unchanged from the antebellum level. (See Table 14.) Since hill real estate was less desirable than black belt real estate, the competition was less severe, and the price was lower; land in the hills was easier to acquire. And, since this land was less valuable, it was not as easy for hill merchant landowners to leave their stores to become farmers or small planters. Landholding among hill merchants increased between 1860 and 1870, while the landholding of black belt merchants showed no such increase: this may simply be a consequence of the fact that many black belt merchants who became landowners during the late sixties gave up the merchant profession by 1870, while hill merchant landholders had to remain merchants because their land was not as productive as black belt land. Aside from the differences in landholding, black belt and hill merchants were similar in their social characteristics. There were few elderly merchants in either black belt or hills at any time, evidence for the view that this was an occupation at which young men earned money so that they would not have to be merchants when they got old.

Table 14. CHARACTERISTICS OF BLACK BELT AND HILL MERCHANTS

	1860 (percentage)		1870 (percentage)		1880 (percentage)	
	Black Belt	Hill	Black Belt	Hill	Black Belt	Hill
Family structure:						
Spouse:						
Present	75	67	57	75	NA	NA
Not present	25	33	43	25	NA	NA
Sons:						
None	63	60	71	48	NA	NA
At least one	37	40	29	52	NA	NA
Four or more	3	4	3	11	NA	NA
Age:						
30 and under	34	36	34	28	36	40
31–54	60	61	53	61	53	51
55 and over	6	3	13	10	12	7
Place of Birth:						
South	73	82	68	80	70	83
North	11	5	9	8	7	6
Foreign	16	12	23	12	22	9
Sex:						
Male	100	100	100	100	99	100
Female	0	0	0	0	1	0
Real Estate:						
Some	37	44	35	60	NA	NA
None	64	56	65	40	NA	NA
Number	146	97	247	92	148	108

In 1880, a single female merchant appears in the census, the only one in eleven counties in thirty years. She was Elisa Sirbert of Sumter County in the black belt. She does not seem to have been the widow of an 1870 black belt merchant. She was fifty years old, foreign-born, and had no children in her household.

Persistence rates tended to be higher for all subgroups of the black belt merchants than the hill merchants, suggesting that the black belt was a more desirable place to operate a country store. It has been argued here that landless merchants had an opportunity to acquire real estate in the black belt up to 1871, when restrictions went into effect, but that there were no such restrictions in the hills. Indeed, the persistence rate of landless merchants in the black belt fell rather sharply from the decade of the sixties to the seventies, declining by ten percentage points. (See Table 15.) At the same time, the persistence rate of landless merchants in the hills increased by five percentage points.

Family structure had little effect on persistence for the sixties in either the black belt or the hills. But merchants with wives and sons were more likely to persist for the seventies in both regions. The difference was particularly pronounced in the hills between 1870 and 1880, when only 9 percent of merchants without wives persisted, in comparison with 26 percent of those with wives. There were some differences in the persistence rates of nonsouthern-born black belt and hill merchants, but the number of such merchants who persisted in either region was too small to warrant firm conclusions. Similarly the persistence rates of elderly merchants varied between black belt and hills, but the numbers were extremely small.

Dun's Mercantile Register was a reference book for wholesalers; it gave credit ratings of an amazing number of merchants, including crossroads supply merchants in rural Alabama.[13] Investigators for Dun's traveled through Alabama, checking up on the state of business in each small town, estimating the net worth of thousands of small businessmen. The *Register* was published quarterly, and the Alabama coverage began in 1867. Since there was competition

13. The Library of Congress run of *Dun's Mercantile Register* goes from 1867 to 1879.

Table 15. FACTORS IN BLACK BELT AND HILL
        MERCHANT PERSISTENCE

| | Percent Persisting | | | |
| | Black Belt | | Hills | |
	1860–1870	1870–1880	1860–1870	1870–1880
Family Structure:				
Wife:				
Present	37	30	28	26
Not present	33	23	19	24
Sons present:				
None	38	22	26	14
At least one	35	34	31	29
Four or more	80	38	25	30
Place of Birth:				
South	36	26	27	22
North	44	18	0	14
Foreign	35	23	50	27
Age:				
30 and under	32	25	23	23
31–54	41	25	29	23
55 and over	25	27	67	0
Real Estate:				
Some	39	29	35	20
None	33	23	19	24
Number Persisting	54	62	27	20

between Dun and other credit rating services, Dun constantly expanded his coverage, claiming to rate more businesses than the competition. Thus the number of rural merchants in the South who received credit ratings in Dun's increased every year. Since it was businesses that were being rated, not individual merchants, it is difficult to follow particular merchants for more than a few years; new businesses were added each year, and almost all businesses eventually changed names. Indeed, a good deal of Dun's own business was keeping track of what merchants who were known credit risks were calling their latest enterprise. This information was not published, but was recorded in private ledgers kept by Dun's field investigators.

The evidence from Dun's credit ratings of general stores in the Alabama black belt town of Demopolis indicates that Alabama black belt merchants did much better before the 1871 law restricting merchant crop liens went into effect than they did after. Of 36 merchants who operated general stores in and around Demopolis between 1867 and 1876, 72 percent started business before the antimerchant lien law was passed. And, of 23 Demopolis general merchants who went out of business between 1867 and 1876, 61 percent went out of business after the new lien law was passed.

Dun's listings also provide a measure of the persistence rate of general stores, rather than that of merchants, which the census provides. There were 36 general stores in and around Demopolis in 1867. The mean store was in business for 4.6 years; the median was 3.5 years. Twenty-two percent of the general stores went out of business after a single year of operation, and 57 percent of the 1867 stores were still open in 1870, the year before the merchant lien restrictions were passed; a year after the restrictions became law, only 38 percent of the general stores opened in 1867 were still in business. By 1874, only 19 percent were left, and at the end of a decade only 5 percent of these stores remained open.[14]

These figures give some idea of the tenuousness of the mercantile business in the postwar South. But a merchant who went out of business in Demopolis in 1872 may well have opened another store, perhaps in the same county, the next year; if that failed, he may have moved to a different county and tried again. The life of

14. The disappearance rate of southern stores on the basis of Dun's reports is 30 percent every five years, according to Roger Ransom and Richard Sutch, *One Kind of Freedom: The Economic Consequences of Emancipation* (New York: Cambridge University Press, 1977), Table 7.7.

many crossroads merchants in the immediate postwar South was an unstable one at best. Dun's also provides a glimpse of the transformations small-town southern merchants went through in the late sixties and seventies. In 1867, Dun lists David Rudisell as a Demopolis merchant in the business of "tin & c." Rudisell's credit rating was low in 1867, and fell steadily through 1871, when he left the tin business and opened a carpentry shop with his brother "A. L." and a mill with one "Dupertius." His credit rating was still at the bottom a year later, but he had added an undertaking business to his carpentry shop. The undertaking side of this mini-conglomerate improved the "pecuniary strength" rating of the whole from the $2,000–5,000 range in 1872 to the $10,000–25,000 range in 1874. But Rudisell's prosperity was brief. Between 1876 and 1879 his credit rating fell to the lowest Dun assigned. The combination of milling, carpentry, and undertaking kept him in business through the hard times to the end of the decade.

The Brietling family went through similar changes. In 1872 Dun listed C. K. Brietling as the operator of a Demopolis livery stable, with Mrs. C. K. Brietling down as "agent sewing machines," apparently a female V. K. Ratliff; like that Faulkner character, she also seems to have been an immigrant from eastern Europe. At the same time, "Brietling and Bro." had a "grocery & billiards" establishment. The following year, the brothers gave up the grocery but opened a "restaurant and bar" in its place; their credit rating promptly fell half a notch. In 1876, Mrs. Brietling gave up the sewing machine concession, and in 1877, the brothers abandoned the bar and billiard parlor and went back into the grocery business, holding on to their restaurant; their credit rating dropped another notch, to the bottom of the scale, but they were still in business at the end of the decade.

If the Rudisells and the Brietlings held on by changing businesses, another group accomplished the same thing by changing partners. In 1867, D. D. Royal operated a general store in Demopolis; six months later he added a partner and became "Royal and Bonner." Six months after that they parted ways, with Bonner forming the firm of "Bonner and Reis, General Store," and Royal going it alone. In 1871 Bonner and Royal disappeared from Dun's ratings, and Reis became "Reis and Gundersheimer, General Store," which existed very low in the credit ratings for four years. At the same time, a new firm, "P. Gundersheimer and Bro., General Store" came into existence in 1873. In 1875, Reis left Gundersheimer and opened his own general store; Gundersheimer stayed with his brother until 1877, when the brother was cast aside and a new firm, "Kohn and Gundersheimer, General Store," appeared on the streets of Demopolis. That same year Morris Reis's one-man general store disappeared, but Kohn and Gundersheimer stayed in existence with the lowest possible credit rating through the end of the decade.

A similar pattern of switching partners was pursued by the Demopolis merchants Marx, Mayer, and Enners. In 1867, "Isaac Marx & Co." operated a "dry goods and grocery" business. In 1869, the firm became "Marx and Enners," and their credit rating went up a notch. The same year, "M. Mayer and Co., General Store" went into competition with them, and the following year Mayer had become "Mayer and Enners" while the competition had returned to "Isaac Marx & Co." The year after that, "Mayer and Enners, General Store" underwent a reorganization and emerged as "Enners and Mayer, General Store," rising a notch in the credit ratings. In 1876, Enners left Mayer, as he had left Marx seven years earlier, and the firm became "Mayer and Brother, General Store." At the end of the decade, both Marx and Mayer were still in business, with "good" credit ratings. Given this kind of movement, it is a wonder that any merchant persisted for a full decade.

Part III

PLANTERS AND INDUSTRIAL

DEVELOPMENT

5

Before Birmingham

The power of Alabama's postwar planters was challenged by the freedmen and by the merchants; it was also challenged by the state's industrialists, that small group in antebellum society that was tied to the planter elite but remained socially distinct. In the view of many historians, the defeat of the planter regime in war struck down the antebellum obstacles to southern industrial development; the North's victory unleashed southern industrialists, who, in this view, moved quickly to make themselves the region's new ruling class.

Alabama is a crucial case for the argument that the war unleashed southern industry, because eventually the state would become the site of the South's most impressive industrial development, Birmingham iron and steel. But the story of the industrial development of Alabama is more complex than the view sketched above. The planters never opposed industry *per se*, not even under the slave regime. The slaveholders favored limited industrial development, development to the extent that it served their own interests and occurred under their own auspices, which is to say, industrial development without a bourgeois revolution, without the rise of an independent and powerful class of industrialists. A clear conception of the planters' relationship to industry in antebellum Alabama is a prerequisite to understanding the developments of the postwar period.

Industry and Society under the Slave Regime

Slavery created insuperable obstacles to industrialization in the antebellum South; a premodern social structure was the basic impediment. In the North and West, a society consisting primarily of farmers who produced for the market spurred regional industry by demanding—and possessing sufficient purchasing power to pay for —a wide variety of advanced agricultural equipment and manufactured goods. In the antebellum South, a society of planters and slaves created an extremely limited demand; they required coarse cotton cloth and simple tools for the slave laborers, jute bagging and cotton gins for preparing the cotton for market, and a small number of luxury goods for the planter families. Southern towns were few and far between, by comparison with developing areas of the country; an English traveler in the Alabama black belt in 1855 wrote, "The more fertile the land, the more destitute is the country of villages and towns." The towns were cotton markets, not centers of production.[1]

Alabama planters, especially after 1840, found that limited industrial development served their own interests. By supplying the plantation with some manufactured goods, local industrialists could reduce planter dependence on northern manufacturers. But the industrial expansion was to take place strictly within the confines of a planter-dominated, agrarian society; there was to be no move to-

---

1. Eugene D. Genovese, *The Political Economy of Slavery* (New York: Pantheon Books, 1967), Chap. 8; Douglass C. North, *Economic Growth of the United States, 1790–1860* (Englewood Cliffs: Prentice-Hall, 1961), 132; Raimondo Luraghi, "The Civil War and the Modernization of American Society: Social Structure and Industrial Revolution in the Old South before and during the War," *Civil War History*, XVIII (1972), 236; Robert E. Gallman and Ralph V. Anderson, "Slaves as Fixed Capital: Slave Labor and Southern Economic Development," *Journal of American History*, LXIV (1977), 24–46; Robert Russell, *North America, Its Agriculture and Climate* (Edinburgh: n.p., 1857), 289, quoted in Lewis E. Atherton, *The Southern Country Store, 1800–1860* (Baton Rouge: Louisiana State University Press, 1949), 19; Clanton R. Williams, "Conservatism in Old Montgomery, 1817–1861," *Alabama Review*, X (1957), 96–110. The argument that slavery created insuperable obstacles to industrialization was put forward by antislavery southerners including Cassius Clay and Henry Ruffner—David L. Smiley, *The Lion of Whitehall: The Life of Cassius M. Clay* (Madison: University of Wisconsin, 1962), 47; Carl N. Degler, *The Other South: Southern Dissenters in the Nineteenth Century* (New York: Harper & Row, 1974), 55–56—and by Republican ideologists like Olmsted and Seward—Frederick Law Olmsted, *A Journey in the Seaboard Slave States* (New York: Dix & Edwards, 1856), 712; Olmsted, *A Journey in the Back Country* (New York: Mason Brothers, 1860), 306; Eric Foner, *Free Soil, Free Labor, Free Men: The Ideology of the Republican Party before the Civil War* (New York: Oxford University Press, 1970), 40–51. Tocqueville had the same analysis: Alexis de Tocqueville, *Democracy in America*, ed. J. P. Mayer (New York: Doubleday & Company, 1969), 318.

wards a general industrialization, southern advocates of industrial development promised.[2]

Cotton mills were by far the biggest employers among Alabama manufacturing enterprises in the late antebellum period. In 1860, 1,312 laborers worked in Alabama cotton mills, out of a state population of 964,000, and $1.3 million in capital was invested in these mills. But even Daniel Pratt, operator of Alabama's largest cotton mills, manufactured only osnaburgs, a "cheap, coarse cloth for slave use." Pratt himself made less money in cotton manufacturing than in his mercantile business, the four company stores in his company town of Prattville.[3]

In 1860, the state's second biggest "industrial" employers were the manufacturers of boots and shoes, who employed around 400 laborers, an average of three or four per establishment. This figure suggests that boots and shoes were made primarily in small artisan shops rather than factories. Virtually all Alabama-manufactured shoes were for slave use; most shoes worn by Alabamians, black and white, came from New York. There were seven blast furnaces in the state in 1860, with a total maximum daily output of forty tons of iron for the twenty to thirty weeks per year when flood or drought did not idle the furnaces. The iron they produced was strictly for local consumption; iron manufacturers limited their products to such simple items as kettles, ovens, stoves, saws, and skillets. At the other end of the manufacturing spectrum stood Churchill and Company in Montgomery, manufacturers of "silk, cassmere and soft hats." The South manufactured silk hats for planters and rough shoes for slaves, but very little in between—a consequence of the inadequate demand arising out of the South's premodern social structure.[4]

2. Genovese, *Political Economy*, 183; see also Fred Bateman, James Foust, and Thomas Weiss, "The Participation of Planters in Manufacturing in the Antebellum South," *Agricultural History*, XLVIII (1974), 277–97; Fabian Linden, "Repercussions of Manufacturing in the Ante-Bellum South," *North Carolina Historical Review*, XVII (1940), 313–31, and Richard W. Griffin, "Cotton Manufacturing in Alabama to 1865," *Alabama Historical Quarterly*, XVIII (1956), 289–307.

3. Weymouth T. Jordan, *Ante-Bellum Alabama: Town and Country* (Tallahassee: Florida State University Press, 1957), 152, 156; Randall M. Miller, "Daniel Pratt's Industrial Urbanism: The Cotton Mill Town in Antebellum Alabama," *Alabama Historical Quarterly*, XXXIV (1972), 19–20.

4. Minnie Clare Boyd, *Alabama in the Fifties: A Social History* (New York: Columbia

The one industry in which the South produced advanced goods was cotton gin manufacturing. Daniel Pratt's cotton gin factory in Prattville was the leading gin factory in the South. Pratt sold 14,000 gins between 1832 and 1861; his salesmen had offices in eight southern cities, and he said he had sold gins to "Prussia, South America, and the French in Africa." The gross income from Pratt's cotton gin manufacturing company was $303,000 in 1860.[5] Pratt's cotton gin factory provides the clearest case of the southern manufacturer's dependence on plantation demand. It was the only machine factory of any large proportions in Alabama; and while Pratt was completely dependent on planters for his market, the planters could purchase gins manufactured outside the South. Pratt, and the rest of the South's manufacturers, needed the planters much more than the planters needed them.

Southern railroad construction was a crucial case where development was confined to that which advanced planter interests. Railroad development in the North had opened the more remote areas to commerce, and helped create the tremendous demand for manufactured goods among the North's farmers; in the antebellum South, railroad development was limited to connecting the plantation areas with the ports from which cotton was shipped, and to extending the political hegemony of the black belt over the rest of the state.[6]

In northern Alabama a political movement arose during the 1850s demanding the region withdraw from the state and join Tennessee. The planters' response was to seek state aid to build a railroad linking the northern counties with the black belt. Their purpose, according to a contemporary newspaper editor, was in "promoting closer political sympathies between the upper counties and those where the cotton plantations and negro slaves were found." In the elections in which state aid for the north-south railroad was an issue, the black belt supported aid and the hills generally opposed

University Press, 1931), 48–49, 50, 53, 54; C. Vann Woodward, *Origins of the New South 1877–1913* (Baton Rouge: Louisiana State University Press, 1951), 200.

5. Jordan, *Ante-Bellum Alabama*, 155–56.

6. Charles S. Davis, *The Cotton Kingdom in Alabama* (Montgomery: Alabama State Department of Archives and History, 1939), 119, 125; Lewy Dorman, *Party Politics in Alabama 1850–1860* (Wetumpka, Ala.: Wetumpka Printing Co., 1935), 16.

it, fearing they would be dominated when the regions became "closer."[7]

Potentially, the most important railroad project for Alabama industrialization was the South and North Railroad, given state funds in 1850 to connect the Tennessee River in north Alabama with the port of Mobile. While this route crossed the mineral region of northern Alabama, a contemporary authority reports that "it had not been located, except incidentally, to develop the coal trade." Instead, "it was intended to make easy connection . . . for the advantages of commerce in cotton."[8]

If the planters were willing to support construction of some railroads, the industrialists were deeply discouraged. Their historian, writing for the Birmingham Chamber of Commerce, said of the antebellum period, "The indifference on the part of the public and the state itself was practically suicidal. Up to the outbreak of the Civil War, indeed, the railroad system here was barely opened. . . . Alabama's railroads were small, detached lines supported by individual subscriptions. They were as a consequence always trembling on the verge of extinction."[9] Thus the planter-dominated antebellum state government was not hostile to all railroad development; it merely restricted the investment of public funds to railroads that served planter interests.

Not only did southern industries, like railroads and cotton mills, serve planter interests; to a considerable extent they were owned by planters. "Cotton Mills by Cotton Planters," the title of an article in De Bow's Review, the leading voice of southern industry, summed up the prevailing situation. The effort to use the planter as organizer and financier of the cotton mills was the most important scheme of the antebellum industrial crusaders, according to one authority. William Gregg, foremost mill-builder of the antebellum South, relied almost completely on local planter capital in his industrial enterprises. In Alabama, some planters invested

7. Dorman, Party Politics, 16; see also Eugene D. Genovese, "Yeoman Farmers in a Slaveholders' Democracy," Agricultural History, XLIX (1975), 331–42.

8. John Witherspoon DuBose, Alabama's Tragic Decade, 1865–1874, ed. James K. Greer (Birmingham: Webb Book Co., 1940), 143.

9. Ethel Armes, The Story of Coal and Iron in Alabama (Birmingham: Chamber of Commerce, 1910), 105.

heavily in iron, while others spread their investments among several industries.[10]

Although planters owned a considerable proportion of the South's industrial enterprises, individual planters' investments in industry "usually formed a minor interest, rarely large enough to influence significantly their social outlook," or to change their fundamental allegiance to an agrarian order. Industrialists' investment in plantation land is a further example of planter domination; even the manufacturers sought the status of plantation-owner. And many industrialists who did not own plantation land were tied to the planter class through marriage to planter daughters.[11]

The industrialists of Alabama, like those of other southern states, joined with the planters in a political coalition in which they were the junior partner. "Agrarians" did not oppose "industrialists" in antebellum state politics; the primary division instead was black belt planters allied with industrialists and urban commercial groups against farmers and smaller planters. The political organ of this black belt alliance was the Whig party. Whig planters owned between two-thirds and three-fourths of the slaves in the South. In Alabama, the Whigs were "the party of the wealthier and more cultivated people," and the Whigs' greatest strength was in the black belt.[12]

The South was preoccupied with the same political issues as the rest of the country; up to 1850 banking and the tariff were central. While southern farmers joined northern farmers in opposing a

10. *DeBow's Review*, VII (1849), quoted in Herbert Collins, "The Southern Industrial Gospel before 1860," *Journal of Southern History*, XII (1946), 399; Broadus Mitchell, *William Gregg, Factory Master of the Old South* (Chapel Hill: University of North Carolina Press, 1928), 149; George W. Smith, "Ante-Bellum Attempts of Northern Business Interests to 'Redeem' the Upper South," *Journal of Southern History*, XI (1945), 185; Armes, *Coal and Iron*, 61, 70; Matthew William Clinton, *Tuscaloosa, Alabama: Its Early Days, 1816–1865* (Tuscaloosa: Zonta Club, 1958), 102–104, 134; Tuscumbia *North Alabamian*, March 13, 1841, quoted in Miller, "Daniel Pratt," 8.

11. Genovese, *Political Economy of Slavery*, 187, 191.

12. Arthur C. Cole, *The Whig Party in the South* (Washington, D.C.: American Historical Association, 1913), 104; Clanton W. Williams, "Early Ante-Bellum Montgomery: A Black Belt Constituency," *Journal of Southern History*, VII (1941), 522; Charles S. Sydnor, *The Development of Southern Sectionalism 1819–1848* (Baton Rouge: Louisiana State University Press, 1948), 318–19; Dorman, *Party Politics*, 13. Some historians have attempted to challenge the view that the southern Whigs had a class basis: Charles Grier Sellers, "Who Were the Southern Whigs?," *American Historical Review*, LIX (1954), 335–46; Grady

national bank they saw as exploitative and corrupt, southern planters and businessmen joined northern businessmen in calling for a
national bank which they hoped would facilitate financing and marketing staple crops like cotton.[13]

If the southern Whigs vacillated on specific political issues of
industrial development, like the tariff, their arguments for local
development were consistently framed in terms of strengthening
the planter regime. Some powerful southern Whig elements were
always protariff: sugar planters, hemp producers, manufacturers,
and even some secessionists who wanted to build up the South's
military-industrial base. In the early 1840s, the southern Whig
party officially abandoned its traditional support for free trade, and
came out in favor of a protective tariff for manufactured goods.
The Whigs argued that free trade had brought only low cotton
prices, and that a protective tariff would encourage the development of a southern textile industry, creating a home market for
some raw cotton and thus making the planters' prosperity less dependent on conditions in the international market. It was argued
that, if the South manufactured cotton textiles for export, then
cotton, and the planter who grew it, would indeed be king. A protective tariff to increase planter prosperity: that was the core of the
southern Whigs' tariff policy in the early forties.

Later, as the sectional conflict sharpened, the southern Whigs
backed off from their support for a protective tariff, but again
argued their position in terms of maximizing planter interests.
The Richmond *Whig* wrote in 1850, "Whilst the southern Whigs
are undoubtedly in favor of any provision which will maintain existing manufactures in the southern states, there is not the same disposition to protect the general manufacturing interests of the
union."[14] They were not interested in strengthening the enemies

McWhiney, "Were the Whigs a Class Party in Alabama?," *Journal of Southern History*
XXIII (1957), 510–22; Thomas B. Alexander, "Who Were the Alabama Whigs?," *Alabama
Revi. v*, XIX (1966), 5–19. Genovese criticizes Sellers in *Political Economy of Slavery*, 180.
A study using quantitative techniques to analyze the Alabama Whig vote by county con-
cluded that the counties "in the main stream of the national and world economy"—i.e., the
black belt—were the Whig base. Thomas B. Alexander, et al., "The Basis of Alabama's
Ante-Bellum Two-Party System," *Alabama Review*, XIX (1966), 243–76.

13. Sellers, "Who Were the Southern Whigs?," 340.

14. Richmond *Whig*, December 11, 1850, quoted in Cole, *Whig Party*, 220.

of the planter regime by supporting tariff legislation that would develop northern industry.

This position was developed by the Whig press in the 1850s into a call for the exclusion of both northern and foreign manufactured goods from the South. The planter regime would be strengthened by promoting the development of its own manufacturing capacity while at the same time stopping the flow of plantation profits out of the region and into the hands of the enemies of slavery. The Whig press insisted that it sought only "a complete development of the opportunities afforded the region by its great staple," rather than a general move towards industrialization. Increasingly, as the sectional division of the fifties widened, the Whigs framed their program for limited industrial development in terms of southern nationalism. If the South manufactured cotton textiles, it could "dictate terms not only to the North but to the entire civilized world," the Whig press argued.[15]

The call for regional industrial development was accompanied by a defense of slavery. Daniel Pratt, Alabama's foremost manufacturer and a leading Whig, gave speeches proclaiming that "African slavery in North America has been a greater blessing to the human family than any other institution except the Christian religion." In 1859 Pratt wrote that he had "no patience to listen to a class of persons who speak of fencing in or penning up slavery." Repeatedly he assured his readers that he was not opposed to "the planting interest," which he considered "the bone and sinew of our country." And he assured the planters that the industrialization which would make them more capable of seceding would not create a class-conscious urban proletariat antithetical to the southern social order. The key was to avoid creating industrial cities by establishing small manufacturing villages, which would be secure from the disruptive influences of northern urban life.[16]

Because the politics of the southern Whig party were class poli-

15. Cole, Whig Party, 206–207, 209.

16. Montgomery Tri-Weekly Alabama Journal, September 8, 1851; American Cotton Planter & Soil of the South, New Series, III (1859), 115; Montgomery Tri-Weekly Flag & Advertiser, June 5, 1847; Prattville Southern Statesman, May 26, 1855; all quoted in Miller, "Daniel Pratt's Industrial Urbanism," 11–12, 16, 32. Despite all this, Pratt was attacked for not supporting secession strongly enough. The class-conscious Montgomery Daily Alabama

tics, uniting southern with northern dominant classes in a defense of big property across regional lines, the party disintegrated as the interests of the South's ruling class diverged from those of northern businessmen. But while the Whig party *per se* disappeared from electoral contests in Alabama after 1853, the coalition of planters, industrialists, and businessmen, whose interests it had pursued, continued to participate in state politics in an organized and systematic way.[17]

Thus the structural position of industrialists in the slave South was one of subservience to planter interests, which allowed for limited industrial development within the context of a planter-dominated, agrarian society. The economic situation was essentially one of limited demand, created by the South's premodern social structure. Southern industry was confined to producing goods for the plantation; the small number of southern railroads linked the black belts to the ports and extended the political hegemony of the black belts over the state. The plantation was practically the only market for manufactured goods, planters were among the leading stockholders in manufacturing enterprises, and the politics of development was controlled by planter-dominated state legislatures; as a consequence, southern industrialists "accepted the prevailing social system despite the restrictions it imposed on the expansion of their wealth and power as a class." Alabama industrialists joined with planters in the Whig party, and, in various

Journal told Pratt that his industrial reputation was "no evidence of your ability to mark out a path for the Southern people." It suggested that Pratt's wealth, acquired in manufacturing rather than agriculture, "has made you step above your *station*." Montgomery *Daily Alabama Journal*, November 22, 1850, quoted in Miller, "Daniel Pratt's Industrial Urbanism," 16. See also Jordan, *Ante-Bellum Alabama*, 159.

17. Thomas B. Alexander, "Persistent Whiggery in Alabama and the Lower South, 1860–1867," *Alabama Review*, XII (1959), 35–36; Genovese, *Political Economy of Slavery*, 232. See also W. Darrell Overdyke, *The Know-Nothing Party in the South* (Baton Rouge: Louisiana State University Press, 1950), and John Vollmer Mehring, "Persistent Whiggery in the Confederate South: A Reconsideration," *South Atlantic Quarterly*, LXIX (1970), 124–43. On the old-line Alabama Whigs in the secession crisis, see especially William L. Barney, *The Secessionist Impulse: Alabama and Mississippi in 1860* (Princeton: Princeton University Press, 1974), 66; also Thomas B. Alexander and Peggy J. Duckworth, "Alabama Black Belt Whigs during Secession," *Alabama Review*, XVII (1964), 181–97, and Ralph A. Wooster, *The People in Power: Courthouse and Statehouse in the Lower South, 1850–1860* (Knoxville: University of Tennessee Press, 1969), 123–26. For Georgia developments, see Michael P. Johnson, *Toward a Patriarchal Republic: The Secession of Georgia* (Baton Rouge: Louisiana State University Press, 1977), 71–77, 94–101.

political and organizational guises, sought the limited industrial development that served planter interests. For the antebellum planters, the existence of an agrarian rather than an industrial society was, in Raimondo Luraghi's well-chosen words, "the most precious issue, the issue over which none of them was ready to compromise."[18]

When secession came, the South's manufacturers chose to continue to serve the planter class in war, as they had in peace, thereby passing the ultimate test of their subservience, and demonstrating the potential for development by way of the Prussian Road. In 1862, the Confederate government, desperate for ordnance and munitions, passed a subsidy for coal and iron mining and iron manufacturing. The government agreed to finance half the cost of erecting factories, and to advance one-third the value of the contracts to cover the purchase of coal and iron ore. The industrial development that resulted has been described as "almost incredible" by Luraghi. The guns cast by Selma's cannon foundry were "almost the best in the world," and in 1864 Alabama produced four times as much iron as any other Confederate state. Southern wartime industrialization was a qualitative as well as a quantitative triumph.[19]

Even more extraordinary than the Confederacy's industrial achievement was the extent to which the planters never lost control over the process of industrialization. No independent class of industrialists was allowed to rise; the planters prevented such a development by the "quasi-nationalization" of southern industry. All factories were operated under strict government control, which included limits on profits and a requirement that factories sell two-

18. Genovese, *Political Economy of Slavery*, 181; Luraghi, "Civil War and Modernization," 240–41. Robert W. Fogel and Stanley Engerman, "The Specification Problem in Economic History," *Journal of Economic History*, XXVII (1967), 295, criticize Genovese's argument for being "weakly specified." Fogel, however, conceals the extent to which he has used impressionistic and intuitive estimates of values in the equations which specify his problems: Thomas L. Haskell, "The True and Tragical History of *Time on the Cross*," *New York Review of Books* (October 2, 1975), 34.

19. Frank E. Vandiver, "The Shelby Iron Company in the Civil War," *Alabama Review*, I (1948), 18; Luraghi, "Civil War and Modernization," 244–45; E. Merton Coulter, *The Confederate States of America* (Baton Rouge: Louisiana State University Press, 1950), 204; Walter L. Fleming, "Industrial Development in Alabama During the Civil War," *South Atlantic Quarterly*, III (1904) 260–72.

thirds of their production to the government. Alabama's Shelby Iron Company operated during the war "almost entirely on mandate of the Confederate Iron Agent at Selma." The planter-ruled government's domination of industry and the railroads and its effective control of the labor supply contributed to preventing the rise of an independent industrialist class.[20]

The government not only controlled privately owned industry; it also started its own industrial enterprises, which surpassed private ones in virtually every field. In 1863 the government impressed Alabama's iron manufacturing establishments into military service. The blast furnaces were put under military jurisdiction, the owners given military commissions, and the skilled laborers were made noncommissioned officers. The Confederacy's treatment of privately owned industry amounted to a "ruthless violation of the sacred rights of private property," which the planters found preferable to allowing an independent class of industrialists to arise.[21]

By the time the war broke out, the planters were vigorously campaigning for slave-based industrialization, and were investing their own capital in regional industrial enterprises. But they insisted that the process of industrialization be controlled by planters, and that planters organize to operate the new wartime industrial enterprises, intending thereby to preserve their own position as a ruling class and prevent the rise of potential challengers from the industrial sector. The planters' objective in the wartime industrialization campaign was to prevent the creation of a "slaveless industrial bourgeoisie independent of planter control."[22] Even in wartime, there was no real development of the southern industrialists' independent power.

Early in 1865, General J. H. Wilson was ordered to take 9,000

20. Luraghi, "Civil War and Modernization," 245; Genovese, *Political Economy of Slavery*, 185; Vandiver, "Shelby Iron Company," 15, *n.* 10; Coulter, *Confederate States*, 201. See also Emory W. Thomas, *The Confederacy as a Revolutionary Experience* (Englewood Cliffs: Prentice-Hall, 1971), 134.

21. Charles W. Ramsdell, "The Control of Manufacturing by the Confederate Government," *Mississippi Valley Historical Review*, VIII (1921), 231; Luraghi, "Civil War and Modernization," 245–46; Joseph H. Woodward II, "Alabama Iron Manufacturing, 1860–1865," *Alabama Review*, VII (1954), 201–202.

22. Robert Starobin, *Industrial Slavery in the Old South* (New York: Oxford University Press, 1970), 231.

men and destroy the Alabama iron industry. His major objective was the Selma arsenal, and in addition to destroying it, he reported the destruction of 7 iron works, 2 rolling mills, 5 coal mines, 3 factories, 35 locomotives, 565 railroad cars, and 3 railroad bridges. It took him twenty-eight days. Only one blast furnace in Alabama escaped destruction.[23]

Postwar Industrial Development: The Reconstruction Constitutions

The end of the war did not unleash southern industry; it did not release southern industrialists from their subservience to planter interests. The early postwar politics of industry did not indicate that "a new order dominated by businessmen" had begun.[24] After the war, two constitutional conventions were held within two years in Alabama—the first in 1865, to establish Presidential Reconstruction, and the second in 1867, when the Radicals took command. The constitutional questions of greatest importance for the industrial development of the state concerned revision of Alabama's archaic antebellum structure of corporate law. The different solutions of the two conventions reveal that the conflict over the nature and extent of Alabama's industrialization did not come to an end in 1865, that the planter class continued to seek limited rather than all-out industrialization in the postwar period.

Under Presidential Reconstruction, for the brief period of 1865 to 1867, the former Whig planters "came into their own," in the words of one authority. The convention delegates included many leaders of the old planter order: two former governors, two former members of Congress, a former minister to Belgium, and a former Mississippi appeals court judge. Benjamin Fitzpatrick was elected president of the convention; he was a planter and a Democrat, had been governor from 1840 to 1844, and had served as a United

23. U.S. War Department, *The War of the Rebellion: A Compilation of the Official Records of the Union and Confederate Army* (Washington, D.C.: Government Printing Office, 1897), Ser. 1, Vol. 49, Pt. 1, p. 365; Woodward, "Alabama Iron," 207; James P. Jones, *Yankee Blitzkrieg: Wilson's Raid Through Alabama and Georgia* (Athens, Ga.: University of Georgia Press, 1976).

24. Woodward, *Origins of the New South*, 22; Sheldon Hackney, *Populism to Progressivism in Alabama* (Princeton: Princeton University Press, 1969), 226.

States senator from 1848 until secession, which he opposed. One student of the convention concluded from all this that "the traditional governing classes . . . dominated the convention just as they had regularly dominated southern society and politics before the war"; at most, there was a "tendency to abandon those within the ruling classes of the South who had consistently agitated the sectional question" and replace them with leaders who had been moderate or indecisive on sectional issues.[25]

When the Radicals in Congress ended Presidential Reconstruction and inaugurated Radical Reconstruction, a new constitutional convention was held in Montgomery in November of 1867. This convention, dominated by Radicals, was organized by the Republican party and the Freedman's League. All of the black belt was represented by Radicals; the planters were completely excluded. A comparison of the actions of the two constitutional conventions, the first dominated by Whigs and the second by Radicals, shows sharp differences in regard to industrial development, and illuminates the persistence of the Whig-industrialists' subservience to planter interests even after the war.

Corporate law was a central issue at both conventions. Two laws were prerequisites for the development of competitive laissez-faire capitalist industry: limited liability of stockholders for corporate debts, and an end to the requirement that state legislatures charter each new corporation individually.[26] The principal advantage of incorporation is the ability to raise large amounts of capital by limiting the liability of stockholders for corporate debts. Historically, the corporation has been created when partnerships have been unable to raise enough capital for large-scale enterprises.

Early in its history, Alabama had placed major restrictions on

25. Allen W. Trelease, "Who Were the Scalawags?," *Journal of Southern History*, XXIX (1963), 465; Montgomery *Daily Advertiser*, October 1, 1865; New York *Times*, September 25, 1865; Walter L. Fleming, *Civil War and Reconstruction in Alabama* (Cleveland: A. H. Clark Company, 1911), 358, 401; James Garnett, *Reminiscences of Public Men of Alabama for Thirty Years* (Atlanta: n.p., 1872), 715–18; Dorman, *Party Politics*, 146, 152, 158, 166–67; Donald Hubert Breese, "Politics in the Lower South During Presidential Reconstruction, April to November, 1865," (Ph.D. dissertation, U.C.L.A., 1963), 166–69.

26. John W. Cadman, Jr., *The Corporation in New Jersey: Business and Politics, 1791–1875* (Cambridge: Harvard University Press, 1949), 39.

business enterprises by creating a form of unlimited liability for bank stockholders. The Alabama constitution of 1819 held these stockholders liable for business debts "in proportion to their stock holdings therein." If a person owned half the stock in a bank, he was liable for half the debts; this was unlimited liability and was "the first instance of a constitutional provision for stockholder liability" in the nation.[27]

The Alabama constitution of 1865, written at a convention dominated by planter-Whigs, did not establish limited liability of stockholders; that convention retained the antebellum constitutional provisions for stockholder liability. It was not until the Radical constitution of 1867 that limited liability for stockholders in Alabama corporations was created.[28]

The second legal requirement of modern corporate development was the ending of special laws of incorporation. In the first part of the nineteenth century, the charter of each corporation required a separate legislative act. The establishment of general laws of incorporation was a precondition for competitive laissez-faire capitalist industrial development—first, because many more corporations could come into existence; second, because legislatures would not be able to establish monopolies, or grant more favorable terms to one corporation than another. (State-chartered monopolies are a premodern form of corporate enterprise, not to be confused with the private monopolies of industrial capitalism.) And general laws would also reduce the power of the legislature to interfere with or supervise corporate activity. While still allowing for governmental regulation, general laws would end the legislature's power to review or revoke corporate status, or to set the conditions under which particular corporations could hold their charters.

The history of incorporation law in Alabama is one of restrictions on incorporation and discouragement of corporate enterprise. The constitution of 1819 was passed at a time when special chartering provisions were the rule in the nation; Alabama, however, was the first state to require more than a majority vote in the legislature for

27. *Ibid.*, 89.
28. *Ibid.*, 191.

granting corporate privileges. Moreover, Alabama's constitution contained the most detailed provisions regarding bank charters of any state constitution.[29]

The planter-Whig-dominated constitutional convention of 1865 did not require that the legislature establish general laws of incorporation; it continued the antebellum procedure. It was not until the Radical constitutional convention that special acts of incorporation were prohibited and the legislature was required to establish a general law.

The Radical constitutional convention passed another provision regarding industrial development: it prohibited the building of highways or railroads directly by the state, but permitted state aid to corporations engaged in internal improvements. Only private enterprise would be allowed to build railroads and highways under Radical rule. In the prewar period and during Presidential Reconstruction, the state had been permitted to construct by itself needed railroads; although no such railroads were completed, that possibility existed until the Radical convention banned such state activity. The Radicals sought to use state power for the development of privately owned corporations and of the social class that controlled them.

The Radical constitutional convention established two new offices, which had not existed under the Whig planters' 1865 constitution: commissioner of industrial resources and commissioner of immigration. The duties of each new official were limited to collecting information and publicizing the advantages of Alabama for industry and for immigrants, who were to serve as the labor force in new industry. These were minor developments in relation to the future of the state's industry, but they are important as an indication of the difference in ideological orientation between the Radical constitutional convention and the Whig-dominated 1865 convention. Planter spokesman F. S. Lyon subsequently called for the abolition of these offices on the grounds that they were "unnecessary."[30]

29. *Ibid.*, 88.
30. Marion *Commonwealth*, July 1, 1875.

Thus, from a constitutional and legal point of view, Radical Reconstruction marked a sharp departure from Presidential Reconstruction for the industrial development of Alabama. In 1865, even though the planter regime had been defeated in war by an expanding capitalist state, the Whig-planter-businessmen who dominated the 1865 convention failed to institute the major legal requirements of modern corporate development, thereby indicating their intention to continue to hold back the industrialization of the state. They did not establish limited liability for corporate stockholders, they did not create general laws of incorporation, they did not abolish special chartering of corporations by the legislature, they did not prohibit the state from competing with private enterprise in the construction of internal improvements, and they did not create the new offices of commissioner of industrial resources and immigration—all of which the Radical constitutional convention did.

Not only did the Whigs fail to create laws favoring corporate development; when the Radicals finally established such laws, the leading local manufacturers and industrial promoters attacked the Radicals' constitutional convention. Concluding that the interests of Alabama industry still lay in an alliance with the planters rather than against them, Daniel Pratt denounced the Radical constitution in spite of its proindustry provisions, as did J. L. M. Curry, the state's leading antebellum industrial promoter, and the Birmingham *Iron Age*, the leading voice of industrial interests. The Radical Demopolis *Southern Republican* taunted Pratt for betraying his true class interests, writing that, as "a large manufacturer," he was "a regular New England Yankee."[31] Local industrialists thus remained subservient to planter interests, even after their defeat in war, even after the Radicals used state power to weaken the planter class.

The Politics of Industry after Reconstruction

It was against a background of national capitalist crisis and the collapse of local development—before virtually any new industry

31. Malcolm Cook McMillan, *Constitutional Development in Alabama, 1798–1901: A Study in Politics, the Negro, and Sectionalism* (Chapel Hill: University of North Carolina

had appeared in the region—that Reconstruction was overthrown and the old Alabama planter ruling class met in Montgomery to write a new constitution for the state. "Redemption," Woodward writes, speaking of the period which followed Radical Reconstruction, "was not a return of an old system nor the restoration of an old ruling class. It was rather a new phase of the revolutionary process begun in 1865." And elsewhere he speaks of the "growing attachment between representatives of the New Order and the few survivors of the old planter class who entered its service."[32] A close look at the constitutional convention that began Redemption suggests different conclusions.

"Bourbons with an agrarian outlook" controlled the Redemption constitutional convention of 1875. The planters did not conceal their anti-industrial intentions. A black belt newspaper argued that "a few giant corporations, rich, powerful, mercenary, and heartless" were establishing "a yoke as galling and far more degrading than that of a military dictatorship." Leroy Pope Walker, president of the convention and former Confederate secretary of war, said of corporations that "their power, like that of King George III, has increased, is increasing, and ought to be diminished."[33]

The Democrats held that the need to ban government aid to corporations was the most important reason for calling the convention. And the key provision of the new constitution was a prohibition of state, county, or municipal aid to corporations. The ban provoked bitter partisan debate; instead of attacking industrialists directly, the planter-Democrats attacked the Republican party for allowing the state to aid corporations. In fact, as some historians have observed, the industrialists were within the Democratic ranks as well as the Republican; Democratic Governor Robert Lindsay (1870–

Press, 1955), 153–54; Birmingham *Iron Age*, May 20, 1875; Demopolis *Southern Republican*, June 20, 1870.

32. Woodward, *Origins of the New South*, 21–22, 17. Also relevant is William B. Hesseltine, "Economic Factors in the Abandonment of Reconstruction," *Mississippi Valley Historical Review*, XXII (1953), 191–210. For a critique of Woodward's interpretation as it applies to Tennessee, see Roger L. Hart, *Redeemers, Bourbons, and Populists: Tennessee, 1870–1896* (Baton Rouge: Louisiana State University Press, 1975).

33. McMillan, *Constitutional Development*, 210; Selma *Southern Argus*, December 29, 1876; Albert Burton Moore, *History of Alabama* (Tuscaloosa: Alabama Book Store, 1934), 595.

1872) was responsible for many railroad bond endorsements. Woodward takes this to mean that the Democratic party cynically professed anti-industrialism but in fact was just as committed to full-scale industrialization as the Republicans. It is more correct to say that the anti-industrial planter-Democrats hoped to discredit the industrialists in their own ranks by linking industry to the Republicans. At the same time, they maintained the façade of party unity, which both pro- and anti-industrial Democrats knew was crucial to the defeat of Radical rule.

In addition to prohibiting state, county, or local aid to corporations, the convention also passed several explicitly antirailroad laws. Railroads were forbidden to grant free passes to public officials or to charge more per mile for a short haul than a long haul. Rebates were forbidden. Several drastic proposals for writing railroad regulations into the state constitution were turned down; the convention adopted a provision recognizing the need for railroad regulation and directed the legislature to pass such laws. The convention also expressed its hostility to industrialism by abolishing the office of commissioner of industrial resources, staffed by what the convention called "useless clerks and offices" during the Radical period. Finally, the convention required that corporations be taxed at the same rate as individuals, prohibiting tax reductions as a means of attracting corporations to the state.[34]

Along with state aid to corporations, the most important issue facing the 1875 convention was adjustment of the state debt to railroad bondholders. The election of George S. Houston, Democrat and friend of the railroads, as governor in 1872 had led to the appointment of a commission to arrive at a settlement acceptable to the bondholders, but the convention itself had the power to set the rate of taxation, which would effectively determine how much money would be available to the state to pay interest on the debt. There was a move at the convention for outright repudiation of the debt; in October, 1875, the convention was reported to be on the

34. McMillan, Constitutional Development, 209; Allen Going, Bourbon Democracy in Alabama, 1874–1890 (University, Ala.: University of Alabama Press, 1951), 111; Alabama Constitution of 1875, Art. IV, Sect. 43; Art. XI, Sect. 6.

brink of complete repudiation. An alliance of black belt conservatives with hill country Radicals was making the proposal.[35]

The convention rejected a proposal to ban the use of tax money to pay interest on the state debt, and set the maximum tax rate at the same level that had been in effect during Radical Reconstruction. This rate supposedly would have been sufficient to meet interest payments on an adjusted debt, but could not possibly have brought in enough money to pay the entire debt at its face value. Thus, the action of the constitutional convention helped the commissioners convince Alabama's creditors of the necessity of reducing their demands. When the convention finally adopted the taxation rate recommended by the commissioners, Republicans declared that the tax limit agreed upon amounted to debt repudiation, and the northern and foreign press agreed.[36]

The conservative lawmakers had made it clear that they were opposed to industrial development of the state. Alabama constitutional historian M. C. McMillan summarizes: "A conservative agrarian-minded policy, which showed a distrust of Republican interests in Alabama's railroads, mining and industrial resources, dominated the work of the convention." Sections of the new constitution against railroad abuses, against state, county, and city aid to corporations, the office of commissioner of industrial resources, and the general mood of restriction and economy, "all

35. *Commercial and Financial Chronicle*, September 18, 1875, quoted in Horace Mann Bond, *Negro Education in Alabama: A Study in Cotton and Steel* (Washington, D.C.: Associated Publishers, 1939), 60. The leaders of the repudiation movement were William C. Oates and George P. Harrison. Oates, a lawyer and editor of a Democratic newspaper, was chairman of the convention's judiciary committee; beginning in 1880 he was elected to Congress seven times, and he resigned in 1894 to become governor. Harrison, a black belt lawyer from a planter family, was a "worker for the rescue of the state from militarism 1867–1874." After the convention, he went on to be a state senator from 1878 to 1884, and again from 1900 to 1904. In the 1901 constitutional convention he was chairman of the committee on corporations. Going, *Bourbon Democracy*, 71; Thomas McAdory Owen, *History of Alabama and Dictionary of Alabama Biography* (Chicago: The S. J. Clarke Publishing Company, 1921), III, 760; IV, 1293.

36. Going, *Bourbon Democracy*, 71; Montgomery *Alabama State Journal*, October 27, 1875, cited in McMillan, *Constitutional Development*, 205. McMillan regards the debt adjustment issue to have been the only victory for the industrial and prorailroad forces at the convention.

indicated that Bourbons with an agrarian outlook controlled the convention."[37]

Industry and Plantation Labor

Although the planters wished to defend their position of status and power in a fundamentally agrarian society against industrialists, there was a crucial economic issue dividing planters and industrialists in the postwar period: the allocation of Alabama's black labor supply. Cotton culture was highly labor-intensive, and the planters' greatest fear was that they would find themselves lacking sufficient black labor to operate their plantations. The threat of a labor shortage was a key political issue for the planter class through the end of the nineteenth century and into the twentieth.

The rivalry between industrialists and planters over black labor seems to have begun almost as soon as the war ended. Swayne wrote in 1866 that "a considerable portion of the land goes untilled" because "there are more calls for [black laborers] at other kinds of labor—on railroads which are being restored, and other works of that kind." These developments led the planter-dominated provisional legislature to pass the law prohibiting "enticement" of black laborers away from the plantation on which they had contracted to work. The law was intended not to control the blacks— there were other statutes that did that—but rather to control competition among employers; the guilty party was the one who lured the black off the plantation, often to industrial labor. The industrialists hired blacks for unskilled mining and railroad construction jobs, and saved the skilled jobs for whites, at least until they went on strike, at which point an attempt would usually be made to use blacks as strikebreakers.[38]

The planter press complained regularly about the industrialists' threat to the plantation labor supply. "Our railroads absorb hosts of the very pick of the plantation force," the Selma *Southern Argus* complained in 1869; this practice was "swiftly and surely exhaust-

37. McMillan, *Constitutional Development*, 210. See also Birmingham *Iron Age*, October 14, 1875; Marion *Commonwealth*, May 27, August 1, October 28, 1875.

38. Fleming, *Civil War and Reconstruction in Alabama*, 381; *Acts of Alabama 1865–1866*, 111–12; Paul B. Worthman, "Black Workers and Labor Unions in Birmingham, Alabama, 1897–1904," *Labor History*, X (1969), 375–407; see Chap. 2, herein.

ing the supply of African labor." According to an 1871 article in the Mobile *Register*, "It is difficult now to equip plantations with hands, and will be more so hereafter, when the railroad will employ a majority of the able-bodied hands at wages no planter can afford to pay." The statewide planters' convention of 1871 passed a resolution stating that "the supply of labor throughout the state is not sufficient to meet the demands and requirements . . . of agriculture, manufactories and the opening up and utilizing the various mineral sections of the state."[39]

Somers reported that, in a typical black belt county in 1870, it was almost impossible to secure labor; "those negroes who wished to work went to the railways." The Selma *Times*, published deep in the heart of the black belt, went so far as to propose in 1866 that the mineral region would be "better off if all its furnaces were torn down, its mines filled with dirt, and its inhabitants put to planting cotton."[40] A clearer expression of agrarian antagonism to industrial development would be difficult to imagine.

The planters were correct in assuming that the state's industrialists were seeking black laborers from the plantation districts. The Radical *Alabama State Journal* wrote, "Colored men: . . . the railroads of the state will be glad to get and put you to work, at better wages than you are now paid." John C. Stanton, superintendent of the Alabama and Chattanooga Railroad, said in 1870, "We were employing . . . all the colored labor we could secure, but owing to the demand of the planters for labor, [there was an] inadequate supply in the country of that class of labor." Industrialist John T. Milner, who had just leased the Montevallo coal mines in 1873, visited the black belt the same year and wrote that while "Alabama is making her first marks in mineral development . . . want and gaunt, haggard despair have prevailed everywhere in the Black Belt since 1867. . . . Now Negro labor does better in coal and iron business than farming."[41]

The Democrats' overthrow of Alabama Reconstruction in 1874

39. Selma *Southern Argus*, June 16, 1869; Mobile *Daily Register*, January 28, 1871.
40. Somers, *Southern States*, 159; Selma *Times*, June 27, 1866, quoted in Going, *Bourbon Democracy*, 47. See also Montgomery *Alabama State Journal*, February 10, 1871.
41. Montgomery *Alabama State Journal*, September 30, 1870; Demopolis *Southern Republican*, August 24, 1870; Armes, *Coal and Iron*, 269.

turned out to be a further spur to the state's black population to head for Mississippi, where Radical Reconstruction was still in power, and where Reconstruction had always been more radical than in Alabama. Alabama black belt newspapers expressed new alarm in 1874 and 1875 over an imminent labor crisis, reporting the daily departure of hundreds of blacks on trains and wagons. The first Alabama legislature which met after the 1874 planter victory over the Radicals passed a series of laws designed to increase planters' control over black tenants and to prevent "desertions" by laborers or tenants. Black belt newspapers and politicians favored severe measures.[42]

Increasingly, when blacks left the black belt, they were heading for industrial employment. During the early 1880s, thousands of blacks were abandoning Alabama plantations for the mines and railroads; in the black belt, it is reported, often only the "older and less energetic" remained. In response, Alabama planters organized meetings at which they decided to take matters into their own hands. Some announced that anyone caught attempting to "decoy away" laborers would be "shot on the spot," while other black belt groups threatened tar and feathers for the "enticers." Alabama Senator John T. Morgan said in an 1883 speech in Congress that if industrial development were "to raise the price of farm labor all over the state . . . the farmers will have to give up cotton planting. . . . If industry in Alabama is to draw the labor from the cotton plantations continually by additional temptations, I do not see how we are to conduct our great agricultural enterprises." Morgan added, "I shall begin to believe after a while that it is more a curse than a blessing to have these great bestowments of coal and iron in the bosom of our state." Black belt newspapers repeatedly deplored the blacks' seemingly universal desire to desert the farm for the daily wage in the mines and factories.[43]

42. Vernon L. Wharton, *The Negro in Mississippi, 1865–1900* (Chapel Hill: University of North Carolina Press, 1947), 108; Going, *Bourbon Democracy*, 96; Edward King, *The Great South* (Hartford: American Publishing Company, 1875), 300; Charles Nordhoff, *The Cotton States in the Spring and Summer of 1875* (New York: D. Appleton and Company, 1876), 93; *House Reports*, 43rd Cong., 2nd Sess., No. 262, p. 8; William Warren Rogers, *The One-Gallused Rebellion: Agrarianism in Alabama, 1865–1896* (Baton Rouge: Louisiana State University Press, 1970), 87.

43. Moore, *History of Alabama*, 507; Wharton, *Negro in Mississippi*, 111; Going, *Bour-*

When the U.S. Senate Committee on the Relations between Labor and Capital came to Alabama, some witnesses argued that the most pressing conflict was between planters and the industrial capitalists who threatened their labor supply, not between capitalists and proletarians. One planter described for the senators the "biggest problem" facing his class: "You have your farm, and your supplies, and your calculations made, and think you are going to get along all right, but suddenly some man comes and says to your laborers, 'I want so many men to build a railroad, I will pay 1.50 a day, and pay the money every Saturday night'; and your laborer . . . makes up his mind to leave you. . . . There ought to be some way to compel him . . . not to desert you when you need him most."[44]

Another planter spokesman repeated the complaint: "The owner of the land makes his contracts with his laborers, and he undertakes to supply those negroes with what they may need during the season . . . in May or June, . . . the negro not unfrequently leaves the plantation . . . and goes off to work on a railroad . . . or a coal mine." Former governor Robert M. Patton agreed: "Parties will want labor, and an agent will come here and will drum up any number of these black men . . . a great many of them go off to work on the railroads." And a Tennessee Valley planter whose laborers had "gone down to Birmingham" could only conclude that the Negro race "seems to be of a restless, roving disposition."[45]

Industrialists had a different view; they freely admitted their preference for black labor for some kinds of work. One of the state's leading industrial developers said, "I began after the war by taking a railroad contract in which I employed about 40 Negro men. The men all left their homes. . . . from that day to this I have had great numbers of Negroes in my employ. . . . I believe they are the best laborers in the world, stronger, more active, more willing than whites." J. W. Sloss, one of Alabama's leading industrialists, described the different jobs blacks found in industry:

bon Democracy, 47, 96; Congressional Record, quoted in Mobile Daily Register, January 9, 1883; Senate Documents, 46th Cong., 2nd Sess., No. 693, pp. 401, 471; Mobile Daily Register, December 28, 1880, January 9, 1883.

44. Senate Documents, 48th Cong., 1st Sess., No. 1262, IV, 32.

45. Ibid., 69–70, 52, 145.

"They come down here, they work on the streets, they work in the coal mines and largely in the ore mines and about the furnaces and rolling mills." The industrialists, however, were no less racist than the planters. One industrialist explained the racial mixture desirable among employees of the coal and iron mines: "There has been a great deal of the bleaching process going on for a great many years. . . . Take a Congo negro of pure African blood, and he is one thing, but one of these colored men with a large infusion of good white blood is another thing. . . . We find that the best among them are men who are pretty well mixed."[46]

In the face of planter intransigence on the question of sharing black labor, Alabama's industrialists renewed their efforts in the early eighties to obtain a state commissioner of immigration, who would recruit white immigrant laborers to work in the mines and factories. The planters, apparently content that the plantations would not need outside labor, opposed the expenditure of state funds to bring a white industrial proletariat into the state. The planter-dominated legislature responded to industrial demands for a commissioner of immigration by declaring that the task of attracting labor belonged to the commissioner of agriculture—a subtle but clear indication that agriculture took precedence over industry in the planters' political priorities, even in 1883.[47]

Many Radicals had clearly understood that successful Reconstruction required a social and economic transformation of the South from an agrarian to an industrial society. One carpetbag industrialist in Selma wrote Wager Swayne in 1867, "My idea in coming South was to engage in a business that would aid in Reconstructing the Rebellious States on a more substantial basis than 'niggers and cotton.' . . . I felt that we should develop *all* the resources of these states. This done, . . . Alabama, like 'a greasy mechanic' will embrace proud old Pennsylvania."[48]

46. *Ibid.*, 102–103, 287, 134.

47. Going, *Bourbon Democracy*, 122–23; *Acts of Alabama 1882–1883*, 190. The use of convict labor in the mines was a solution to the industrialists' rivalry for plantation labor: see William Cohen, "Negro Involuntary Servitude in the South, 1865–1940: A Preliminary Analysis," *Journal of Southern History*, XLII (1976), 31–60.

48. R. M. Moore to Wager Swayne, April 15, 1867, in Wager Swayne Papers, Alabama Department of Archives and History. This position was associated with Horace Greeley and

But, as the Radical *Alabama State Journal* explained in a brilliantly concise paragraph, the prebourgeois planter class was the obstacle to the state's industrial development. The article was titled, "Why southern manufacturers do not succeed":

> Manufactures require educated and skilled operatives to run them, and the whole power of the "best society," as it pretentiously calls itself, is exerted to repeal that most needed class of skilled workmen. The ignorant aristocracy of the South are attempting to conduct a new era of freedom on the same principles which ruled in the days of slavery. Southern society knows only two classes, and they are separated by the widest social gulf that can be made between . . . absolute power on one side and the most abject dependence on the other. The Southerner's idea of independence and superiority is to live in idleness while pushing another to do his work. . . . Doubtless these truths will be assented to by many of the more intelligent and liberal men of the South. . . . But unfortunately the old oligarchs have come to the surface again, and so long as they rule, manufactures cannot be built up at the South.[49]

"Pig Iron" Kelley: Earle D. Ross, "Horace Greeley and the South," *South Atlantic Quarterly*, XVI (1917), 333–34; William D. Kelley, *Speeches, Addresses and Letters on Industrial and Financial Questions* (Philadelphia: H. C. Baird, 1872), 182–83; Robert P. Sharkey, *Money, Class and Party: An Economic Study of the Civil War and Reconstruction* (Baltimore: The Johns Hopkins Press, 1959), 165–66; Eric Foner, "Thaddeus Stevens, Confiscation, and Reconstruction," in Stanley Elkins and Eric McKitrick (eds.), *The Hofstadter Aegis: A Memorial* (New York: Alfred A. Knopf, 1974), 166. Northern workers were among the strongest supporters of Reconstruction. A trade union leader speaking before thousands of workmen in Boston in 1865 said, "We rejoice that the rebel aristocracy of the South has been crushed, we rejoice that beneath the glorious shadow of our victorious flag men of every clime, lineage and color are recognized as free. . . . The workingmen of America will in the future claim a more equal share in the wealth their industry creates in peace and a more equal participation in the privileges and blessings of those free institutions, defended by their manhood on many a bloody field of battle." Quoted in David Montgomery, *Beyond Equality: Labor and the Radical Republicans, 1862–1872* (New York: Alfred A. Knopf, 1967), 90–91.

49. Montgomery *Alabama State Journal*, April 4, 1871. Du Bois made the same argument: the planters' "exploitation of labor reduced it to a wage so low and a standard of living so pitiable that no modern industry in agriculture or trade or manufacture could be built upon it; it made ignorance compulsory and had to do so in self-defense; and it automatically was keeping the South from entering the great stream of modern industry where growing intelligence among workers, a rising standard of living among the masses, increased personal freedom and political power, were recognized as absolutely necessary." W. E. B. Du Bois, *Black Reconstruction in America, 1860–1880* (New York: Atheneum, 1969), 52.

6

The Birmingham Case

The agonizingly slow and incomplete development of Birmingham, the South's one genuine center of heavy industry, indicates that southern industry was not liberated or unchained as a result of the defeat of the planter regime in war. The story of Birmingham's development has been told many times, but the Alabama planters' opposition to the growth of a genuinely industrial society in their midst has been overlooked.

Although development of the mineral region was not part of the state's plan to build a south and north railroad in 1850, geological discoveries had changed matters by 1858. That year the legislature authorized money to be spent to survey a new route for the "South and North," in an effort to find "the most practicable route with reference to the development of the mineral region."[1] This first clear declaration of planter support for such development came two years before secession.

The planters, however, were not calling for genuine industrial development when they authorized the new routing for the railroad. The planters' strategy was to mine the coal and iron ore, and then ship the ore to Mobile to be transported to industrial centers outside the state. According to a contemporary newspaper editor, "to make an export and import harbor of Mobile, for the mineral commerce . . . was the plan of the legislature of slaveholders and cotton planters."[2] Mobile was to be the beneficiary of opening the

1. John Witherspoon DuBose, *Alabama's Tragic Decade, 1865–1874* (Birmingham: Webb Book Co., 1940), 143.
2. *Ibid.*, 146.

mining region, and there is no mention of creating the kind of industrial center that Birmingham would eventually become.

Although the existence of the mineral fields of northern Alabama had been known in the late 1850s, the railroads that were the key to their development were not built. The Confederate government had authorized funds to be spent on construction of Alabama's South and North Railroad into the mineral region, but the track was unfinished at the war's end. With the end of the war, Alabama's planters were confronted with the unavoidable question of the development of the mineral region. It was obvious that the railroad itself was going to be completed, sooner or later; the issue in 1865 was what kind of development would take place in the mineral region, and under whose control.

Two Strategies of Development

Planters wanted northern Alabama's ores mined, the coal used for fuel, and the iron ore shipped out of the state, to be manufactured into iron elsewhere—the same plan they had advocated in 1858. Local industrialists, on the other hand, wanted to develop a great new industrial center to manufacture pig iron within the mineral region itself. The Montgomery *Advertiser*, consistently a leading spokesman for planter interests, repeatedly put forward the former alternative: Alabama coal should be delivered to Mobile to fuel ocean steamers. In a discussion of the state's developing railroad system, another planter newspaper reported that for this reason "Mobile is moving heaven and earth to reach the mineral region of this state."[3]

Politically, these alternatives took the form of competition be-

3. Montgomery *Daily Advertiser*, October 9, 1866, September 19, 1868; Selma *Southern Argus*, July 7, 1869. Mobile was to become more noteworthy for unloading bananas than for loading coal. In the twentieth century the Mobile and Ohio banana wharf unloaded 40,000 bunches of bananas daily, while the nearby state docks and refrigerated warehouse had banana conveyors with a capacity of 260 refrigerated railroad cars. The bananas were shipped to Mobile by United Fruit Company from its Central American plantations. Workers of the Writers' Program of the Works Projects Administration in the State of Alabama, *Alabama: A Guide to the Deep South* (New York: Richard H. Smith, 1941), 215. Mobile's rival in this enterprise was, of course, New Orleans. Thomas Karnes, *Tropical Enterprise: Standard Fruit and Steamship Company in Latin America* (Baton Rouge: Louisiana State University Press, 1978).

tween two groups of railroads for state aid. One group, dominated by antebellum industrialists, proposed that their railroads cross at a new city, between a mountain of iron ore and a mountain of coal, which would become the major new industrial center for manufacturing pig iron in the South. The other group consisted of leading planters allied with Boston and New York financiers. They sought to limit the development of the Birmingham region to mining and shipping ore, to build a railroad between Birmingham and Chattanooga, and to make Chattanooga the exclusive center for manufacturing pig iron from the ores of northern Alabama. The Montgomery *Advertiser* quoted the New York *Journal of Commerce* in 1871 as reporting that the Alabama and Chattanooga Railroad would "furnish facilities for reaching every market with the ores."[4] It is notable that the report mentioned ore rather than manufactured products and pig iron.

The struggle between these two groups—local industrialists seeking the full development of Birmingham, and the alliance of planters and eastern financiers planning to limit Birmingham to mining—began under Presidential Reconstruction and continued through Radical Reconstruction, as each group maneuvered to win state aid for their cause and keep it from their opponents. The provisional legislature that met in 1866, before Radical Reconstruction began, passed a law requiring the governor to endorse the bonds of any railroad chartered by the legislature which completed twenty miles of road, at the rate of $12,000 per mile for the portion completed, to be paid for twenty-mile sections. The railroads found this formula unacceptable. The endorsed bonds could be sold for no less than 90 percent of par, the railroad interests complained; the state appointed two members to the directory of all participating railroads, the governor could sell the railroad if the company defaulted on interest payments, the railroads had to purchase rail and track supplies from local producers wherever possible, and all state-aided lines were to carry official state freight free of charge. As a contemporary reported, "The promoters of the roads claimed that [this] law was useless to . . . attract Northern and European

4. Montgomery *Daily Advertiser*, July 21, 1871.

capital." Congress brought Presidential Reconstruction to an end before any railroads could receive aid under the law.[5]

When the Radical legislature met, they eliminated these restrictive conditions, raised the endorsement from $12,000 to $16,000 per mile, permitted it to be paid for five-mile sections instead of twenty-mile sections, and provided aid for construction of roads twenty miles outside of state lines. The Radical legislature also created a new form of governmental aid to railroads, one that had not existed previously: they passed a law permitting railroads to apply to city and county governments for capital stock subscriptions, which were to be financed through local bond issues.[6] Needless to say, it was much easier for a railroad to influence a city council than a state legislature.

The planter press followed the railroad controversy closely. The position of the leading planter newspapers was not opposition to railroad development, but rather support for railroads which served planter interests—precisely their antebellum position. Railroad projects were consistently evaluated in terms of their contribution to planter prosperity and power. The railroad was offered as a contribution to solving the planters' number one problem, the labor shortage: "If we had a great truck road to the Tennessee Valley," the *Advertiser* argued in 1867, "our landlords would no longer have to drum for tenants." Explaining the value of a south and north railroad, the *Advertiser* wrote in 1868, "Agriculture will not

5. John F. Stover, *The Railroads of the South, 1865–1900: A Study of Finance and Control* (Chapel Hill: University of North Carolina Press, 1955), 88; Hilary A. Herbert, *Why the Solid South? Or, Reconstruction and Its Results* (Baltimore: R. H. Woodward & Co., 1890), 52. Stover's interpretation is challenged in Maury Klein, "The Strategy of Southern Railroads, 1865–1893," *American Historical Review*, LXXIII (1968), 1052–68. For another view, see Horace Mann Bond, *Negro Education in Alabama: A Study in Cotton and Steel* (Washington, D.C.: Associated Publishers, 1939), 43, 46.

6. Walter L. Fleming, *Civil War and Reconstruction in Alabama* (Cleveland: A. H. Clark Company, 1911), 589, 604–605; Stover, *Railroads*, 89. See also A. B. Moore, "Railroad Building in Alabama during the Reconstruction Period," *Journal of Southern History*, I (1935), 421–41; Sarah Van V. Woolfolk, "Carpetbaggers in Alabama: Tradition versus Truth," *Alabama Review*, XV (1962), 140; Woolfolk, "Five Men Called Scalawags," *Alabama Review*, XVII (1964), 42–52; James F. Doster, *Railroads in Alabama Politics, 1875–1914* (University, Ala.: University of Alabama Press, 1957). To compare developments in Alabama with Georgia, see Elizabeth Studley Nathans, *Losing the Peace: Georgia Republicans and Reconstruction, 1865–1871* (Baton Rouge: Louisiana State University Press, 1968), 118–20, 207–12.

only be enlarged in area, but will be immensely stimulated all over the state. . . . lands will sell at a continually increasing price . . . a cultivated and refined society will follow." The lack of interest in developing the mineral region expressed in these statements is striking. For the Mobile *Register*, the conflict over northern Alabama railroad development was a contest between Mobile and Chattanooga over which would become the transshipment point for Alabama ore. If Chattanooga got the ore, the port of Mobile would follow Antwerp and Venice into decline, it was argued.[7]

Because planter representatives were excluded from the Radical legislature, they lacked the power to decide which of the competing railroad systems and groups of capitalists would be permitted to develop the state's industrial potential under the new railroad aid law. Practically the only way the planters could influence railroad development during Radical Reconstruction was by becoming stockholders in the various railroad development enterprises. In the conventional view, the presence of planters on railroad boards of directors is evidence that they had entered the service of the new industrial order; but the planter role in the South and North Railroad, the single most important project for Alabama's industrialization, suggests the opposite conclusion.[8]

While the first Radical legislature was meeting in June, 1868, a new president of the South and North Railroad was elected. A sharp struggle broke out between planter and industrialist stockholders over the fate of the road, and with it, Alabama's industry. The new president, John Whiting, was a Montgomery banker and a member of the planter establishment. He proposed to change the route of the South and North so that, instead of going north from the site of Birmingham, it would go straight to Chattanooga. The Montgomery planters backing Whiting favored this route; Ethel Armes, the historian of Birmingham, observes that "Montgomery then, as now, was in the main a cotton market. By this arrangement she would get a competing commercial line to New York. As for

7. Montgomery *Daily Advertiser*, September 22, 1867, May 24, 1868; see also March 23, 1866; Mobile *Daily Register*, June 11, 1871.
8. C. Vann Woodward, *Origins of the New South, 1877–1913* (Baton Rouge: Louisiana State University Press, 1951), 17.

any mineral region in Alabama, [the planters felt that] the thing was mainly talk after all. Alabama was a cotton state."[9]

Whiting, William Garrett recalled, was a man of "wealth and affluence. He was a Virginian, well-bred, intelligent, high-toned, and honorable. . . . His election as President [of the South and North] secured a large subscription to the road by the city of Montgomery, the citizens of which had unbounded confidence in Mr. Whiting."[10] That is, Whiting's plan to have the South and North serve planter interests, rather than develop the mineral region, gained him extensive support in the heart of the black belt.

The industrialists among the railroad stockholders were led by the head engineer of the South and North, John T. Milner. He later recalled that the planters' plan "meant the ruin of our great railroad enterprise forever, and the transfer of everything to Chattanooga, an irretrievable loss to Alabama." "Whiting was stubborn," Milner recalled; "he wanted what was good for cotton." Fortunately for the industrialists, Whiting died unexpectedly, and in November, 1869, the former South and North president, Frank Gilmer, came up with enough proxy votes to get himself elected president. The new board returned to the task of industrial development of the Birmingham district.[11] Although the planters lost this struggle, they had made it clear where they stood on the issue of Birmingham's future; in taking over a key railroad, they were not entering the service of the new industrial order, but rather fighting in an effective way against it.

The climax of the struggle between the Birmingham group and the planter-Chattanooga group, between the South and North Railroad and the Alabama and Chattanooga Railroad, came shortly after the Radical legislature met. The Birmingham group persuaded the Radical legislature to provide $1.2 million in state aid for their project. But in the meantime the Chattanooga group had purchased a majority of the South and North bonds, and now demanded that the railroad either pay the back interest on the bonds,

9. Ethel Armes, *The Story of Coal and Iron in Alabama* (Birmingham: Chamber of Commerce, 1910), 216.

10. James Garrett, *Reminiscences of Public Men of Alabama for Thirty Years* (Atlanta: n.p., 1872), 591.

11. Armes, *Coal and Iron*, 217.

which was impossible for it, or else "transfer . . . the complete and total . . . South and North railroad to the Nashville and Chattanooga Railroad Company," which "meant the transfer to Chattanooga of all the interests and industries then centering in Birmingham. Practically, it meant the murder of the town in cold blood." John T. Milner, president of the South and North, called this "the most critical and dangerous period in the history of Birmingham."[12]

Planter hopes were dashed by the last-minute intervention of Albert Fink, president of the mighty Louisville and Nashville Railroad (the L&N), who proposed to save Birmingham's future by paying off the bondholders, incorporating the South and North Railroad into the L&N system, and tying Birmingham to Louisville rather than Chattanooga. The L&N would obtain a through line from Louisville to Montgomery, giving them control of a large area of southern trade, for which Louisville wholesalers were eager. The Alabama industrialists would continue developing Birmingham into a major industrial center, with a strong regional railroad to protect them against northeastern financiers and their planter antagonists.[13]

Birmingham in the Seventies

Up to this point—1872—Birmingham was a real estate boomtown at a railroad crossing. In spite of its well-known mineral riches, and in spite of the railroad development in the region, local promoters had great difficulty in attracting northern capital to develop the iron and coal mines, and initially were forced to depend on Alabama capital almost completely. In 1870, the stockholders, officers, and directors of the leading iron and coal companies of Alabama were all local men, with the now elderly Daniel Pratt the most prominent. D. S. Troy, one of the state's most prominent

12. *Ibid.*, 243–44.

13. Maury Klein, *History of the Louisville and Nashville Railroad* (New York: Macmillan, 1972), 112–22, 129–36, 264–76, relies on Armes; see also Kincaid A. Herr, *The Louisville and Nashville Railroad, 1850–1947* (Louisville: L&N Magazine, 1943); Thomas D. Clark, *The Beginning of the L and N* (Louisville: The Standard Printing Co., 1933); Jean E. Keith, "The Role of the Louisville and Nashville Railroad in the Early Development of Alabama Coal and Iron," *Bulletin of the Business Historical Society*, XXVI (1952), 165–74.

developers, was unable to obtain northern capital to rebuild the Oxmoor furnaces in 1872; they had been the biggest in the region in the antebellum period, and had been out of operation since Wilson's Raiders destroyed them in 1864. The industrialists were forced to turn to Daniel Pratt for financing.[14]

These indications of a lack of enthusiasm among northeastern investors for developing Alabama coal and iron during the early 1870s contradict the argument that "quite early northern capital became prominent in southern mineral industries."[15] The impressive fact is not the prominence of northern capital in developing the mineral region, but rather the unwillingness of New York or Boston or Philadelphia capitalists to undertake the development of Alabama coal and iron mines in the seventies.

The planter press was also unenthusiastic about the industrial future of Birmingham. Black belt reporters visited Birmingham and sent back descriptions that were sharply at odds with the enthusiasm of the developers. A reporter from the Mobile *Register* wrote, "I stayed there but a short time, and was very unfavorably impressed. . . . the dinner was miserable, and the tablecloth so outrageously dirty as to sicken one, and give a traveller a great disgust with even the memory of the city of Birmingham." Another reporter for a black belt newspaper indicated that "The most interesting sight by far to me, is the crowd that is generally collected here—the victims of the Birmingham fever. . . . All afford a study worthy of a philosopher. When I go to Birmingham again, I intend to tie a piece of asafoetida around my neck to guard against the contagion, and I would advise all visitors to take a similar precaution. . . . the town will . . . probably remain *in status quo* for some years to come."[16] The skepticism of this black belt reporter proved to be a more accurate prediction than the enthusiasm of the developers.

14. Armes, *Coal and Iron*, 202–203; Merrill E. Pratt, "Daniel Pratt, Alabama's First Industrialist," *Textile History Review*, II (1961), 25. See also Carl V. Harris, *Political Power in Birmingham, 1871–1921* (Knoxville: University of Tennessee Press, 1975); Mark H. Elovitz, *A Century of Jewish Life in Dixie: The Birmingham Experience* (University, Ala.: University of Alabama Press, 1974).

15. Woodward, *Origins of the New South*, 128.

16. Mobile *Daily Register*, December 28, August 27, 1871.

The black belt newspapers emphasized the corruption of the railroad developers who were pushing Birmingham, and reported that, as a result, "starvation stares at the employees of the railroads."[17] The planter press did not portray industrial development in rosy or glowing terms; promises of unheard-of wealth to be created by Birmingham are notably lacking in these accounts.

At the same time that the planter press criticized Birmingham for the corruption, foolishness, and bad manners of its industrial boosters, it expressed interest in the agricultural prospects of the region. The Selma *Southern Argus* described the virtues of the region late in 1869: "The [farm] lands . . . will yield a rate of return unsurpassed by any locality in Alabama"; the "advantage of this section above all others of our knowledge is its peculiar adaptability to the growth of cotton, corn, wheat, rye, oats, rice, potatoes, both Irish and sweet, sugar cane, clover and other grains, . . . apple, peach, and grapes equal to any country in the world, and without failure one year in ten." The account concluded, "in addition to the above mentioned inducements there is no country in America or Europe that possesses such quantities and qualities of minerals as this."[18] The mineral wealth came as a postscript to the agricultural potential of the region.

The railroad from Birmingham to Louisville was completed in 1872. The same year the first iron furnaces built since the end of the war were opened. Then the Panic of '73 struck, dropping the bottom out of the iron market. The town's real estate boom collapsed, the new iron works shut down, and Albert Fink, the L&N president who had supported the development of Birmingham, was forced to resign. Fink came upon John Milner, one of the industrialists who had persuaded him to support Birmingham against the Chattanooga financiers, and shouted, "You have ruined me, you fool, me, and the Louisville and Nashville Railroad Company! The railroad cannot pay for the grease that is used on its car wheels! Where are those coal mines and those iron mines you talked so much about that morning, and write so much about? Where are they? I look, but I see nothing! All lies! Lies!" In 1873 and 1874, pig

17. *Ibid.*, July 20, 1871.
18. Selma *Southern Argus*, October 13, 1869.

iron production in the state fell to zero, and no iron ore was mined. Armes writes, "Certain it is that the company, the railroad, the blast furnaces, and the town were barely breathing in the year of 1873."[19]

With the collapse of the Birmingham region following the Panic of '73, and the hostility of the Redemption lawmakers to industrialization, the restoration of state government to conservative rule in 1875 did little to revive the enterprises of the industrial promoters. Their most important activity in this period was development of the technology of pig iron production based on coke. Pig iron was first produced experimentally using Alabama coke in 1876, demonstrating at last the commercial potential of the Alabama iron industry. The technological experiments, however, were not financed by northeastern capitalists, but rather by old Daniel Pratt. Once again the lack of enthusiasm of northeastern capitalists in the Birmingham region delayed development; New York and Boston financiers showed little interest in supporting the technological experiments that would open the Birmingham region to massive development.

Other outside capitalists did. Milton Hannibal Smith of the L&N saw that his railroad was not going to make money in Birmingham until something happened to the local iron industry. He therefore persuaded the company to invest $125,000 in the experiment to manufacture pig iron with local coke. Another outside investor in the new iron-making process was David Sinton of Cincinnati, who had made a fortune from pig iron during the war.[20]

Even the demonstration that pig iron could be manufactured with locally produced coke did not lead to a rush of investment in Birmingham industry. The district continued to stagnate for three more years. Up to 1879, the "industry" of the Birmingham region consisted first of mining coal, which continued to be shipped out of the region to be used as a fuel instead of in iron manufacture, and

19. Armes, *Coal and Iron*, 252, 254. Robert H. McKenzie, "Reconstruction of the Alabama Iron Industry, 1865–1880," *Alabama Review*, XXV (1972), 178–91, argues that financial problems, rather than wartime destruction, were the most important cause of the slow recovery.

20. John Leeds Kerr, *The Story of a Southern Courier: The Louisville and Nashville* (New York: Young & Ottley, 1933), 65; Armes, *Coal and Iron*, 261.

second, manufacturing pig iron in a few small furnaces which used the old charcoal method. Ethel Armes describes Birmingham in 1879, a full fifteen years after the war's end:

> Although two railroads mingled their energies upon its ground, they got no sustenance. Cattle grazed upon their tracks. Although millions of tons of iron ore flaunted wine-red in the very face of the town, Red Mountain served as but fruit to Tantalus, and the far, long swell of the Warrior coal fields, indeed, as the bitter, receding waters. Although two furnaces in Shades Valley had made brave trial, neither had been able to carry its own weight, much less lend a hand to the struggling town.[21]

The Take-Off of 1879

Birmingham industrial development began in 1879, and the key to its development was the organization of the Pratt Coal and Coke Company, which mined coal for local iron manufacture rather than for export from the region. But even the Pratt Company did not initially receive outside investment; it was financed by the fortune of Daniel Pratt, who had at last died, leaving his son-in-law Henry DeBardeleben as heir and the "one big-money man in this part of the state." DeBardeleben was president of the new company; James Sloss, the Alabama railroad man who had brought in the L&N to defeat the Chattanooga interests, was secretary-treasurer, and Thomas H. Aldrich, the New York-born engineer and coal miner, was superintendent and mine manager. The company mined coal but neither mined nor manufactured iron. When the Pratt Coal and Coke Company began operations in 1879, "then, and not until then, was there any sign of life in the city of Birmingham," industrialist John T. Milner said. Armes concludes that "but for the opening of these Pratt mines the little town of Birmingham might indeed have utterly collapsed."[22] Now, with a new industrial process that took advantage of the region's coal resources, development proceeded. Eight new mining and manufacturing companies were founded between 1880 and 1884 in the region.

In 1883, a U.S. Senate committee held hearings in Birmingham

21. Armes, *Coal and Iron*, 274.
22. *Ibid.*, 233, 282–83.

on the "relation between labor and capital." The senators patiently listened to happy white workers, happy black workers, and even happy convict laborers, and asked questions like "To what forms of vice do you find the Negroes addicted?" Occasionally an industrialist would admit that all was not well with the city's economy. T. H. Aldrich himself conceded that "there is a dearth of capital here. . . . Northern capital has not come down here."[23]

Willard Warner, once a carpetbag United States senator from Alabama, had founded Birmingham's Tecumseh Iron Company in 1871 with $200,000 in capital. He told the committee the hard facts about Birmingham's industrial failure. In ten years, Warner revealed, "We have not had any return, we have never had a dividend." He proceeded to demonstrate that the record of his own firm was the rule rather than the exception, listing for the skeptical the fate of the major Birmingham iron manufacturing firms: Pratt & DeBardeleben, biggest in the region, "stock now below par"; Shelby Iron, paid dividends of 5 percent twice in ten years; Eureka Iron, out of business; the Selma Iron Works, closed for a year but still in existence; Rocky Run Iron, sold in a sheriff's sale; Stonewall Iron, "broke and idle"; Aetna Iron, paid one dividend of 10 percent, then sold in a sheriff's sale; and finally the Anneston Iron Works, "successful."[24]

Northern speculators took control of the L&N Railroad in the early 1880s, and the familiar process of stock watering and manipulation began, but with a difference for the Birmingham region. The year 1884 marked the addition of the master-speculators Jay Gould, Thomas Fortune Ryan, and Russell Sage to the L&N board of directors. Under the new board, the L&N pushed the development of Birmingham with renewed energy.

The planter press's coolness towards Birmingham continued during the 1880s. Searching the Mobile *Register* and the Montgomery *Advertiser* for evidence of their attitude towards the development of Birmingham, one is struck by the paucity of articles on the subject. For every mention of industrial development in the

23. *Senate Documents*, 48th Cong., 1st Sess., No. 1262, IV, 106, 479.
24. *Ibid.*, 260–62.

mineral region, there are a hundred articles on agriculture in general, and cotton in particular—detailed, regular reports on the condition of the crop in particularly important Alabama counties and in other states, endless discussions of improving yields, using fertilizer, and dealing with insect pests, advice on the latest farming tools and new machinery, uses for excess seed, and of course information on cotton prices and cotton shipments in all the major world markets. In the mid-eighties the Mobile *Register* had a regular column on "logs and lumber," but none on iron and coal, a regular column on "Mississippi Matters," but none on Birmingham Business. What news there was from Birmingham tended to be the usual reports of crime, accidents, and bad weather, rather than economic developments. Later the Mobile *Register* ran regular news from Birmingham that reported on the farm crops but not on industrial production.[25] The planter press in the 1880s gave little indication that Birmingham believed it had at last reached "take-off"; the planters were hostile, or looked the other way, or honestly believed that nothing of significance would come to pass there.

In 1880, as the industrial development of Birmingham was getting under way, the *Register* reminded its readers that agriculture was the true basis of Alabama's economy: "no country has been found that can successfully compete without Cotton States as to the quality of staple. . . . Cotton is entirely a southern plant . . . the very perfection of cotton soil may be said to be the canebreaks of Central Alabama." An 1880 article urging immigration from the North listed as the state's most attractive features "the possibilities of our farming lands, and the railroads which penetrate the best cotton lands."[26] Industry was not mentioned among the potential inducements; railroads were portrayed as serving the plantation districts, and no mention was made of their role in developing the mineral region.

When the planter press discussed industry, it was often to point out its economic instability and financial problems. The Mobile

25. See for instance Mobile *Daily Register*, September 23, 1882, January 26, 1883, January 23, 28, February 21, May 1, 1884.
26. *Ibid.*, March 22, June 23, 24, 1880.

Register reported, "The whole sum paid as dividends on capital invested in making pig iron . . . has not amounted to 5 per cent. of the capital sunk and lost in the same business during the last 15 years." The *Register* also reported on strikes in Birmingham's mines and mills, and on the problems of particular industrial enterprises: "The financial situation of the Stonewall Iron works . . . is such, that Mr. Jackson, the manager, called a meeting of the creditors to ask an extension."[27]

The planter press had a variety of critical remarks about Birmingham. The Montgomery *Advertiser* ran a report in 1883 that "the coal mines . . . are, without exception, the most wretchedly opened I have ever seen." In what could only have been a stinging insult to the South's new industrial center, a black belt newspaper reported in 1883 that "The people of Birmingham will soon have to burn wood if the supply of coal is not better." "None of the men employed around the blast furnaces are paid enough to enable them to live decently," the Montgomery *Advertiser* indicated in 1883, and implied that things were better in the plantation districts. "A few months ago iron went up with amazing rapidity. The furnaces came again into blast and dying corporations rapidly obtained credit and paid off their liabilities. The advance was spasmodic and baseless . . . the bottom dropped out, and soon we saw . . . 800 laborers thrown out of employment. 800 wives stood with tears at 800 doorsteps, and 2,000 children looked at their fathers with hungry eyes." This vivid picture painted by the planter press of the human suffering created by an industrial economy was at sharp odds with the way the industrialists of the day were describing their achievements. And one writer for the authoritative Montgomery *Advertiser* concluded in 1883, "that [Birmingham] will ever be a second Pittsburgh, as is confidently claimed by the hopeful men doing business here, I do not believe."[28]

When the planter press was not criticizing or ignoring Birmingham, it would sometimes damn the city with faint praise. An 1882

27. *Ibid.*, August 14, September 1, 1882, February 21, 1883, June 1, August 13, 1884.
28. Montgomery *Daily Advertiser*, January 26, February 1, 1883; Mobile *Daily Register*, July 25, 1880. This is not to say that the planter press never ran pro-Birmingham articles; see for instance Mobile *Daily Register*, October 4, 1882, April 17, 1883, January 9, 1884, February 11, 1885; Montgomery *Daily Advertiser*, January 17, 1883.

article in the Mobile *Register* bore the headline "Birmingham's Boom"; the report was two sentences long. A black belt reporter traveling in northern Alabama in 1883 devoted more space to the new agricultural settlement at Cullman than to Birmingham, whose principal achievement he believed to be the laying out of "two new avenues parallel to the railroads."[29]

During the 1880s the Mobile press continued to dream about shipping coal for steamships and home heating rather than for iron manufacture. If Birmingham would only ship its coal south, "the problem of Mobile's destiny" would be solved, the *Register* argued in 1882. If a direct railroad were built from the coal mines to Mobile, "nothing in any country will surpass it as a great mineral road." "Suppose we have a war with a colonial European Power, the South Atlantic and gulf squadrons would be able to coal in Mobile." This could lead to "the reestablishment of the grand emporium on the Gulf of Mexico"—Mobile, for the uninitiated. Dissatisfied with Birmingham's shipments, the Mobile Board of Trade in 1883 purchased 160,000 acres of mineral lands, "the coal mines to be worked on a lease, the coal to be sold in Mobile . . . and thus make Mobile a great coal shipping port." But even these dreams of greatness did not destroy other plans; the *Register*, examining Mobile's future in 1881, gave equal billing to "Mobile as a Coal Fueling Station" and "Mobile as a Winter Health Resort."[30]

The Iron Tariff and the Politics of Industrial Development

Tariff legislation is a subject that causes many eyes to glass over. But the debate over lowering the iron tariff in 1883 and 1884 went to the heart of the question of industrial development in Alabama. The industrialists of Birmingham were unqualified in their support for high tariffs on iron, which they argued were essential to Birmingham's economic take-off, while planter spokesmen firmly and consistently argued for lower iron tariffs. The debate on the iron tariff gave planter spokesmen an opportunity to reveal once again the depth of their hostility to industrial development in Alabama.

29. Mobile *Daily Register*, October 4, 1882, January 10, 1883.
30. *Ibid.*, May 22, 1881, January 12, March 22, September 21, 1882, April 2, 1883, December 28, 1884. See also May 6, 1882, January 6, 24, 1883.

The Birmingham press insisted that high iron tariffs were the basis of the region's economic promise. The strength of high tariff "lies in the prosperity which it has given the . . . great industrial cities it has built and in the diversified industries it has founded," the Birmingham *Chronicle* wrote in 1884; "in all it enobles industry and adds to its earnings, lies the strength of this American system." Birmingham was united around this argument. In 1883 a "mass meeting" in Birmingham passed a resolution urging "ample and adequate protection" for the city's fledgling industry; those participating in the meeting included "the iron capitalists of the city." A meeting of "the representative iron men of Alabama," held to organize "concerted action," it passed a resolution stating, "We, the iron producers of Alabama, . . . need the tariff to secure the American market;" they did not neglect to point to the notoriously low profits of Birmingham iron producers. A representative was selected to lobby in Washington for the group, and others were assigned the task of organizing southern iron manufacturers outside Alabama. In 1884 the Birmingham *Age* reported the organization of the "Industrial League" with over 3,000 members in the Birmingham region; it was dedicated to continued tariff protection for Alabama industry.[31]

The planter representatives who led the fight to lower the iron tariff seldom challenged the argument that Birmingham's survival depended on keeping tariffs high; they nevertheless opposed the continuation of high tariffs. Black belt congressman William C. Oates was perfectly explicit: "If manufacturing will not pay when the manufacturer in this country finishes his goods at the same cost that the Englishman does with the advantage to the American of the intervention of an ocean 3,000 miles wide, then it had better be abandoned, for the government cannot afford to continue the perpetration of the great wrong of taxing one class of its citizens for the benefit of another." Oates, who later became governor, correctly described the high iron tariff as a legacy of the Civil War, and argued that the tariff Birmingham sought would eventually

31. Birmingham *Chronicle*, quoted in Eutaw *Mirror*, October 14, 1884; see also Demopolis *Southern Republican*, May 4, 1870; Montgomery *Daily Advertiser*, February 6, 13, 1883; Mobile *Daily Register*, February 26, 1884.

produce "discontent, lawlessness, and communism"—the characteristic disorders of northern industrial society.[32]

Hilary Herbert, who represented Montgomery in Congress, saw the issue in equally stark terms; he suggested that the Birmingham high-tariff advocates "want to break up agriculture and drive the toilers from the field and the farmers from their homes." To industrialists who argued that high tariffs meant high wages for Birmingham workers, Herbert replied that "it is capital, not labor, that you are seeking to protect," and concluded that the high tariff on iron was similar to the British navigation acts, which provoked the American Revolution. Senator John T. Morgan described how the tariff Birmingham sought had brought misery to the poor people of the state. In a speech remarkable for its disconnected but purple prose, Morgan said the iron tariff had created "a people so poor that the clamoring cries of many of them for bread and fuel and clothing come up during these wintry blasts and howl down the very storms that rage and reverberate and are now beating upon the walls of the Senate Chamber."[33]

Other advocates of tariff reduction were more coherent. The *Register* wrote, "We see no justice in legislation being exclusively devoted to the development of our manufacturing interests. . . . We object to the great agricultural interest of the country being forced to pay tribute to men who have made colossal fortunes in the past while whining about infant industries, many of whom are so greedy for gain that any reduction in their large profits causes them to seek to grind the faces of their poor employees." The Montgomery *Advertiser* also denounced the iron tariff as "an organized system for robbing the people, . . . an outrageous device of [those who seek] . . . the advantage of a few classes of monopolists." As the vote in Congress drew closer, the Birmingham press complained that "very few journals in this state . . . favor a policy of encouragement to the growing industries of Alabama, . . . threatening destruction of the iron industries of the state." Defenders of

32. *Congressional Record*, 48th Cong., 1st Sess., 3849.
33. Montgomery *Daily Advertiser*, February 16, 1883; *Congressional Record*, 48th Cong., 1st Sess., 3231, 341; see also Hugh B. Hammett, *Hilary Abner Herbert: A Southerner Returns to the Union*, Memoirs of the American Philosophical Society, CX (Philadelphia: American Philosophical Society, 1976).

the high tariff denied that "those engaged in industrial pursuits" were "robbers and outlaws" who had "committed an unpardonable sin."[34]

But the arguments of the state's industrialists did not persuade Alabama's representatives in Congress. The entire Alabama delegation in the House voted to lower the iron tariff. However, northern Republican strength defeated the proposal. A bitter Mobile *Register* commented that the proposed reduction "aroused the moneyed interests and drove into closer alliance the various manufacturing communities with their millions of voters and hundreds of millions of capital."[35]

Birmingham thus kept the high tariff it believed it needed to survive, but it did so only because of northern Republican support and against the wishes of the entire Alabama congressional delegation as well as the leading planter newspapers of the state. If the planters had not denied the industrialists the tariff they claimed they needed to survive, they had made their intentions clear.

The depression of 1884–1885 saw a fateful development for the Birmingham iron industry; for the first time, southern iron made a successful invasion of the northern market. A concerned Andrew Carnegie finally came to Birmingham in 1889 to look over his competition. After his tour he declared that "the South is Pennsylvania's most formidable enemy," a statement with ominous implications when coming from an industrialist as powerful as Carnegie. It was not unexpected in Birmingham: six years earlier, in a discussion of the desirability of tariff protection for the city's fledgling industry, a leading industrialist said, "It is not the English competition that we fear. . . . That Pittsburgh competition is the competition that Birmingham fears."[36]

34. Birmingham *Iron Age*, quoted in Mobile *Daily Register*, January 20, 1884; Mobile *Daily Register*, April 20, 1882, May 7, 1884; Montgomery *Daily Advertiser*, February 14, 1883. See also Mobile *Daily Register*, October 21, 1880, February 5, 1881, January 7, 25, 1883; Montgomery *Daily Advertiser*, February 22, 1883; Eutaw *Mirror*, October 28, 1884.

35. Mobile *Daily Register*, May 8, June 3, 1884. For the 1884 debate on lowering the iron tariff, see *Congressional Record*, 48th Cong., 1st Sess., 3908. HR 5893 was debated in the House on April 22 and May 5, and defeated May 6. The key vote was on a motion to strike out the enacting clause of the bill to lower iron tariffs by 20 percent; thus a "nay" vote is a vote in favor of a lower tariff.

36. Quoted in Woodward, *Origins of the New South*, 127; *Senate Documents*, 48th Cong., 1st Sess., No. 1262, IV, 257.

Technological backwardness continued to plague the Birmingham region in the late eighties. The market for pig iron was declining as Pennsylvania-produced steel grew in importance. In 1889, Birmingham produced its first experimental steel with local iron at the Henderson furnaces; Henry Grady was jubilant, proclaiming that Birmingham's era had finally begun. But once again capital investment was the major stumbling block; "the necessary capital could not be raised to enlarge and improve the Henderson steel plant," the company "failed commercially," and it was eventually dismantled and sold for scrap.[37]

Birmingham was not alone in Alabama; during the 1870s, the state's industries as a whole failed to reach the fabled "economic take-off." The census statistics on the work force show that the proportion of Alabamians engaged in "manufacturing, mechanical, and mining" occupations did not increase between 1870 and 1880, and that the proportion engaged in "trade and transport"—which included the railroads—actually decreased during the same decade. As late as 1880, only 5 percent of Alabama's work force was employed in "manufacturing, mechanical and mining" occupations, and only 3 percent in "trade and transport."[38]

In 1895, six years after the failure of the Henderson steel operations, the Tennessee Company, now the dominant force in Birmingham, succeeded at making a basic pig iron good enough to be converted into open-hearth steel. Again there was general jubilation, but once again development passed Birmingham by; the new iron was sold to "the Carnegie people" for them to manufacture into steel in Pennsylvania, instead of spurring development of a local steel industry.

Finally, at the end of 1899, Birmingham produced its first commercially successful steel. Colonel Shook, promoter of the project, complained that if steel had not supplanted iron, Birmingham would have prospered: "If Sir Henry Bessemer had never invented the Bessemer process for making steel, the Birmingham district

37. Armes, *Coal and Iron*, 410–11; Justin Fuller, "From Iron to Steel: Alabama's Industrial Evolution," *Alabama Review*, XVII (1964), 137–48.

38. U.S. Bureau of the Census, *10th Census* (Washington, D.C.: Government Printing Office, 1883), "Report on Occupations."

would have been the leading iron center in the world for the last quarter century. . . . The next quarter of a century [1900–1925] will give it the development it is entitled to, and that has been retarded and held back for the last quarter of a century."[39] Shook was speaking thirty-four years after the end of the war and twenty-seven years after the founding of Birmingham.

When U. S. Steel purchased the Tennessee Coal and Iron Company in 1907, the indefatigable industrial spokesman once again predicted that Birmingham was about to become "the largest steel manufacturing center in the universe," but U.S. Steel was more interested in controlling Birmingham's competition with Pittsburgh than with developing the full potential of the north Alabama steel industry. Carnegie effectively removed "Pennsylvania's most formidable enemy" from the competition by raising prices on Birmingham steel; in the ensuing years, Birmingham's iron production remained almost stationary, while that of the United States as a whole increased by more than 70 percent. The South's proportion of national iron production fell from 22 percent in 1893 to 11 percent in 1913.[40]

Conclusion

"The cause of southern industrialism demanded, above all, the destruction of the slave regime," Genovese writes. The key impediments were the immobility of southern capital, tied up as it was in slaves, and slavery's stifling effects on purchasing power.[41] The removal of these obstacles was necessary for the development of southern industry but not sufficient. What is impressive about the progress of Birmingham's industry after the war is how incomplete and partial the movement toward industrialization was, and how persistent was the pattern of industrial weakness and planter strength.

The planters did not oppose any and all industrialization enterprises in the postwar period, just as they had not done so before

39. Armes, *Coal and Iron*, 466–67.
40. Victor S. Clark, *History of Manufactures in the United States, 1860–1914* (New York: McGraw-Hill Book Company, 1929), III, 26.
41. Eugene D. Genovese, *The Political Economy of Slavery* (New York: Pantheon Books, 1967), 191.

the war. Instead they sought industrial development which served their interests, and which they could control. From the viewpoint of the planter class, the object of development was not the creation of an industrial economy, but rather the strengthening of agriculture in general and plantation agriculture in particular.[42] The vertical integration of the cotton industry, under planter control, was the limit of industrial development favored by the planters; cotton mills kept the profits from manufacturing in the state and acted as a safety valve for white agrarian discontent by providing an alternative source of employment. But the creation of an iron and steel industry in north Alabama did little to advance planter interests. The potential harm resulting from competition for black labor was greater than any benefit regional industry might bring. As long as agricultural tenants had no real alternative sources of employment in industry, the planters' coercive system of labor allocation and control was secure. But the rise of a vigorous free market in labor would threaten the basis of the planter-dominated Prussian Road.

The development of Birmingham's heavy industry was agonizingly slow and incomplete; the fifteen-year period following the end of the war saw virtually no economic growth. Many historians have noticed this delay in the beginning of postwar southern development, but few have devoted more than a sentence or two to it. Woodward writes only that "the business revival of 1879 opened the war for the southern iron industry, until then largely a hopeful potentiality." Stanley Coben interprets the slow start of southern industrialization as a consequence of the opposition of northeastern capitalists to Radical Reconstruction. "Eventually," he writes, "northerners invested huge sums in southern factories, mines, railroads, and real estate; but it is significant that only a small number did so as long as Radicals controlled southern state legislatures."[43] But northeastern capitalists failed to show much support for industrialization in the Birmingham region after the overthrow of the Alabama Radicals. Outside capitalists persistently

42. Robert L. Brandfon, *Cotton Kingdom of the New South* (Cambridge: Harvard University Press, 1967), 2.
43. Woodward, *Origins of the New South*, 126; Stanley Coben, "Northeastern Business and Radical Reconstruction: A Reexamination," *Mississippi Valley Historical Review*, XLVI (1959), 67–90.

refused to support rapid development of Birmingham's technology and industrial capacity, and northeastern steel interests opposed the development of southern industry, which would compete for markets. These factors, along with planter political opposition and the financial weakness of the local industrialists, were responsible for the slow development of Birmingham.

When outside capital finally was obtained by Birmingham developers, around 1880, it came not from the centers of finance in New York, Boston, and Philadelphia, but from the periphery, from Nashville and Cincinnati and Louisville, from the second and third string of industrialists and financiers. Northeastern capitalists first refused to invest in mines and blast furnaces as the mineral region was being opened; then they refused to support the technological innovations in coking coal that could make the region a major pig iron center. Once the pig iron was in production, they failed to invest in conversion to steel; once the technology of making basic pig iron good enough for steel was perfected, the northeastern interests bought the iron for their own manufacturing, further delaying the development of southern steelmaking capacity; and, when Birmingham had at last converted to steel, northeastern capital finally bought in, but with the purpose of holding back southern steel production, retarding the growth of southern manufactured goods which competed with their own.

The roots of this situation lie in Radical Reconstruction. There is no indication that the congressional Radicals, or their northern supporters, wanted to create a new southern industry capable of supplying this southern yeomanry they proposed to bring into existence. If northern industry needed anything from the South, aside from cotton, it was new markets, rather than new industrial competition or new opportunities for investment.[44] The North did not fight the war to create markets for industrial goods; no such argument is being made here. But successful Radical Reconstruction would have served the interests of northeastern industry by establishing a new western-styled yeoman farmer class, not by a general southern industrialization.

44. Henry R. Swint, "Northern Interest in the Shoeless Southerner," *Journal of Southern History*, X (1950), 457–71.

The refusal of northeastern financiers to pour capital into the development of Birmingham may have been as much a consequence of the splendid opportunities for profit in their own region as it was a consequence of particular features of Birmingham itself. These financiers were engaged in the first stages of the consolidation of capitalist enterprises in their own rapidly developing region—a consolidation that absorbed a great deal of capital and paid an embarrassingly handsome return.

Alabama industrialists thus faced two powerful antagonists between the end of the war and the beginning of the twentieth century. The planters wanted to keep black labor tied to the plantations, to preserve the state's fundamentally agrarian society, to keep Alabama on the Prussian Road; northeastern finance and industry wanted to prevent the rise of competition in iron and steel production. Alabama industry was able to find some important allies among Kentucky and Tennessee financiers and industrialists, which temporarily counterbalanced the opposition of the planter class and enabled Birmingham industry to get off the ground; but these regional allies were no match for Carnegie, Frick, and U.S. Steel.

Some historians have argued that the South followed the same general pattern of industrial development as the northeast had a few decades earlier; first, a cotton textile industry, then an iron industry, and finally, the construction of a railroad network. The key to Alabama industrial development, however, is not its similarity to, but rather its divergence from the northeastern and British pattern. In Alabama, the combination of textiles plus iron plus railroads did not add up to a case of general and sustained industrialization. In this respect, Alabama has much in common with the developing world in the twentieth century, as C. Vann Woodward has observed. In Alabama, the limited nature and extent of industrial development were shaped by a dominant nonbourgeois planter class, and by external "imperialist" corporations seeking raw materials and markets, which strengthened the local forces leading the region down the Prussian Road. Like most developing countries in the contemporary world, in late nineteenth-century Alabama the development of railroads, textiles, and iron occurred in the midst of an economically stagnant, politically repressive agrarian society. The state did not move off the Prussian Road and onto the classic capitalist path to modern society until well into the twentieth century, and the process is by no means complete today.[45]

45. Edward C. Kirkland, *Industry Comes of Age: Business, Labor, and Public Policy 1860–1897* (New York: Holt, Rinehart and Winston, 1961); C. Vann Woodward, "The Irony of Southern History," in *The Burden of Southern History* (Baton Rouge: Louisiana State University Press, 1960); see also Douglas F. Dowd, "A Comparative Analysis of Economic Development in the American West and South," *Journal of Economic History*, XVI (1966), Supplement, 558–74; George B. Leighton, "Birmingham, Alabama: The City of Perpetual Promise," *Harpers*, CLXV (1937), 225–42. For a different perspective from the one presented here, see Stanley Engerman, "Some Factors in Southern Backwardness in the Nineteenth Century," in John F. Kain and John R. Meyer (eds.), *Essays in Regional Economics* (Cambridge: Harvard University Press, 1971), especially p. 316. Engerman does not distinguish different types of economic growth, and defines wealth in terms of per capita income, overlooking inequality. The Birmingham elite did not begin buying the great antebellum plantation homes of the black belt until the 1930s; some are still owned by the original antebellum planter families—personal communication from J. Mills Thornton III.

The Struggle for Hegemony

The rise of a class of industrialists was accompanied by the development of their self-consciousness, by the growth of a distinctive world view, and by the appearance of intellectuals who developed the new world view into a coherent program. This became the ground on which the ideologists waged their battle against the ideals and values of the old order. It was a struggle for hegemony, in which fundamentally antagonistic ideologies "come into confrontation and conflict, until only one of them . . . prevails, gains the upper hand, propagates itself throughout society—bringing about not only a unison of economic and political aims, but also intellectual and moral unity, posing all the questions around which the struggle rages not on a corporate but on a 'universal' plane, and thus creating the hegemony of a fundamental social group over a series of subordinate groups." The concept is based on the assumption that latent class antagonisms are fundamental in society; hegemony is the ability to confine the conflicts that arise to issues acceptable to the dominant class, in a way that prevents the emergence of an effective challenge to the ruling groups.[1]

Neither the planters nor the industrialists were a hegemonic class within the South during the 1870s and 1880s. This was one of

1. Quintin Hoare and Geoffrey Nowell Smith (eds.), *Selections from the Prison Notebooks of Antonio Gramsci* (New York: International Publishers, 1971), 181–82; see also 12–13, 228–29, 261–64; Perry Anderson, "The Antinomies of Antonio Gramsci," *New Left Review*, No. 100 (1976), 5–80; Gwynn Williams, "Gramsci's Concept of *Egemonia*," *Journal of the History of Ideas*, XII (1970), 587; John M. Cammett, *Antonio Gramsci and the Origins of Italian Communism* (Stanford: Stanford University Press, 1967), Chap. 10; Eugene D. Genovese, "On Antonio Gramsci," in Genovese, *In Red and Black* (New York: Pantheon Books, 1971), 391–412; Eugene D. Genovese, *Roll, Jordan, Roll: The World the Slaves Made* (New York: Pantheon Books, 1975), 658. For a critical test of the slaveholders'

the moments in southern history when the question of "the basis of society" was openly and hotly debated. Since the South's new industrialists were weak, and since the planter class proved to be unexpectedly tenacious, the postwar planters and their intellectual allies fought vigorously to turn back the assault on their moral sensibilities and their notions of order, to defend the Prussian Road with a nonbourgeois agrarian ideology. (Since ideological conflict crossed state lines, this discussion will do the same.)

Bourgeois Ideology in the Postwar South

The ideologists of the New South were attempting to cast off the cultural domination of the planter class, to spread their own conception of reality throughout southern society in a way that would replace the planter standards of taste, morality, and culture, with their own. Woodward has a brilliantly concise description of the tasks facing the New South ideologists in their effort to win hegemony: "It was necessary that the acquisitive instincts not only become respectable, but that they be regarded as ambition. Speculation should be awarded the prizes of courage and valor, and the profit motive mile-posted as the road to the good life. . . . It was important that the meaning of life be discovered in the vicissitudes and triumphs attending the competitive struggle for business profits."[2]

The new man and new conception of morality put forward by the New South advocates contained nothing that would have been unfamiliar to, say, Benjamin Franklin; they argued a Social Darwinist

---

hegemony in one state, see Michael P. Johnson, *Toward a Patriarchal Republic: The Secession of Georgia* (Baton Rouge: Louisiana State University Press, 1977), especially pp. 65–78, 85–94. An alternative theoretical approach to viewing the "New South Creed" as a bourgeois ideology is to consider it in terms of the Protestant Ethic: Max Weber, *The Protestant Ethic and the Spirit of Capitalism*, trans. Talcott Parsons (New York: Charles Scribner's Sons, 1958); David Bertelson, *The Lazy South* (New York: Oxford University Press, 1967); C. Vann Woodward, "The Southern Ethic in a Puritan World," *American Counterpoint: Slavery and Racism in the North-South Dialogue* (Boston: Little, Brown, 1971), 13–46.

2. C. Vann Woodward, *Tom Watson, Agrarian Rebel* (New York: The Macmillan Company, 1938), 89. He returned to the topic in 1968: "The range of New South rhetoric left unsounded no maxim of the self-made man, no crassness of the booster, no vulgarity of the shopkeeper, no philistinism of the profit maximizer." Woodward, *American Counterpoint*, 43.

position in unsophisticated language, preaching the bourgeois gospel of work. Alexander McClure, a leading New South ideologist, contrasted the planters with the new men of the New South in powerful and vivid images: "The young men [of the New South] are not the dawdling, palefaced effeminates which were so often visible in the nurslings of the slave. They had keen, expressive eyes; their faces are bronzed; their hands are often the tell-tales of labor; their step is elastic and their habits energetic." The planters, it was said, had been "easy going and oligarchical," lacking all sense of the practical; they had lived a life of "luxurious abandon and hospitable idleness." The new man of the New South, in contrast, was "energetic and enterprising. . . , sensible and shrewd and self-reliant," according to one of the dozens of southern books of the eighties on how to be successful in business.[3]

Benjamin H. Hill made a clear and decisive attack on the Old South ideal in 1871: the region could not afford to waste time and strength in defense of "theories and systems," however valued in their day, which had been "swept down by the moving avalanche of actual events. . . . [We can] live neither *in* nor *by* the defeated past." The Birmingham *Chronicle* explained that a new spirit had swept across the region; "those men who cannot catch this spirit, as it permeates the South, will have to retire from high places and give room to new men." And the Birmingham *Iron Age* contrasted the achievements of the new world's industrialists with the failings of the planters. The industrialists "filled the earth with the most beneficent and utilitarian civilization it has ever witnessed, and strewed the shores of its oceans with mighty cities, reticulated its surface with steam roads, covered the wild seas with the white wings of commerce, and even invaded their unknown depths with the iron-shod pathways of lightning . . . [while the planters] acknowledge that the wheels of their progress are stopped because

3. Mobile *Daily Register*, December 23, 1880; Paul M. Gaston, *The New South Creed: A Study in Southern Mythmaking* (New York: Alfred A. Knopf, 1969), 110. Henry Grady echoed Franklin in terms that Max Weber would have rushed to quote: "we have fallen in love with work." Grady also anticipated Daniel Boorstin by eighty years: "We have sowed towns and cities in the place of theories." Raymond B. Nixon, *Henry W. Grady: Spokesman for the New South* (New York: Russell & Russell, 1943), 345.

the negroes won't work and keep their contracts; a sorry spectacle indeed!"[4]

The program for regional industrialization put forward by the New South ideologists beginning in the 1870s marked a radical departure from the proposals of the antebellum industrial advocates: for the first time, an argument was being made for full industrialization, for the creation of a genuinely bourgeois society in which agriculture would serve the needs of the industrial sector instead of the other way around, for a society producing manufactured goods, populated by industrial workers, and presided over by the captains of industry. But, at the same time, the New South industrial program preserved some key elements of the arguments of the antebellum industrial promoters.

Men like Henry Grady and Richard Edmonds saw clearly how plantation slavery had been a fetter on the development of southern industry—tying up capital in slaves, making the plantation the center of economic power, and forcing the manufacturers to serve the needs of the plantation. They based their hopes for industrialization on the abolition of slavery, the apparent decline of the planter class, and on the region's abundant natural resources.

The New South ideologists' most radical proposal was the abolition of the plantation. Sidney Lanier summed up the argument concisely: "The New South means small farming." The adjectives that went along with the proposal were "inefficient" for plantations and "prosperous" for small farms—prosperous because they would produce a diversified crop whereas the plantations concentrated exclusively on cotton. DeBow had argued for the breakup of large plantations as early as 1867; he hoped the availability of divided plantation land would attract immigrants possessing needed skills. Some spokesmen for northern business agreed. After the Panic of '73, various newspapers proposed dividing the plantations as an alternative to depression. Advocates of the transition to small farming believed they were simply describing a process that was already taking place. Lanier wrote in 1880 that "the quiet rise of the

4. Quoted in Gaston, *New South Creed*, 34; Birmingham *Chronicle*, quoted in Eutaw *Mirror*, October 14, 1884; Birmingham *Iron Age*, October 21, 1875.

small farmer in the Southern states during the last twenty years becomes the notable circumstance of the period," and Wilbur F. Tillet, dean of the Vanderbilt School of Theology, wrote in 1887 that tenant farming had "well-nigh disappeared."[5]

The proposal to replace plantations with farms came from none less than Thaddeus Stevens, whose analysis of the South on this count was essentially what the New South spokesmen were to argue in the 1880s: the disappearance of the planter would mean the end of the antagonism between agriculture and industry, and thus between North and South; the sections would become one continuous capitalist society. There were crucial differences, of course. Stevens wanted the ex-slaves to get the divided plantation land, so they would have a material basis for their political and social freedom; the New South spokesmen felt that the land should go to energetic and thrifty whites, who would form the core of the rural half of New South society.[6] But on the crucial question of abolishing the plantation and thus eliminating the planter class, the position of the New South advocates was remarkably similar to that of Stevens and the Radical Republicans.

In the early days of the New South movement, the attack on the planters was unrestrained. Daniel Harvey Hill wrote in 1866 about the planters: "What factories did they erect? What mines did they dig? What foundries did they establish? What machine shops did they build? . . . The glories of the past were purchased at the expense of the material prosperity of the country."[7]

5. Sidney Lanier, "The New South," *Scribners*, XX (1880), 840; *DeBow's Review*, After the War Series, IV (1867), 94–105; Philadelphia *North American and United States Gazette*, quoted in Eric Foner, "Thaddeus Stevens, Confiscation, and Reconstruction," in Stanley Elkins and Erik McKitrick (eds.), *The Hofstadter Aegis: A Memorial* (New York: Alfred A. Knopf, 1974), 173; New Orleans *Picayune*, quoted in Roger W. Shugg, *Origins of Class Struggle in Louisiana* (Baton Rouge: Louisiana State University Press, 1939), 253; Wilbur F. Tillet, "The White Man of the New South," *Century*, XXIII (1887), 769–76. In large part Lanier and Tillet based their argument on faulty methods of enumeration by the census office.

6. Genovese has pointed out how Stevens's land distribution proposal was connected to his ideas on money and the tariffs: a southern yeomanry would have provided northern farmers and small businessmen with a powerful ally in their struggle against monopoly. Eugene D. Genovese, "Problems in the Study of Nineteenth-Century American History," *Science & Society*, XXV (1961), 48–51.

7. Daniel Harvey Hill, *The Land We Love*, I (1886), 2. The debate on the character of the antebellum planters continues: compare Du Bois: "They became arrogant, strutting,

Although they did not emphasize it, New South ideologists had no doubts about the importance for their program of an end to the domination of the planter class. The disappearance of the planter was the prerequisite to a newly harmonious relationship between agriculture and industry. Later New South ideologists soft-pedaled the notion of abolishing the planters as a class, preferring to speak in terms of the natural process by which inefficient plantations would give way to thrifty, prosperous farms; they assumed that the abolition of slavery would lead to the abolition of the plantation and thus to the disappearance of the planters. In place of a dominant rural class which limited industry to serving its own needs, there would be a subservient rural class, which would prosper by filling the industrialists' needs.[8]

When they assessed the South's potential for industrial development, the New South ideologists concluded that, in view of the region's critical lack of both skilled labor and capital available for investment in manufacture, abundant natural resources were its single asset. This realization led them to argue rather naïvely that possession of natural resources was the key to economic development. Edmonds wrote articles describing "nature's wonderful blessings to the South," arguing that, if a town possessed mineral wealth and a location which made transportation easy, "its future is

quarrelsome kinglets; . . . they expected deference and self-abasement; they were choleric and easily insulted"—with Genovese: "they were tough, proud, and arrogant, liberal-spirited in all that did not touch their honor; gracious and courteous; generous and kind; quick to anger and extraordinarily cruel . . . [they] were heroes"—and with Bertram Wyatt-Brown: "[they had] a rigid formality, an intractable and humorless sobriety, and a basic selfishness . . . stubbornly wrapped up in rural pleasures and dull conformities; [for them,] insularity was a means of shutting out unpleasantries, vulgarities, and contrary forces; . . . carefully confined to chosen boundaries, . . . they easily converted the mediocre into the grand." W. E. B. Du Bois, *Black Reconstruction in America, 1860–1880* (New York: Atheneum, 1969), 52; Genovese, *Roll, Jordan, Roll*, 96–97; Bertram Wyatt-Brown, "Children of Pride and Patriarchy," *Reviews in American History*, I (1973), 103, 105.

8. Gaston, *New South Creed*, 67. A few New South writers criticized diversification and the replacement of planters by yeoman farmers. Tompkins, while urging southern farmers to produce foodstuffs, insisted that cotton would remain the basis of the South's agricultural prosperity. The solution to the region's agrarian problems, he wrote, was not to abolish cotton culture, but to grow cotton more efficiently and scientifically. George T. Winston, *A Builder of the New South: Daniel Augustus Tompkins* (Garden City: Doubleday & Co., 1920), 84–94. A less important writer, John C. Reed, argued that crops should be diversified but that the plantation should remain the unit of production. "A class of new planters," he wrote, "diversify their crops and products." John C. Reed, "The Old South and the New," *International Review*, III (1876), 209–33.

assured."[9] Probably the argument about the importance of natural resources was a case of emphasizing the positive and putting the best foot forward, rather than a failure to comprehend the social and economic requirements of industrial development.

Capital for investment in manufacturing could come from two sources: from the South, or from northeastern and foreign investors. Former governor Patton of Alabama argued as early as 1867 that the changed status of black labor made cotton growing unprofitable, and thus southern capital should be shifted from plantation agriculture to textile manufacturing. John W. DuBose, a leading industrial spokesman, wrote in 1886 that the question facing Birmingham was whether the city would be developed by Alabama capital, created by local planters "from the ground," or "foreign capital," capital from the North. DuBose opposed the latter alternative, arguing that the Republican party from its inception had conspired to make the South a colony of the North; he viewed northern capitalists as amoral, which distinguished them from Alabama planters.[10] Most of the New South industrial advocates, however, concentrated their efforts on attracting outside capital; it was to northern capitalists that they directed their glowing descriptions of the South's natural resources.

Attracting an industrial proletariat was a project to which New South ideologists devoted considerable effort. One group concluded that the South should imitate the Northeast and recruit immigrant labor to fill southern factories. They advanced various proposals to attract immigrants: some favored making land available to immigrants, while others, like John C. Delavique, had more contorted plans. Delavique argued in *DeBow's Review* that white immigrants would not come south until the blacks were forced out of the region. Daniel Harvey Hill disagreed; he thought the blacks would not have to be driven out because they could be left to "degenerate." New South advocates argued that factory workers could

9. *Manufacturers' Record*, March 19, 1869, February 1, 1888.
10. Robert M. Patton, "The New Era of Southern Manufactures," *DeBow's Review*, After the War Series, III (1867), 56–68; John W. DuBose, "A Practical Question," Birmingham *Weekly Iron Age*, February 11, 25, 1886; Hugh C. Davis, "An Analysis of the Rationale of Representative Conservative Alabamians, 1874–1914" (Ph.D. dissertation, Vanderbilt University, 1964), 180, 198.

also come out of the ranks of the poor white farmers. The factories, by providing employment, would offer an alternative to tenancy for the poorest and most abject of them. The industrialists would get a cheap, dependable labor force, and the ruling class as a whole would be relieved of the responsibility of dealing with the agrarian problem. *DeBow's Review* said it in 1868 with revealing simplicity: "the state must build a poorhouse and a prison, or a cotton factory in every county or parish."[11]

The proposal to put poor white farmers to work in factories was nothing new in 1868; it had been a favorite scheme of antebellum industrial advocates, whose central task was always to demonstrate how the planters' interests would be served by their proposals. De-Bow had written almost thirty years before the war that "it is to the interest of the slaveholder that a way of wealth and respectability be opened to [the poorest white farmers], and that encouragement should be given to interest and enterprise." He was proposing that, since there was no place for the poor whites in the slavehold-ing economy, a separate industrial society be created for them. The South as a whole should remain an agrarian society dominated by planters; the whites for whom there was no place would find work in a small industrial sector. This program for antebellum industry had been supported even by slave ideologist George Fitzhugh. "If there were to be industrial growth," Fitzhugh argued, "let the slaves be the unskilled laborers, and the whites the skilled. Let white labor be privileged and imbued with caste pride; let it benefit from the more lowly labor of the Negro."[12] Fitzhugh had

11. John C. Delavique, "Cotton," *DeBow's Review*, After the War Series, IV (1867), 562–71; Daniel Harvey Hill, "Education," *The Land We Love*, I (1866), 1–11, 83–91. On the immigration campaigns, see Allen Going, *Bourbon Democracy in Alabama 1874–1890* (University Ala.: University of Alabama Press, 1951), 120–24; William Warren Rogers, *The One-Gallused Rebellion: Agrarianism in Alabama, 1865–1896* (Baton Rouge: Louisiana State University Press, 1970), 80–89; see also Rowland T. Berthoff, "Southern Attitudes towards Immigration, 1865–1914," *Journal of Southern History*, XVII (1951), 259–60; *De-Bow's Review*, After the War Series, V (1868), 837; William W. Rogers, "A Monarch Reinstated: Cotton Production and the Textile Industry in Alabama, 1865–1900," *Cotton History Review*, II (1961), 211–20.

12. Richmond *Enquirer*, February 2, 1832, cited in William Henry Yarbrough, *Economic Aspects of Slavery in Relation to Southern and Southwestern Migration* (Nashville: George Peabody College of Teachers, 1932), 64, 72; Richard W. Griffin, "Poor White Laborers in Southern Cotton Factories," *South Carolina History Magazine*, LXI (1960), 26–40; Randall M. Miller, "Daniel Pratt's Industrial Urbanism: The Cotton Mill Town in

recommended limited industrialization subordinate to a broadly based plantation regime.

The South's most important antebellum industrial advocates had assured the planters that they "neither desired nor expected a general industrialization."[13] The program of the antebellum industrialists, in brief, had called for a small industrial sector that served planter needs, the most important industry of which would be cotton textile manufacturing. By bringing the factories to the fields, the planters would be less dependent on the international cotton market, and gain for themselves the profits from manufacturing cotton textiles as well as those associated with growing cotton. Thus, argued the antebellum industrial promoters, the planter regime would be strengthened by the existence of a small industrial sector. It was precisely this form of the argument, stated in terms of planter interests, that was rejected by the industrial ideologists of the New South.

The New South program for factory employment of poor white tenant farmers gained a new urgency for planters in the later 1880s as agrarian unrest increasingly threatened social peace. In the language of the mill builders, the argument for social peace was that "corruption, idleness, and misery cannot be dispelled until the poor people are given an opportunity to become productive"—in the cotton mills.[14]

The best of the New South advocates understood that radical changes in agriculture would have to accompany the rise of industry. Henry Grady observed that, in the North, a prosperous farming class found a substantial market for diversified foodstuffs in the new industrial cities; the hope for the South's farms, he concluded, lay in developing urban industrial centers that would provide a new market for southern farms, enabling them to produce diversified foodstuffs and escape from cotton monoculture. Daniel A.

Antebellum Alabama," *Alabama Historical Quarterly*, XXXIV (1972), 9; Eugene D. Genovese, *The World the Slaveholders Made* (New York: Pantheon Books, 1969), 208.

13. *DeBow's Review*, XI (1851), 130.

14. Broadus Mitchell, *The Rise of Cotton Mills in the South*, Johns Hopkins University Studies in History and Political Science, XXXIX, No. 2 (Baltimore: The Johns Hopkins Press, 1921), 135. See also Herbert Collins, "The Idea of a Cotton Textile Industry in the South, 1870–1900," *North Carolina Historical Review*, XXXIV (1957), 372.

Tompkins agreed, writing that "the factories will require operatives, who in turn must have foodstuffs, which will make a market
for the farmers' supplies. . . . diversified crops can then be sold for
cash." Benjamin Hill put the argument for diversification simply:
"You will ever grow poor who produce cotton."[15]

Diversification had been the heart of the antebellum agricultural
reformers' programs. Grady, however, realized that without the
appearance of an urban, industrial demand for foodstuffs, diversification would mean only that individual farms would become self-
sufficient—a move out of the market, and thus a backward step.
The Old South agricultural reformers had indeed concentrated
almost exclusively on farm self-sufficiency, arguing that southern
farmers should grow their own feed for livestock and cultivate
products for their own tables.[16] Grady too favored such measures,
but he put diversification into the much larger context of social
change toward industrialization—a significant advance over the
Old South argument, possible because he rejected what the Old
South reformers accepted, the permanence of a planter-dominated
agrarian society.

Other New South advocates justified crop diversification on
more opportunist grounds. One writer proposed in *DeBow's Review* in 1867 that the South retaliate against Radical Reconstruction
by refusing to grow cotton for northern mills, and instead produce
diversified foodstuffs for regional consumption, refusing to purchase food from the North. Diversification was often considered a
remedy to the labor shortage. The Selma *Southern Argus* wrote in
1870, "The present scarcity of labor, the extraordinary and unsup-
plied demand for labor, is because planters persist in the cultivation of cotton, which . . . can be profitable only when labor is
superabundant."[17]

15. Atlanta *Constitution*, quoted in Gaston, *New South Creed*, 69; Daniel A. Tompkins,
"Cotton Manufacture in the South," quoted in Winston, *Tompkins*, 128; Hill quoted in
Edwin DeLeon, "The New South," *Harpers*, XLVIII (1874), 270.

16. Eugene D. Genovese, *The Political Economy of Slavery* (New York: Pantheon
Books, 1965), 131–36.

17. C. Deranco, "The South: Its Situation and Resources," *DeBow's Review*, After the
War Series, IV (1867), 441–47; Selma *Southern Argus*, February 10, 3, 1870. Stephen J.
DeCanio, *Agriculture in the Postbellum South* (New Haven: Yale University Press, 1975),
129–39, argues that there was approximately equal sentiment for and against diversified

Planter Antibourgeois Ideology

The New South ideologists' bid for hegemony provoked the most explicit opposition from the planter community. Before the Civil War, ideologists like George Fitzhugh had developed a powerful moral critique of industrial capitalism. Genovese goes too far when he writes of the planters' antebellum ideology that its "defeat was indeed total" in the war. Although postwar defenders of the planter regime no longer argued for slavery, they proclaimed that they were "heirs to a great reactionary tradition," and this time they attacked not the northern industrialists, but the southern Yankees in their midst, the advocates of the New South creed.[18]

Edward A. Pollard was the earliest of the defenders of planter hegemony in the postwar period. In 1866 he published a book whose title, *The Lost Cause*, came to label the values planter ideologists were defending. In it Pollard argued,

> The danger is that [southerners] will lose their literature, their former habits of thought, their intellectual self-assertion, while they are too

farming, which he takes to be evidence that "literary sources" are contradictory and unreliable. Ransom and Sutch argue that he has "seriously misinterpreted" the literature, pointing out that DeCanio is surely wrong in characterizing Grady's endorsement of diversification as "half-hearted." Roger Ranson and Richard Sutch, *One Kind of Freedom: The Economic Consequences of Emancipation* (New York: Cambridge University Press, 1977), Chap. 8, *n.* 18.

18. Genovese, *World Slaveholders Made*, 234, 162. Louis Hartz argues similarly that after the war "the feudal dreamers of the South . . . all but forgot themselves." Hartz, *The Liberal Tradition in America: An Interpretation of American Political Thought Since the Revolution* (New York: Harcourt, Brace & World, 1955), 172. Woodward, on the other hand, notes that a "running critique of Yankee morals" was put forward after the war by those who sought to "define [the South's] identity and keep the image clear:" C. Vann Woodward, *The Burden of Southern History* (Baton Rouge: Louisiana State University Press, 1960), 109. William J. Cooper, Jr., *The Conservative Regime: South Carolina, 1877–1890* (Baltimore: The Johns Hopkins Press, 1968), 17, 132, argues that the conservatives "looked forward not to a better world, but to a recreated one"; however Cooper believes there was no conflict between agriculture and industry over this issue. See also Carl N. Degler, *Place Over Time: The Continuity of Southern Distinctiveness* (Baton Rouge: Louisiana State University Press, 1977); George Brown Tindall, *The Persistent Tradition in New South Politics* (Baton Rouge: Louisiana State University Press, 1975), 16–19; William B. Hesseltine, *Confederate Leaders in the New South* (Baton Rouge: Louisiana State University Press, 1950), and T. Harry Williams, *Romance and Realism in Southern Politics* (Athens, Ga.: University of Georgia Press, 1961), 46–47. Genovese has revised his position somewhat in *Roll, Jordan, Roll*, 111: after the war the antebellum ideology "declined slowly; . . . to a decreasing extent it lingered on well into the twentieth century."

intent upon recovering the mere *material* prosperity. . . . There are certain coarse advisors who tell the Southern people that the great ends of their lives now are to . . . make themselves rivals in the clattering and garish enterprise of the North. . . . But there are . . . loftier aspirations than the civilization of material things.[19]

Robert L. Dabney, a Presbyterian minister, was more concise. In reply to those who said the past was dead, Dabney asserted, "There are issues that cannot die without the death of a people, of their honor, their civilization and their greatness." He went on: "In this world of sin, the spirit of heroic self-sacrifice is the essential condition of national greatness and happiness. The only sure wealth of the state is in cultured, heroic men, who intelligently know their duty and are calmly prepared to sacrifice all else, including life, to maintain the right."[20]

John C. Calhoun Newton, a Protestant theologian, was even more apocalyptic. "When this mammonism has once invaded the Church of God, made the pews vain and worldly, frivolous and luxurious . . . then we shall wish that the iron furnaces had never come. . . . The new wealth of the New South is to be a curse, drowning men's souls in the perdition of grovelling sense and avarice." Newton expressed a concern over the moral consequences of factory labor that was similar to that of Tocqueville. The proletariat "is engaged in work so monotonous, so constant from morn till night," Newton wrote, that "there is a danger that these human operatives shall become little better than walking machines." He favored agricultural labor over factory work, arguing that farming

19. Cited in Gaston, *New South Creed*, 156; see also Jack P. Maddex, Jr., *The Reconstruction of Edward A. Pollard: A Rebel's Conversion to Postbellum Unionism* (Chapel Hill: University of North Carolina Press, 1974), especially pp. 33–42. Perhaps the most powerful twentieth-century critique from the planters' perspective was Faulkner's portrayal of the New South as "the age of the Snopeses." Flem Snopes, Faulkner's "New South Man," "with his pure and simple nose for money like a preacher's for sin and fried chicken," was "doomed to respectability like a feller in his Sunday suit trying to run through a field of cockleburs and beggarlice." Faulkner, *The Mansion* (New York: Vintage Books, 1955), 56, 57.

20. Robert L. Dabney, *The New South* . . . (Raleigh: Edwards, Brighton & Co., 1883), 13–14. See also George M. Fredrickson, *The Black Image in the White Mind: The Debate on Afro-American Character and Destiny, 1817–1914* (New York: Harper & Row, 1971), 219, which points out that Dabney's *Defense of Virginia* was the "only thoroughgoing defense of slavery published *after* the war."

elevated the soul through "close contact with nature." Albert Bledsoe agreed that "virtue and innocence sprang from close connection with the soil."[21]

Sidney Lanier attacked the New South ideologists directly. Apparently referring to Grady, Lanier wrote: "Listen how he brags, in newspaper and pamphlet! Are not your ears fatigued with his . . . stentorious vaunting of himself and his wares? . . . Crudity, immaturity, unripeness, acidity, instability—these things characterize all our thought, our politics, our social life."[22]

The paternalistic sensibility of the slaveholding class got a new lease on life in the postwar planters' ideological struggle against the New South creed. To those who argued that the South should model its economy and society on that of the Northeast, planter newspapers like the Selma *Southern Argus* replied by referring to the virtues of traditional paternalism:

> No other laborers in any part of the United States are in so good a condition as the negroes of the South. . . . They are oppressed by no grinding monopolies. They are the victims of no unfriendly combinations. They are antagonized by no hostile interests. Their employers are without capital, without credit, ground down by poverty; but their employers *must*, by hook or by crook, stand between them and want. . . . There is suffering in the manufacturing cities of New England. There are want and destitution in the coal and iron regions of Pennsylvania and New York. . . . On the plantations of the South, there are well-fed, well-clothed, and contented Negro laborers.[23]

The Mobile *Register* made the same comparison between the South's paternalistic labor relations and the North's capitalistic

21. John C. Calhoun Newton, *The New South and the Methodist Episcopal Church* (Baltimore: King Bros., 1887), 26, 24; Gaston, *New South Creed*, 157; Alexis de Tocqueville, *Democracy in America*, ed. J. P. Mayer (New York: Doubleday & Co., 1969), II, Chap. 20. Tocqueville was not popular with planter ideologists: "He philosophizes over us, but his commentaries are now utterly obsolete. He simply accepted the ultra-views of Jefferson's administration and clothed them in superior language." Mobile *Daily Register*, October 19, 1882.

22. Sidney Lanier, *Retrospects and Prospects: Descriptive and Historical Essays* (New York: C. Scribner's Sons, 1899), 95–96.

23. Genovese, *Roll, Jordan, Roll*, 111; Selma *Southern Argus*, February 19, 1875. On paternalism in the postwar South, see Jay R. Mandle, *The Roots of Black Poverty: The Southern Plantation Economy After the Civil War* (Durham: Duke University Press, 1978), Chap. 3; James L. Roark, *Masters Without Slaves: Southern Planters in the Civil War and Reconstruction* (New York: W. W. Norton Co., 1977), 144–47, 198–203.

ones: "there is more consideration and sympathy for colored labor at the South than there is consideration and sympathy for employees in some of the stores on Fulton Avenue, Brooklyn, or Broadway, New York, or Washington Street, Boston, or Chestnut Street, Philadelphia." In a separate editorial, the newspaper commended the article for "an elegant and powerful argument" in defense of the planters, "a just and noble tribute to our people." The paternalist argument was also made by Albert Bledsoe, who founded the *Southern Review* at the war's end and made it one of the two or three most important reactionary journals. Against those New South ideologists who argued that black labor was useless and that the blacks should be allowed to deteriorate or forced to emigrate, Bledsoe insisted that, under the Christian paternalism of the planters, the blacks would learn to be of economic value.[24]

All of this amounted to a postwar version of Fitzhugh's argument that paternalistic planters treated slaves better than capitalists treated free wage laborers—that there was an element of "consideration and sympathy" present in the planters' attitudes towards their tenants that was missing from industrialists' attitudes towards their laborers. These planter ideologists seized upon one of the New South program's major weaknesses—the lack of a coherent scheme of what role the former slaves would play. There is also a hint here that the New South would move toward more virulent forms of racism than had prevailed while the paternalist ethic was dominant; if planters' professed paternalism was defeated by the forces of the New South, how would the blacks' subservient status be enforced, if not by a harsher racism?[25]

24. Mobile *Daily Register*, June 25, 1880; Albert Bledsoe, "Review of *Nojoque*," *Southern Review*, II (1867), 485–90. Bledsoe's intellectual work for the planter cause had official status during the Civil War. Jefferson Davis sent him to England to search the British archives for documentary justification of secession. The results were published in 1866 as *Is Davis a Traitor: or Was Secession a Constitutional Right*. Publication of his work even after the Confederate defeat was a sign that the planter ideologists were not about to give up the fight against capitalist penetration of southern society. Edward Mims, "Albert Taylor Bledsoe," *Dictionary of American Biography*, II, 365.

25. C. Vann Woodward, *The Strange Career of Jim Crow* (New York: Oxford University Press, 1957). Fredrickson has a different analysis; he sees the antebellum paternalists becoming postwar antipaternalists and racists. "For them, the Negro was not what the proslavery writers had predicted he would become after emancipation—a positive menace who must be forcibly contained. Such thinking presaged the extreme racism of the 1890s. . . . To

The planter press developed its own critique of the notion of the "New South Man." Pollard denounced the "coarse . . . material-istic . . . and corrupted" businessmen who "smelt of trade." Arti-cle after article described the fate that awaited those who embraced the New South creed: "The prosperous businessmen, . . . who is possessed with the thirst for riches, [is] reduced to poverty, . . . the evil results of wild and reckless speculation . . . hate and malice awful and sensual vice disgusting ones; men, as they shud-der at these little realize that the darling passion they hug to their breasts has strewn the sea of life with the wrecks of fortune, home, and happiness." The typical New South businessman "is never satisfied; he never knows when to quit. . . . the shores of life's ocean are cumbered with wrecks, and the whirlpool of speculation has dragged down many a gallant bark. . . . Can the life of a reckless speculator be a happy one? Can he ever be himself sufficiently to consider his duty to his God and his fellow men? Can he find peace even in the home circle, living as he does in a state of feverish excitement? We think not."[26]

"Business life," the Mobile *Register* proclaimed in 1881, "has become to a great extent feverish, and constant strain and anxiety, . . . recklessness and unhealthy speculation [grow]. . . . such a revel of wreckers must bring a certain and fearful reckoning." The warning was sounded with strident but monotonous regularity:

> No nation has ever existed for any length of time where the majority of people neglected the soil. Abnormal has always been, and must ever be, the forerunner of extinction. Shall the prophetic warning be lost on America? We are not alarmist, but we see in the signs of the times indications of a willingness to foresake the paternal acres and rural respectability of our fathers for the petty strifes and excitements of the metropolis. An insatiable desire for wealth is taking the place of the "earth-hunger" . . . of our fathers.[27]

---

these representatives of the old aristocracy, segregation was . . . a deliberately repressive mechanism to hold the Negro in a permanently inferior position. Any other policy . . . would threaten the whites with biological contamination or race war." Fredrickson, *Black Image*, 219, 221.

26. Edward A. Pollard, *The Lost Cause* (New York: E. B. Treat, 1866), 49; Edward A. Pollard, *The Second Year of the War* (New York: Charles B. Richardson, 1864), 305; both cited in Maddex, *Pollard*, 39; Mobile *Daily Register*, March 15, 1882, May 4, 1884.

27. Mobile *Daily Register*, January 27, 1881, October 24, 1880.

The moral for young men in agrarian society was clear: in the words of a headline in the Huntsville *Advocate*, "Stay Where You Are!" "One of the greatest drawbacks to prosperity is the restive, roving and unsettled spirit of our people. Each one imagines that there is an El Dorado somewhere. . . . The idea unsettles him . . . he is forever thinking about it and neglects to improve his present home and farm." The Tuskegee *Weekly News* added, "Many a young man has been hopelessly ruined by leaving his father's quiet home and finding employment in the city. . . . 'There is no employment more honorable, more enobling than tilling the soil.' " And an 1882 article in the *Register* argued, "The farmer living among the beauties of God's creation has little of the temptations to viciousness which allure others to destruction. Love of home, too, is something which is distinctly characteristic of a farmer's life."[28]

The planter ideologists realized that the New South program entailed the abolition of the planters as a class. The Mobile *Register* reprinted an article from the staunchly Republican Chicago *Tribune* in 1881 which held that "the Southern people do not realize that, to the extent that manufacturing is introduced in that section, their political and social system will be revolutionized. . . . Oligarchies, aristocracies, and 'first families' will have to get out of the way." The *Register* replied in an editorial that it was well aware of the situation, and that "it is among the shoddy aristocracy of the North and the *nouveaux riches* of the West that we now look for contempt of honest labor, not among the 'first families' of the South. Of course there will always be different grades of society, and social distinctions will, and always should exist."[29] This was class-consciousness in a well-developed form.

Planter spokesmen denounced the New South program for regional industrialization. The view of postwar southern economic development put forward by planter ideologists was remarkably similar to their antebellum program: limited industrial develop-

28. Huntsville *Advocate*, May 18, 1875; Tuskegee *Weekly News*, June 19, 1877; Mobile *Daily Register*, October 24, 1880. See also Mobile *Daily Register*, September 21, 1882, January 14, 1883.
29. Mobile *Daily Register*, January 14, 1881.

ment in the context of a planter-dominated, cotton-producing plantation South; in short, the Prussian Road.

Railroad development was desirable to the extent that it increased the value of plantation land and reduced planters' transportation costs, the Montgomery *Advertiser* argued in 1866. The construction of factories in Alabama was desirable "in order that planters may find a safe investment for their money," the *Advertiser* wrote in 1867. But a move toward full industrialization was undesirable. The *Advertiser* observed in 1867 that there had been "many efforts in this and the adjoining states to start manufacturing companies. . . . most of them have failed, either utterly, or partially." The planter paper explained this failure as the result of overly ambitious planning by industrialists; "it were far better to begin with a few spindles, barely sufficing to keep looms in the neighborhood farming district busy."[30] Needless to say, factory construction scaled to the needs of neighborhood farms is nothing like the development of heavy industry.

The New South program of cotton factories as a solution to the problem of agrarian unrest was compatible with planter interests; there was little difference of opinion between the two groups over this issue. As early as 1866 the Montgomery *Advertiser* had run an article under the headline "Cotton Factories: Labor for the Indigent in Alabama," which argued, "As our indigent population must be fed and clothed, we know of no better means of doing it and of turning their labor to practical account, than by . . . cotton factories." Later that year the newspaper noted that factories "will afford constant employment to thousands of the worthy poor of both sexes, who, for years to come, will [otherwise] be dependent upon private or public charity."[31]

An 1868 article in the planter press explained more fully the basis on which the planters favored the development of textile factories. They would be "by the side of the cotton field"; they would "furnish a market for all the edibles . . . enabling the planter to divert his labor from cotton . . . and not be compelled to overstock the market with cotton," and "around a manufacturing village

30. Montgomery *Daily Advertiser*, October 20, 1866, August 9, September 21, 1867.
31. *Ibid.*, August 18, October 25, 1866.

would necessarily accumulate a great deal of fertilizing material, that might be profitably taken back in our empty wagons to our exhausted and impoverished fields."[32] Mill towns would be sources of manure for the plantations—a vivid example of industry serving planters' needs.

In 1880 the planter press was making the same argument. An official of the Mississippi Valley Cotton Planters' Association proposed that planters "set up spindles in the cotton fields" so that the planters could earn the profits that accompanied spinning. He proposed that "the planters combine" and put spinning machinery "in every town and township . . . at their own expense"; the planters should "superintend the process, and divide the profits." This was described as getting out of "the old ruts," as "industrial and economic progress."[33] But it was industrial progress of a particularly limited kind, vertical integration of the cotton industry under the control of the planters.

The planter press regularly expressed antibourgeois and antiindustrial sentiments throughout the late sixties and seventies and into the eighties. The Selma *Southern Argus* was the most explicit: "We of the South are not a manufacturing people," the black belt newspaper proclaimed.

> Necessities will, for a long time, perhaps forever, confine our manufacturing to the heavier and coarser fabrics. But an unparalleled development is in store for the South in agriculture. . . . This development will spring from natural causes and be governed by natural laws. . . . It is a delusion to suppose that we are going to manufacture all the raw material that our fertile lands produce, or work up all the products of our inexhaustible mines. We are an agricultural people, par excellence, and neither manufacturing nor mining can ever be made the leading pursuit of the people.[34]

The same year the *Advertiser* wrote, "While we would not lose sight entirely . . . of the spirit of enterprise which is . . . looking to the building of railroads and factories . . . yet we look upon all such as of secondary importance, compared to the agricultural interest

32. *Ibid.*, September 29, 1868.
33. Mobile *Daily Register*, December 19, 1880.
34. Selma *Southern Argus*, June 23, 1869.

of the country. . . . It is the foundation stone upon which the whole fabric rests; shatter it and the whole structure falls to the ground." A county agricultural association in the black belt passed a resolution which declared, "Agriculture, the most ancient, and in the scale of dignity, the most useful and honorable of all the sciences, is the sole substratum upon which the superstructure of development in the line of wealth can be successfully reared. . . . The industries of all other classes of labor, such as merchants and manufacturers . . . , while they constitute useful and honorable agencies for development . . . can only be regarded in the light of non-producers."[35]

Under the headline "Respectability," the *Advertiser* wrote in 1867, "While there is to the capitalist . . . must of respect due; there is still a much higher order of respectability surrounding, like a halo of glory, the sturdy sons of toil . . . forcing from the bosom of mother earth . . . her lavish riches." "The time is not distant," the *Advertiser* wrote in 1866, when "the cotton lands of the South will be more valuable than any other species of property. . . . Our planters should take counsel from this fact."[36] This was a barely concealed argument that investment in industry would not be as profitable as investment in plantation land, and that the planters should act accordingly.

Such arguments continued to appear in the planter press through the seventies and eighties. The Mobile *Register* made explicit its conception of the planter class as a European-styled landed aristocracy in an article comparing Alabama planters with British "landlords . . . who constitute the nobility." The article predicted that the Southern "nobility" would outlast their British counterparts. The abolition of slavery in Cuba in 1880 received extensive coverage in the planter press. The *Register* praised the Spanish government for blocking immediate emancipation, and supporting "gradual emancipation . . . after eight years of provisional servitude under their present masters." Abolition was necessary, the planter paper argued, only "to prevent the expiring flames of insurrection from being kindled afresh for the destruction

35. Montgomery *Daily Advertiser*, March 19, 1869, September 19, 1868.
36. *Ibid.*, August 7, 1867, October 21, 1866.

of the flourishing haciendas" of the island.[37] Slave rebellions made abolition necessary in Cuba, but fortunately the slaveowners had eight more years of servitude due them.

The planter press contained statements that echoed the great antibourgeois thinkers in the European tradition. In an otherwise unremarkable article on conditions in Pike County, a reporter for the Mobile *Register* reported that farmers there "are not burdened with tastes and wishes that cannot be gratified." This was almost precisely the meaning Jean-Jacques Rousseau conveyed in his critique of Parisian bourgeois society in the 1760s.[38]

The planter press also argued specifically against small farms, a key element of the New South program. The National Cotton Planters Association, a leading organization of planter opposition to New South ideology, pointed to the undeniable empirical fact that prosperous small farmers were few and far between in the South; southern prosperity depended upon the plantation's economies of production, and especially on cheap tenant labor, the organization argued.[39]

Railroad development and immigration were desirable, planter ideologists said, because they would promote efficiency in cotton growing, and thus greater profits to the cotton grower, which would in turn enrich southerners of all classes and occupations. The planters supported development of the cotton textile industry on the grounds that vertical integration of the cotton industry was in the interests of cotton growers. Whatever industrial development occurred should be gradual and limited, the planter spokesmen argued. Daniel Harvey Hill, whose journal, *The Land We Love*, was another important reactionary periodical, urged that the growth of big corporations be prevented, because they were "a hundred-fold less respectable and venerable, than the landed aristocracy." Thus the National Cotton Planters Association sought railroad development in the plantation regions, federal expendi-

---

37. Mobile *Daily Register*, January 29, 31, 1880.
38. *Ibid.*, February 5, 1880; Jean Jacques Rousseau, *Letter to d'Alembert on the Theater*, trans. Allen Bloom (Glencoe: The Free Press, 1967).
39. Theodore Saloutos, *Farmer Movements in the South 1865–1933* (Lincoln, Neb.: University of Nebraska Press, 1964), 58–59.

tures on levee construction to end the danger of flooding the black belts, and construction of cotton mills. "In the context of the twentieth century," Robert Brandfon correctly concludes, "this development could hardly be called industrialism." [40]

The planter position on agriculture was endorsed by Ulrich B. Phillips several years later. Arguing against New South advocates of small farming, he wrote that the plantation's "concentration of labor under skilled management made the plantation system . . . practically the factory system applied to agriculture. Since the replacement of domestic manufacturing by the factory has become established in history as the industrial revolution, the counter-replacement of the plantation system by peasant farming . . . seems to require description as an industrial counter-revolution." [41] Here Phillips deftly turned the New South's pursuit of industry against itself by arguing that the most advanced form of capitalist agriculture was not small yeoman farms but plantations.

Planter spokesmen sensitive to the ideological struggle took on the slogan "New South." A black belt newspaper in 1885 referred to it as a phrase of "Yankee invention," and urged its readers instead to be true to the heritage of Washington, Jefferson, and Lee. The Mobile *Register* in 1881 denied that "in some wonderful and miraculous way the nature and disposition of our people has become totally changed," as was implied in the term New South. There was, however, "gradual and steady effort and quiet work. . . . Agriculture especially has made and is making progress," the newspaper reported. In an ingenious attack on the New South program, the *Register* in 1881 called instead for the creation of a

40. *Land We Love*, quoted in Gaston, *New South Creed*, 31; Robert L. Brandfon, *Cotton Kingdom of the New South* (Cambridge: Harvard University Press, 1967), 19–20. Brandfon's excellent book is marred by a misunderstanding of the New South program for agriculture. He writes that "the South's planter community [was] fully in accord with the ideals of Henry Grady." (p. 16) But Grady sought to replace plantations with small farms, and urged crop diversification to replace cotton monoculture.

41. Ulrich B. Phillips, "Decadence of the Plantation System," in Eugene D. Genovese (ed.), *The Slave Economy of the Old South* (Baton Rouge: Louisiana State University Press, 1968), 245; for a fuller discussion of Phillips's position on the plantation in the postwar South, see Genovese, *In Red and Black* (New York: Pantheon Books, 1971), 290–92, and Daniel Joseph Singal, "Ulrich B. Phillips: The Old South as the New," *Journal of American History*, LXIII (1977), 872–91.

"New North," which it argued "is needed in business affairs. It is from the teeming money centers of that section that the spirit of wild speculation spreads its baneful influence over the land. . . . less worship of money, and more independence of thought and action are what should be characteristics of a New North."[42]

The reactionary planter ideology had a social base that was both extensive and well-organized. First were the political organizations dedicated to advancing planter interests, like the National Cotton Planters Association. Then there were the churches. After the war, only the Episcopal church reunited its northern and southern branches; the Southern Baptists, Methodists, and Presbyterians maintained separate southern organizations, which usually clung to prebourgeois ideals. Ministers and theologians took the lead in condemning Social Darwinism and the godless materialism New South ideologists were spreading; the ministers not only had an extensive audience in their Sunday congregations, but were able to spread the traditionalist, reactionary message through the publications of the church presses.[43]

The third arena for the expression of planter ideology was the Confederate veterans' organizations, which had long membership lists, regular meetings, and annual conventions, and which exerted considerable pressure in state politics. Candidates wanted to speak before the veterans' meetings, and leaders of the veterans' organizations pursued political careers. Charles Colcock Jones, president of the Georgia veterans' organization, was the most rabid of the reactionaries; fearing that "mere time and human mortality" would end the veterans' organizations and thus abolish a key base of

42. Hayneville *Examiner*, January 22, 1885, quoted in Going, *Bourbon Democracy*, 47; Mobile *Daily Register*, January 30, March 17, 1881; see also Eutaw *Mirror*, October 28, 1884.

43. Frederick A. Bode, *Protestantism and the New South: North Carolina Baptists and Methodists in Political Crisis, 1894–1903* (Charlottesville: University Press of Virginia, 1975); Kenneth K. Bailey, "Southern White Protestantism at the Turn of the Century," *American Historical Review*, LXVIII (1963), 618–35; Hunter D. Farish, *The Circuit Rider Dismounts: A Social History of Southern Methodism, 1865–1900* (Richmond: The Dietz Press, 1938), 209–33; Rollin G. Osterweis, *The Myth of the Lost Cause 1865–1900* (Hamden, Conn.: Archon Books, 1973), 119, 124–25; Robert Darden Little, "The Ideology of the New South: A Study in the Development of Ideas, 1865–1910," (Ph.D. dissertation, University of Chicago, 1950), 125.

opposition to New South "materialism," he proposed that sons of veterans be admitted to membership. The proposal was adopted, and later the Daughters of the Confederacy was organized. It was to become the principal repository of the official memories of the Lost Cause.[44]

The reactionaries' critique of New South values and culture did not go unanswered. Churchmen associated with the New South movement were eager to reply to charges that godless materialism and a decline of religious virtue were associated with industrialization. Wilbur F. Tillet, dean of the Vanderbilt School of Theology, asserted that "the South is morally better than it was before the war." The masses of people, he wrote, "are freer from public and private vices, take more interest in the Christian religion, contribute twice as much to religious and benevolent objects, build neater and finer churches than they ever did . . . in the best days of slavery." If there was a touch of materialism in Tillet's concern for contributions and church construction, Atticus G. Haygood's Thanksgiving sermon of 1880 was more explicit. Haygood, president of Emory College and a leading Methodist apologist for the New South, gave thanks for the great increase in domestic comforts and conveniences the New South was bringing, praising God especially for blessing his children with "mattresses, stoves, lamps, and parlor organs."[45]

The New South religionists' reply to charges of materialism was summed up in a *Harpers* magazine article. "We are no apologists for that materialistic spirit of the age which we have often so deservedly condemned. . . . Material development, however, promotes moral development, and is needed to protect and preserve it." Methodist Bishop Oscar P. Fitzgerald was willing to admit that northern industry was materialistic and atheistic; the real difference between northern and southern industry, he said, was that southerners "put God into [their] material progress."

44. Little, "Ideology of New South," 137.
45. Wilbur F. Tillet, "White Man of the New South," 776; Atticus G. Haygood, *The New South: Thanksgiving Sermon 1880* (Atlanta: The Library, Emory University, 1950). See also Harold W. Mann, *Atticus Greene Haygood: Methodist Bishop, Editor and Educator* (Athens: University of Georgia Press, 1965).

Haygood took the offensive with the proper Methodist argument: hard work was the only means of achieving virtue; the New South had put an end to the immoral laziness that had characterized the antebellum elite.[46]

The New South Ideologists

Who were the New South ideologists? The most important of them had their social origins outside the mainstream of planter society; they came from southern families that were not enthusiastic about slavery or secession. The ideologists of the New South tended to be the social as well as the intellectual and political descendants of the industrial promoters of the Old South.[47]

Henry Grady, editor of the Alabama *Constitution* in the 1880s, and the most important New South ideologist, was the son of a prominent merchant in Athens, Georgia. Woodward says it best: Grady "came by his businessman's philosophy honestly, for he sprang not from planter stock but from antebellum tradesmen, promoters, and gold prospectors, and he married into a pioneer cotton manufacturing family."[48]

Daniel Augustus Tompkins had a father who was a wealthy South Carolina planter, owning 2,000 acres of land and forty slaves; the son, however, instead of taking over the plantation, went to Rennselaer Polytechnic Institute in Troy, New York, as did many other important figures in the history of southern industry. He became a machinist, worked for iron and steel companies in New York, Pennsylvania, and Germany, and, having learned the business, moved to North Carolina. By 1882 Tompkins was presi-

46. T. M. Logan, "The Southern Industrial Prospect," *Harpers*, LII (1870), 589–93; Frederick A. Bode, "Religion and Class Hegemony: A Populist Critique in North Carolina," *Journal of Southern History*, XXXVII (1971), 427.

47. On the social origins of industrialists, see Genovese, *Political Economy of Slavery*, 207; Justin Fuller, "Alabama Business Leaders, 1865–1900," *Alabama Review*, XVI (1963), 279–86, *Alabama Review*, XVII (1964), 63–75; Broadus Mitchell, *The Industrial Revolution in the South* (Baltimore: The Johns Hopkins Press, 1930), 32, 106; William B. Hesseltine and Larry Gara, "Confederate Leaders in Post-War Alabama," *Alabama Review*, IV (1951), 5–21; E. A. Alderman and A. C. Gordon, *J. L. M. Curry: A Biography* (New York: The Macmillan Company, 1911).

48. C. Vann Woodward, *Origins of the New South 1877–1913* (Baton Rouge: Louisiana State University Press, 1951), 146.

dent of three cotton mills and director of eight others, owner of three newspapers, and "father of the cottonseed oil industry."[49] He alone of the first rank of New South ideologists was an industrialist as well as an intellectual; he wrote articles and pamphlets and was a popular after-dinner speaker.

Walter Hines Page came from a family of respected and self-reliant small proprietors in North Carolina; his father had not been enthusiastic about slavery and had opposed secession, while his grandfather had consistently advocated Jeffersonian politics. Page was a North Carolina newspaper editor. Henry Watterson, editor of the second most important New South newspaper, the Louisville *Courier-Journal*, was the son of a lawyer and politician. His father was an advocate of southern industrialism who lacked sympathy for slavery; in politics he had been a Union man, but finally chose to fight for the Confederacy when war came.[50]

Thus, of the first rank of New South ideologists, all but one came from nonplantation backgrounds, from families that were not supporters of slavery and had been opponents of secession. Some other facts about this group stand out; for their time, they were well-educated. Walter Hines Page attended graduate school at Johns Hopkins University, where he studied under Basil Gildersleeve; Grady had a year of postgraduate study at the University of Virginia; Tompkins attended Rensselaer Polytechnic. Gaston points out that virtually all were born in the early 1850s, growing up to see a planters' South defeated in war and humiliated in Reconstruction; this youthful trauma may have further weakened their allegiance to the old regime.[51]

Of all the New South ideologists, Henry Grady was the most deeply involved in state politics. He was associated with Georgia's "New Departure" Democrats, who acquiesced in the national party's support for Reconstruction, and were opposed by "the great unreconstructed" Robert Toombs within the Democratic party. The New Departure Democrats were dominated by the "Bourbon

49. Gaston, *New South Creed*, 50.
50. *Ibid.*, 50–53. See also Joseph Frazier Wall, *Henry Watterson: Reconstructed Rebel* (New York: Oxford University Press, 1956), especially p. 97.
51. Gaston, *New South Creed*, 48–49, 52.

Triumvirate," three men who rotated the offices of senator and governor among themselves during the late seventies and eighties. Grady invariably supported them for whatever office they sought, providing some insight into the concrete political positions to which New South ideology led.

Governor Joseph E. Brown of Georgia was a typical New South industrialist, with wide-ranging, if occasionally fraudulent, holdings in railroads and mines, an antagonist of traditional southern values and policies. But General John Brown Gordon, second member of the Georgia triumvirate, played exactly the opposite public role. As Georgia's greatest war hero, he was the living incarnation of the aristocracy of the Old South—president of the United Confederate Veterans, and famous for his speech "The Last Days of the Confederacy." Woodward argues that Gordon's involvement in the "Huntington Affair" of 1884, a financial scandal second only to the Credit Mobilier, demonstrated that he possessed the "acquisitive zeal of the rising capitalists."[52] But Gordon's secret acquisitiveness was a far cry from the enthusiastic praise for regional industrialization characteristic of Henry Grady and Governor Brown. Gordon was the political incarnation of the old order and the Lost Cause, with all that implied about opposing industrialization of the region, and Grady supported him.

The third member of the triumvirate was Governor Alfred H. Colquitt, a member of a distinguished black belt family, and one of the largest planters in the state. Woodward says that although Colquitt "seemed to belong to the old aristocratic planter statesmen, . . . his interests were not exclusively agricultural," pointing out that he speculated in railroad, mining, and manufacturing stocks. But stock ownership does not necessarily make one an industrialist; in the antebellum period, most of the big planters had investments in manufacturing.[53] The question of the New Departure Democrats' open or secret involvement in industrial undertakings is separate from the question of their public politics, and Gordon's and

52. C. Mildred Thompson, *Reconstruction in Georgia: Economic, Social, Political, 1865–1872* (Savannah, Ga.: Beehive Press, 1972); Woodward, *Tom Watson*, 57–60, 62.

53. Woodward, *Origins of the New South*, 17; Genovese, *Political Economy of Slavery*, 187–88; Fred Bateman, James Foust, and Thomas Weiss, "The Participation of Planters in Manufacturing in the Antebellum South," *Agricultural History*, XLVIII (1974), 277–97.

Colquitt's public roles did not suggest enthusiasm for industry. At most they were secret industrialists who chose to blur their position in the conflict over the South's social and economic future. Grady himself did not blur the issue, of course; but his support for Gordon and Colquitt made his own proindustry position something less than relentless.

Grady's subservience to New South industrialists and northern capital and his failure to deal with the real agrarian problems facing the South were openly attacked by Populist leader Tom Watson. Notes for a speech of Watson's read, "Mr. Grady . . . thinks that 'plenty rides on the springing harvests!' It rides on Grady's springing imagination. Where is this prosperity?" In an 1883 speech attacking Grady, Watson said:

> The city orators say that . . . the Watchman upon the Tower will sing out "All's well with the Republic." . . . I would first wish to know what the Watchman is—if he is floating with the tide which carries prosperity to certain classes at the expense of others—if he is the known champion of Rail Road kings, and R.R. combinations. If he is cheek by jowl with the heretofore dominant influences which have sought to fasten upon us forever the curse of High Tariff, and has prostituted his paper and his talents. . . . Rather, O my countrymen, listen to those who tell you of the danger which threatens—who warn you to put on your armour, and man the walls.[54]

Watson's description of the New South was significantly closer to reality than Grady's own view, as Woodward observes.

Grady's most quoted and best-known argument about southern politics was simple: "What we need is fewer stump speakers and more stump pullers—less talk and more work—one plow is worth twenty politicians." At first glance this argument seems to have been simply dishonest. Grady knew he was not the only New South ideologist actively involved in state politics; most of the other editors and writers in his movement bombarded state legislatures with proposals to exempt industry from taxation and to provide free building sites for factories.[55]

54. Quoted in Woodward, *Tom Watson*, 126, 128; for Grady's view of the agrarian problem, see his "Cotton and Its Kingdom," *Harpers*, LXIII (1881), 719–34.

55. Atlanta *Constitution*, November 7, 1880, cited in Nixon, *Grady*, 178; Gaston, *New South Creed*, 73.

Richard Edmonds explained Grady's statement of opposition to "politics": "Politics won't attract investors," he wrote; "on the contrary, it often creates such oppressive laws for the benefits of its adherents that capital is kept away." Grady's politics were not likely to keep capital away; but the politics put forward by the proto-Populist opponents of the Georgia triumvirate in 1880 would not attract investors. And investors would be kept out by hostile legislation—provisions for state regulation of industry, or strict tax and incorporation laws like those passed by the Alabama Constitutional Convention of 1875. "Politics" was an activity engaged in by extremists like the Populists and the Radical Republicans; Grady portrayed himself as more of a statesman. The Mobile *Register* had the same view: "politics and politicians are pretty generally ignored," the paper wrote in 1880. "This is the best sign yet [that] our people have gone to work in earnest."[56]

There was another meaning to the New South ideologists' attack on "politics." The context in which Grady first made the statement was the Democratic defeat in the 1880 presidential election. He was to repeat the statement many times in later speeches and articles, but on this original occasion his intention was to persuade militant southern nationalists not to seek political expression for their hatred of the Republican party. Although the Republicans had not only forced Reconstruction on the South, but also had stolen the 1876 presidential election from the Democrats, Grady urged militant and angry southern nationalists to express their hostility for the North by out-producing them in manufactured and agricultural goods. It was an argument against sectional bitterness, for national reconciliation, at the same time promoting regional industrialism in the guise of southern nationalism competing with the North.

Edward Atkinson of Boston was the most important spokesman for New England cotton manufacturers; he is often mistakenly considered a northern ally of the New South ideologists because of his often-expressed interest in southern economic development. Atkinson, however, came south not to praise local industry but to discourage it. His euphemisms were skillfully constructed: "inter-

56. Gaston, *New South Creed*, 109; Mobile *Daily Register*, February 20, 1880.

dependence" of the regions was his term for the neocolonial system in which the South grew cotton and New England manufactured textiles. Atkinson's message was that the southerner should concentrate on "ginning, packing, and pressing cotton," rather than "trying to do it all"—i.e., manufacturing textiles. He told planters that preparation of the staple for the factory was actually "the most important branch of cotton manufacture," and that "a million dollars spent in the right manner in this department will do more to build up the cotton states than any million expended in cotton factories." He even asserted that this initial processing of the staple was "the most profitable branch of cotton manufacturing," that "by light expenditures in improved gins, a little more care in handling the staple, and with no risk, the planter could make more clear profit by adding to the value of his cotton than could be counted on in great factories."[57]

In arguing against the development of southern industry that would compete with the North, Atkinson was expressing the interests of northern manufacturers. What they needed was a South prosperous enough to buy their manufactured goods. By arguing against southern industrialization, Atkinson made himself an opponent not only of the full industrialization sought by the New South ideologists, but also of the planters' plan in which vertical integration of the cotton industry would consolidate production and manufacture in planter hands, increasing their profits.

Yet Atkinson was invited by "leading men of city and state" to address the 1881 Atlanta cotton exposition organized by Henry Grady. That Atkinson would become the "friend of New South spokesmen" was evidence of their pathetic eagerness for attention of any kind from genuine northern capitalists. Their failure to attack his program was a crucial sign of weakness of the New South ideologists, a foreboding of their willingness to accept a subservient, colonial status for southern industry.

57. Gaston, New South Creed, 85; Woodward, Origins of the New South, 143, is closer to the mark. Edward Atkinson, "Address at Atlanta" to state senate, October, 1880, quoted in Mitchell, Rise of Cotton Mills, 118–19; Mobile Daily Register, February 17, 1881; see also February 20, July 30, 1881; Harold F. Williamson, Edward Atkinson: The Biography of an American Liberal, 1827–1905 (Boston: Old Corner Book Store, 1934).

The Politics of the Old South Myth

Planter ideology in the debased form of historical romances about the Old South became the literary rage of the nation in the 1880s. In the South, the Old South myth achieved a "complete conquest" and became "an inviolable shibboleth," dominating not only literature but the classroom, the pulpit, and the political podium, as Paul Gaston shows. The romantic reaction developed simultaneously with the arguments for industrialization, both reaching a peak in the eighties. C. Vann Woodward was the first to observe that "one of the most significant inventions of the New South was the 'Old South'— a new idea in the eighties, and a legend of incalculable potentialities."[58]

The ideology of the Lost Cause, while often lacking political coherence, possessed in its more developed forms a powerful critique of northern capitalist industrial society, and a defense of a planter-dominated agrarian society for the postwar South. Nevertheless, New South spokesmen often honored the Old South myth, and, indeed, were at times among its most vociferous exponents. Henry Grady himself expressed reverence for the "imperishable knighthood" of the old regime, and praise for the planters' "exquisite culture" in which "money counted least in making the social status." He went so far as to say that "the civilization of the old slave regime in the South has not been surpassed, and perhaps will not be equaled, among men." Edmonds similarly wrote that Southerners should forever "hold in tenderest reverence the memory of this Southern land; never forget to give all honor to the men and women of antebellum days."[59]

What is the significance of this embrace of the Old South by New South ideologists? Paul Gaston argues that the New South advocates succeeded in wedding their cause to the Old South myth,

58. Gaston, *New South Creed*, 171; Francis Pendleton Gaines, *The Southern Plantation: A Study in the Development and Accuracy of a Tradition* (New York: Columbia University Press, 1924), 82; Woodward, *Origins of the New South*, 154–55. See also Clement Eaton, *The Waning of the Old South Civilization* (Athens: University of Georgia Press, 1968).

59. Quoted in Gaston, *New South Creed*, 173–74.

and in enlisting the mythic past in the service of their view of the future. The first use to which the New South advocates put the Old South myth, he notes, was to emphasize the heritage of industrialism in the antebellum period, to relate their efforts to the tradition of industrial campaigns in the slave South. Tompkins, for instance, argued that the New South ideologists—himself included—were "keepers of the older, authentic tradition"; before the invention of the cotton gin, the South had been headed for industrialization, and "the years of the spread and dominance of slavery" had been only "an interruption of the true course of southern history." Such an argument was made for Alabama by industrial spokesman John W. DuBose. The development of the new order in Birmingham, he wrote, was "but a continuation of the old." The mineral region was developed with the same spirit, and indeed by the same people, as had first carved plantations out of the canebreak of the black belt. DuBose asserted that, by 1873, 2,500 planters and their black laborers had already come to Birmingham to lead the development of the region; he portrayed this as merely a continuation of the planters' antebellum interest in industry. The evidence offered for this argument was that the first mayor of Birmingham, Robert H. Henley, had come from the "handsome and chivalrous race of the most refined cotton planters in the whole southwestern territory." John T. Milner, another leading Birmingham promoter, made the same argument; the development of Birmingham was part of the continuity of southern economic and social life, and arose out of a sound plantation economy and a viable "patriarchal system." [60]

Although this was an ingenious argument, it was not an argument that used the Old South myth for New South purposes. The Old South myth held up as the ideal precisely the "years of the spread and dominance of slavery"; the notion that these years were only an "interruption" was not the Old South myth, but rather a different myth about the prewar period. Needless to say, the myth

60. *Ibid.*, 162–63; John W. DuBose, *Mineral Wealth of Alabama and Birmingham Illustrated* (Birmingham: N. T. Green & Co., 1886); John T. Milner, *Alabama: As It Was, As It Is, As It Will Be* (Montgomery: Barrett & Brown, 1876), 149–50; Davis, "Rationale of Conservative Alabamians," 194–95, 89. The same argument is made in Robert S. Cotterill, "The Old South to the New," *Journal of Southern History*, XV (1949), 3–8.

of an Old South headed for industrialization did not catch on in the literary field, the school curricula, or in political rhetoric.

Part of the Old South myth was its picture of harmonious race relations based on black subservience, white racism, and noninterference from the North, as Gaston points out; the New South ideologists endorsed this system for postwar society. Certainly that is correct, but there was nothing uniquely self-serving about the New South ideologists' advocacy of white supremacy and northern noninterference. Few prominent southern whites disagreed with that position in the eighties. The New South ideologists here were not using the Old South myth to distinguish their own movement, but rather were simply agreeing with the rest of white society.

Although the apparent content of the Old South myth was undying hostility to the Yankees, because it was just as popular in the North as it was in the South, to espouse the myth was to promote national unity and oppose sectional bitterness, a crucial element of the New South's campaign for northern capital. This is Gaston's most subtle argument. (Woodward also noted the national appeal of the Old South myth.) But there is a crucial difference beneath this apparent unity: in the North, the myth of the Old South had a purely romantic significance. At most it represented a reactionary critique of their civilization, but a critique that had no social basis and no political reality. In the South, the situation was exactly the reverse—the Old South myth was the ideological aspect of the planters' attempt to retain hegemony; it had an organizational base in the churches and Confederate veterans' organizations. The Old South myth was the cultural expression of a social force that was very much alive, that possessed substantial political power, that was able to mobilize tens of thousands of supporters to go to the polls and vote for aristocratic freedom, against tax exemptions for thieving Yankees, for dignity and honor, and against the new scalawags in their midst.

Finally, Gaston argues that the New South advocates were able to unify their cause with that of the Old South by putting Confederate generals on the boards of directors of their new corporations and thereby legitimizing the corporations in the eyes of the southern community. It is undeniable that such an attempt was made;

but, by putting Confederate generals at the heads of their new corporations, the New South advocates were simply abandoning their position that the New South needed new men. In place of the energetic, shrewd, and self-reliant southerners, the New South advocates held up as their model the same figure they were describing as easy-going and impractical, luxury-loving and lazy. If the corporations gained a few dollars in stock subscriptions from Confederate veterans with this tactic, they lost an incalculable amount in their effort to achieve hegemony around the notion of the New South man.

The Birmingham *Iron Age*, voice of the industrialists, made other remarkable concessions to planter ideologists, particularly in the earlier years of Birmingham's history. "To develop our mineral and manufacturing interests we need *home* capital," the newspaper argued in 1875. "It would be better for the state that our mountains of iron and coal should remain untouched than they should be developed for the purpose of building up other sections. . . . the best way to get capital, such as we want, is to build up our agricultural interest." Another article conceded that "the population of towns in the South is by no means the index of prosperity. . . . Now they are entirely too prosperous. . . . When the country begins once again to be attractive *then* the towns will prosper." The newspaper put on page one reports of planters visiting the mineral district and the rare complimentary remarks about the city which appreared in the black belt press, apparently believing that their own legitimacy was enhanced by planter attention. A Birmingham reporter visiting Montgomery found that its streets were "as quiet as those of Birmingham . . . no crowd, no hurry, no bustle."[61] This was a strange observation to be coming from the self-proclaimed center of southern hustle and bustle.

In fact the New South ideologists embraced the Old South myth because they were not strong enough to attack it, even though it posed a sharp critique of their own program. Woodward writes that "the bitter mixture of recantation and heresy could never have

61. Birmingham *Iron Age*, September 23, October 21, 1875, January 27, June 29, 1876. The *Iron Age* printed more news about the cotton crop in the late seventies than it did about the iron industry.

been swallowed so readily had it not been dissolved in the syrup of romanticism," and Gaston admits that "no program of reform could do violence to a universally cherished past and hope to succeed."[62]

But the Old South myth was resisted with remarkable success by the Populists. It was used against them in much the same way it had been used against the industrialists—as a justification for subservience to planter interests. During the political campaigns of the 1890s, anti-Populist newspapers devoted an amazing amount of space to the Confederacy and the Lost Cause; a favorite tactic of the Populists' opponents, as Woodward has noted, was to "get General Gordon to deliver his lecture on the last days of the Confederacy, inviting the country people."[63] Henry Grady had abandoned his position in the face of demands that he honor the reactionary agrarian ideal; the Populists seldom displayed such ideological weakness. Instead, they sought to unmask the oppression which the Old South ideology concealed and justified. The Old South myth was not "universally cherished"; the Populists proved that.

The New South ideologists' profession of allegiance to the Old South myth was thus a sign, not of their strength, but of their weakness; it was not so much a successful use of the past to build the New South program, but rather a strategic attempt at accommodation with an opponent they were unable to defeat—an opponent that was not simply "mythic," but one with extensive economic and political power. By accommodating their position to the Old South myth, the New South ideologists lost a crucial battle in their attempt to win hegemony for their view of society, and betrayed their own class interests.

The bourgeois ideology advocated by the New South ideologists

62. Woodward, *Origins of the New South*, 158; Gaston, *New South Creed*, 154.

63. Woodward, *Origins of the New South*, 156, 158. "What bittersweet tears washed Nashville's grimy cheeks over Page's *In Ole Virginia*! 'Dem wuz good ole times, marster—de bes Sam ever see! Dey wuz in fac'! Niggers didn' hed nothin' 'tall to do.' Embarrassing race conflict dissolved in liquid dialect, angry Populist farmers became merely quaint in Billy Sanders' vernacular, depression rolled aside, and for a moment, 'de ole times done come back again.' " Woodward, *Origins of the New South*, 167. It is disturbing that almost the identical language reappears in the "documentary" W.P.A. slave narratives: see for instance the Alabama narrative of "Aunt Clara Davis": "Dem was de good ole days." George P. Rawick (ed.), *The American Slave: A Composite Autobiography* (Westport, Conn.: Greenwood Publishing Company, 1972), VI, 109.

was not exactly new in the 1880s; their arguments followed a well-trod path that was first laid out in England and France a century or two earlier. Statements that had become self-serving clichés in the North, in England, and in France still had an authentic urgency in the South, tied as it was to the Prussian Road. Yet despite the "world-historical" hegemony of bourgeois ideology outside the South, the New South ideologists surrendered crucial ground to their reactionary antagonists. Can one imagine their predecessors making such concessions? The seventeenth-century English Calvinists who made themselves "new men," the eighteenth-century Parisian revolutionary intellectuals, the northern Republicans of the 1850s calling for "free soil, free labor, free men"—these heroic predecessors of the New South ideologists never for a moment praised the grace and dignity of the traditional landed elite or honored those who had fought to preserve the old agrarian order. [64]

Genovese's analysis of the ideology of the slaveowners applies equally well to their postwar heirs, whose antagonism to bourgeois society "constituted an authentic world-view in the sense that it developed in accordance with the reality of social relations," the reality of the Prussian Road. "If it was nonetheless self-serving and radically false in its fundamental philosophic content, so is every

---

64. Michael Walzer, *Revolution of the Saints* (Cambridge: Harvard University Press, 1966); Frank Manuel, *The Prophets of Paris* (Cambridge: Harvard University Press, 1962); Eric Foner, *Free Soil, Free Labor, Free Men: The Ideology of the Republican Party before the Civil War* (New York: Oxford University Press, 1970). This supports the view that the Radical Republicans were "the last revolutionary flicker that is strictly bourgeois and strictly capitalist." Barrington Moore, Jr., *Social Origins of Dictatorship and Democracy: Lord and Peasant in the Making of the Modern World* (Boston: Beacon Press, 1966), 142. The Abolitionists themselves also drew parallels between their objectives for the South and the French Revolution; see for instance Wendell Phillips, quoted in James M. McPherson, *The Struggle for Equality: Abolitionists and the Negro in the Civil War and Reconstruction* (Princeton: Princeton University Press, 1964), 411. The planters also had a world historical perspective on Radicalism; the Mobile *Register* wrote in 1871, "The history of France during the past twelve months; the history of the U. S. during the past bloody, distracting and miserable decade; the history of Spain during the past two or three years; the state of Italy at the present time, with the radical hell steadily kindling in her bosom; and the fast approaching horror of terrible civil convulsions in England, all demonstrate that the Radical philosophy and teachings, like some awful besom of destruction, are sweeping mankind away from God and reason, to fearful moral and religious infidelities, anarchy, and ultimate ruin." Mobile *Register*, quoted in Montgomery *Alabama State Journal*, May 6, 1871.

other ruling-class ideology, . . . every attempt to justify the exploitation and oppression of others."[65]

But where the slaveowners' ideology had been "an authentic, if disagreeable, manifestation of an increasingly coherent world outlook," the postwar planters' world-view gradually became less coherent as the twentieth century approached. Despite brave attempts to keep a quasi-aristocratic, antibourgeois ideology alive, it deteriorated slowly, increasingly anachronistic in a nation undergoing bourgeois development.

The planters' coercive system of labor allocation and control remained the basis of agriculture. Debt peonage fostered by the crop lien continued to tie tenants to the land, opportunities for employment outside agriculture were sharply limited, and the legal apparatus of labor coercion remained in place; the enticement laws, for instance, were not repealed until well into the twentieth century. But keeping the South on the Prussian Road increasingly required a resort to violence, which is always a sign of the failure of hegemony, the inability of a dominant class to confine conflict to its own chosen political terrain. The openly violent racism and repression of the nineties thus indicate the deterioration of planter hegemony.

It indicates equally clearly the absence of a hegemonic bourgeoisie, powerful enough to reshape southern society on the basis of a new culture and world-view. The New South ideologists' deference to the Old South "myth" was thus neither paradoxical nor ironic; the weakness they displayed when confronted with the planters' critique of their position had its roots in the structural obstacles posed for their program by the Prussian Road.

---

65. Genovese, *Roll, Jordan, Roll*, 86.

Epilogue:
Populism, Progressivism,
and the Planters

The 1890s were a period of decisive class conflict in Alabama; the Populist uprising was the first organized threat to planter rule since the hill counties had opposed secession. The political choices made by planters, merchants, and industrialists in the face of the Populist uprising illuminate their mutual relations during the seventies and eighties.

Sheldon Hackney's *Populism to Progressivism in Alabama* deals with class forces in politics during the 1890s and the early 1900s. The planters judged the Populists as more dangerous opponents than the industrialists. With the white tenants of the hills seeking allies among both black plantation laborers and members of the Birmingham industrial proletariat, the big planters and big industrialists were forced into an uncomfortable alliance, dedicated to the pursuit of social order and political stability: the so-called "Big Mule–Black Belt" coalition, the "Big Mules" being the big Birmingham industrialists.[1]

But there were others in the ruling circles who evaluated the Populist threat differently. The small businessmen, merchants, and smaller manufacturers of the towns had come to the conclusion in the late eighties that big industry was exploiting them and restricting regional economic growth, primarily by means of high railroad freight rates. During the eighties, a movement seeking

1. Sheldon Hackney, *Populism to Progressivism in Alabama* (Princeton: Princeton University Press, 1969); William Warren Rogers, *The One-Gallused Rebellion: Agrarianism in Alabama 1865–1896* (Baton Rouge: Louisiana State University Press, 1970); V. O. Key, Jr., *Southern Politics in State and Nation* (New York: Alfred A. Knopf, 1949), 36–57; Michael Schwartz, *Radical Protest and Social Structure: The Southern Farmer's Alliance and Cotton Tenancy, 1880–1890* (New York: Academic Press, 1976).

effective regulation of railroad rates had arisen among the merchants and small manufacturers of the major urban centers; as the Birmingham Commercial Club was told at an 1895 meeting, "the greatest difficulty that now confronts this club in securing the location of industries in this city is the railroad."[2]

Since the railroads were tied to the coal and iron companies (the L&N had been the key to Birmingham's development), the merchants and small businessmen seeking railroad regulation found themselves opposed to most of the biggest industries in the state. And since the big industrialists now shared control of the state's Democratic party with the big planters, the reform-minded small businessmen included among their issues reform of the Democratic party.

The Big Mule–Black Belt alliance was a mixed blessing from the planters' point of view. The lower railroad rates sought by both business Progressives and Populists would, in fact, serve planter interests. But the planters seem to have decided lower railroad rates would not compensate for the social disorder that might accompany a victorious Populist movement. It was more important for the planters to destroy an alliance of black and white tenants than it was to obtain lower railroad rates; thus the planters lined up with the big industrialists against the Progressive small businessmen.

The issues of corporate regulation and Democratic party reform were shared by the business Progressives and the Populists, Hackney argues. He writes that "Progressivism and Populism were contemporary, rather than sequential," and that Progressivism in Alabama was "a substantially different reaction by a separate set of men to the same enemy Populism faced—the . . . industrial wing of the Democratic Party."[3] Progressive small businessmen argued that the Populist tenant farmers could serve as the political base to defeat the Big Mule–Black Belt coalition of industrialists and plant-

2. Hackney, *Populism to Progressivism*, 128, 134; see also Arthur S. Link, "The Progressive Movement in the South, 1870–1914," *North Carolina Historical Review*, XXIII (1946), 172–95.

3. Hackney, *Populism to Progressivism*, 122. For a critique of Hackney's statistical methods, see J. Morgan Kousser, "The 'New Political History': A Methodological Critique," *Reviews in American History*, IV (1976), 1–15.

ers. This strategy found its political expression in the split of the Silver Democrats from the regular Cleveland party, a process that began in 1893 and reached its culmination in 1896.

In 1893, a group of prominent Alabama Democrats repudiated the gold standard and the Cleveland administration and endorsed the Populist call for free and unlimited coinage of silver. The Silver Democratic League grew rapidly, and a statewide convention was held in Birmingham in September, 1895. Its announced purpose was not only to advocate the silver cause, but also to reform the planter-industrialist Democratic machine.[4]

For a time, the Big Mule–Black Belt coalition took up the challenge, defending the gold standard and Cleveland. The Montgomery *Advertiser*, the most prominent black belt newspaper, said that for the Democratic party to endorse silver would be "subversive of everything in the history and tradition of the Party," by which they meant the history and tradition of planter domination. The small business Progressives' endorsement of silver was "not only Populistic" but "full of socialism," the black belt newspaper added.[5]

Hoke Smith, the southerner in Cleveland's cabinet and leader of Georgia's Gold Democrats, emphasized the connection between gold politics and the economic development of the South. He asked, "Shall we involve our land in financial convulsion . . . at the very hour that we seem at last about to receive the benefits of investment that we have so long asked?" Here Smith was conceding that the South hadn't gotten much northeastern investment in industry. Alabama's Governor William Oates added that, because of the strength of the gold faction among Alabama Democrats, the state "had a higher reputation among eastern capitalists than any other" in the South.[6] The Gold Democrats of the Big Mule– Black Belt alliance were telling the Progressive small businessmen that the way to prosperity was through the social stability of the

4. Allen J. Going, "Critical Months in Alabama Politics, 1895–1896," *Alabama Review*, V (1952), 272–73; Hackney, *Populism to Progressivism*, 127, 90.

5. Montgomery *Daily Advertiser*, July 14, 1896.

6. Dewey W. Grantham, Jr., *Hoke Smith and the Politics of the New South* (Baton Rouge: Louisiana State University Press, 1970), 102; John B. Clark, *Populism in Alabama* (Auburn, Ala.: Auburn Printing Company, 1927), 164.

Prussian Road and subordination to outside capitalists, not through movements which mobilized oppressed tenant farmers.

The Democratic National Convention's nomination of Bryan and endorsement of silver put the Alabama Gold Democrats in a difficult position. The national party had saddled them with a candidate and a platform that were anathema to everything the party regulars stood for. A small group of diehards from the Big Mule–Black Belt group responded by splitting from the regular Alabama Democrats, forming the Gold Democratic party, committed to principled opposition to the Populists and repression rather than the concessions and cooperation the national party was forcing on the Alabama regulars.

The Alabama Gold Democrats held a convention in Montgomery, the heart of the black belt, in August, 1896, and nominated Congressman Richard Clarke of Mobile as their candidate for governor. Among the more prominent sources of support for the gold gubernatorial campaign was the Montgomery *Advertiser*, the leading planter newspaper in the state. To provide balance, Big Mule ex-governor Thomas Goode Jones campaigned actively for Clarke and the antireform cause. Jones had been one of the L&N's two top attorneys in Alabama before being elected governor in 1890. Hackney describes him: "Joining with the president of the railroad in land speculation, lobbying with Congressmen on the railroad's behalf before the ICC, distributing free railroad passes to probate judges and other officials, advising his superiors when to buy opposing newspapers and when to support friendly ones— Jones was completely identified with his railroad employers."[7]

The Gold Democrats' gubernatorial campaign illustrated the fact that the split in the party was really over who would control state politics. After all, to make the currency issue the basis of a campaign for governor was a little foolish; the governor of Alabama would have no control over the metallic standard the federal government adopted. The issue between the small business Progressives and the planter-industrialist party regulars was how to deal with the Populist tenants and what the state's economic future should be. The Republican party of Alabama, previously allied

7. Rogers, *One-Gallused Rebellion*, 320; Hackney, *Populism to Progressivism*, 12.

with the Populists, dissolved that coalition to run a slate of Mc-
Kinley electors. They sensed that the anti-Bryan vote of the Democratic diehards would go to the Republicans rather than to the
Gold Democratic slate, even in Alabama, where Republicanism
had been analagous to hill country radicalism.

On election day in 1896, the Alabama Democrats succeeded in
building a winning coalition of Progressive small businessmen and
Populist tenants. The Republicans took the votes of antireform
Democrats away from the Gold Democratic slate. The Democrats
won 56 percent of the vote, the Republicans 28 percent, the Populist party 13 percent, and the Gold Democrats 3 percent.[8]

The small business Progressives thus elected their gubernatorial
candidate in 1896, but their alliance with the Populist tenants
proved to be short-lived; they lost their support in the next election, 1900, to the Big Mule–Black Belt coalition. In Hackney's
perceptive analysis, the small business Progressives concluded
from this experience that the only way for them to stay in power
was to give up on the Populist tenants and seek planter support.
Planters opposed the business Progressives as long as a political
coalition of black and white tenants challenged prevailing class
relations. The small business Progressives thus joined the planters
in supporting disfranchisement of black and white tenants at the
Alabama constitutional convention of 1901.[9] Disfranchisement was
passed, and the Progressives went on to assemble a winning coalition from the purged electorate, with the planters as their principal
allies.

The spread of tenancy had made the New South industrialists'
agrarian program of diversified, independent small farming an im-
possibility. The New South ideologists, implicitly admitting this
fact, revised their program so that by the nineties it was an exclusively industrial one. With the rise of the Populist movement,
planters realized that white tenants were not their allies in a struggle between agrarian and industrial society, but in fact were their

8. Hackney, *Populism to Progressivism*, 99–104.
9. *Ibid.*, 126; C. Vann Woodward, *Origins of the New South, 1877–1913* (Baton Rouge:
Louisiana State University Press, 1951), 327–31; Key, *Southern Politics*, 541; J. Morgan
Kousser, *The Shaping of Southern Politics: Suffrage Restriction and the Establishment of
the One-Party South, 1880–1910* (New Haven: Yale University Press, 1975), 165–71.

worst enemies. Industrialists recognized that the repressive system presided over by the planters was necessary in the context of popular unrest. Once the industrialists had dropped their antiplanter agrarian program, once they had conceded that the planters would remain a dominant class and that the South would develop along the Prussian Road, a coalition between the two became possible. It was the threat from below that at last brought the planters and the industrialists together.

Appendix:
The Manuscript Census

The scholar using the manuscript schedules of the United States census faces a number of choices regarding kinds of data and kinds of errors present in the various parts and different years of the census. The problem is to determine which set of statistics provides the best measure of wealth in landholding: the census of population, which gives the value of real estate owned by each resident of the county, or the census of agriculture, which gives the value of each farm, along with a variety of statistics on acreage and production.

I have chosen to use the census of population.[1] The crucial difference between the two censuses is that the population census gives data for individual *planters*, while the agriculture census gives data for individual *plantations*. Many planters, especially the biggest, owned more than one plantation, or had their plantation divided into several noncontiguous units. For instance, among Alabama planters, Sellers found that Gaious Whitfield in 1860 owned

1. These are described in Katherine H. Davidson and Charlotte M. Ashby, "Records of the Bureau of the Census," *The National Archives, Preliminary Inventories*, No. 161 (Washington, D.C.: Government Printing Office, 1964), especially p. 101, and were first discussed in Joseph A. Hill, "The Historical Value of the Census Records," American Historical Association *Annual Report*, I (1903), 199–202. The instructions to census enumerators in 1850 read, "You are to obtain the value of real estate . . . owned by each individual enumerated . . . by inquiry of each individual who is supposed to own real estate, be the same located where it may. . . . No abatement of the value is to be made on account of any lien or encumbrance thereupon in the nature of a debt." The 1860 and 1870 instructions added that "the value meant is the full market value." Carroll D. Wright and William C. Hunt, *The History and Growth of the United States Census* (Washington, D.C.: Government Printing Office, 1900). The alternative to my procedure, using the census of agriculture, is presented in Roger Ransom and Richard Sutch, *One Kind of Freedom: The Economic Consequences of Emancipation* (New York: Cambridge University Press, 1977). For a study based on

229

three plantations in Marengo County and one in Lowndes County, Mississippi; Samuel Townsend owned seven plantations in Madison County and one in Jackson County, all in Alabama; Francis Gilmer owned five plantations in Lowndes and Montgomery counties, Alabama, and James Tate owned five plantations in Alabama and one in Mississippi. There are reports in the literature of planters who owned as many as twelve different units. While the extent of multiple holdings is not accurately known, the census of population provides the only measure of the total plantation holdings of individual planters. The census of agriculture, by giving separate statistics for each plantation or contiguous landholding, overlooks the existence of noncontiguous and multiple holdings, and gives a false impression that there were more planters and smaller plantations than in fact existed.[2]

The war transformed the plantation labor force from slaves into tenants. The agriculture census of 1870 failed to take account of the development of tenancy; it did not record the tenure of the farm operator—whether he was the owner, renter, or sharecropper of the land he worked. Some census enumerators reported all tenants as being landowners.

The 1880 census of agriculture corrected this deficiency by carefully listing the tenure of each farm operator as owner, renter, or sharecropper. But it failed to ascertain the ownership of land which was rented or sharecropped. If the owner of a plantation had sharecroppers or tenants working on it, the tenant, rather than the

slaveholdings reported in the 1860 census of slave inhabitants, which defines a "large planter" as one holding 50 or more slaves used in agriculture, see Joseph K. Menn, "The Large Slaveholders of the Deep South" (Ph.D. dissertation, University of Texas, 1964). Menn lists every owner of more than 50 slaves in 1860 in Alabama, as well as Georgia, Louisiana, and Mississippi, by county; he combines the population, agricultural, and slave data for individual planters onto the same tables. For Marengo County, Alabama, for instance, he lists 155 "large planters" in 1860; my study included 76. Menn, "Large Slaveholders," 412–32. Chalmers Gaston Davidson, *The Last Foray: The South Carolina Planters of 1860, A Sociological Study* (Columbia: S.C.: University of South Carolina Press, 1971), defines a "planter" as an owner of 100 or more slaves; he found 440 such planters.

2. James B. Sellers, *Slavery in Alabama* (University, Ala.: University of Alabama Press, 1950), 29–32; Fabian Linden, "Economic Democracy in the Slave South: An Appraisal of Some Recent Views," *Journal of Negro History*, XXXI (1946), 165; Herbert L. Weaver, *Mississippi Farmers 1850–1860* (Nashville: The Vanderbilt University Press, 1945), 52, 76; Charles S. Sydnor, *Slavery in Mississippi* (New York: D. Appleton-Century Company, 1933), 193.

owner, was listed as the "farm operator," and several tracts owned by a single planter but worked by different tenants were registered as different "farms," even though they were contiguous.[3] Thus, beginning in 1870, it is impossible to determine the actual ownership of land by using the census of agriculture; the data on individual real estate holdings in the census of population provides the only figures on landownership for the post-Civil War period.

The agriculture census continued to count tenants but not owners of plantation land in the censuses of 1880, 1890, and 1900, but it was finally decided in 1910 that this had been an error. A special census study was conducted as part of the 1910 census to determine the ownership of southern plantation land, in addition to surveying the tenants. In the meantime, historians had used the 1870–1900 figures to argue that a revolution in landholding had occurred after the Civil War, that the plantation had disappeared, and that a new class of black yeoman farmers and small holders had arisen. It was not until 1937, when Roger Shugg published his article "Survival of the Plantation," that it became clear to many historians that the predominant form of land ownership in the postwar South was the plantation.[4]

Although the census of population contains more accurate figures than the census of agriculture for the antebellum period on the number of planters and the size of individual planters' holdings, and although it contains the only data on ownership of plantation land after 1860, it has some serious problems. Most serious is the question of the reliability of the data on the value of

3. Roger W. Shugg, *Origins of Class Struggle in Louisiana* (Baton Rouge: Louisiana State University Press, 1939), 235. Fleming noted defects in the agricultural census as early as 1911: Walter L. Fleming, *Civil War and Reconstruction in Alabama* (Cleveland: A. H. Clark Company, 1911), 725, *n*. 1.

4. U.S. Bureau of the Census, *Plantation Farming in the U.S.*, *Report of the Bureau of the Census* (Washington, D.C.: Government Printing Office, 1916); historians who studied census reports and concluded that the old plantation system had been destroyed by an agrarian revolution included Charles A. and Mary R. Beard, *Rise of American Civilization* (New York: The Macmillan Company, 1927), II, 269; Samuel E. Morison and Henry S. Commager, *The Growth of the American Republic* (Rev. ed.; New York: Oxford University Press, 1937), II, 23–24; Arthur Meier Schlesinger, *Rise of the City 1878–1898* (New York: The Macmillan Company, 1933), 3–4; Allan Nevins, *The Emergence of Modern America* (New York: The Macmillan Company, 1927), 20–21, 24–25. Shugg's article, "Survival of the Plantation," 234–73 in *Origins of Class Struggle in Louisiana*, originally appeared in *Journal of Southern History*, III (1937), 311–25.

landholdings. In 1870, the director of the census indicated that people might have tended to underreport or refuse to report real estate holdings, especially large holdings, because they feared increased property taxation. For this reason, the 1870 data on population wealth were not published, and the questions were omitted from the 1880 census.[5]

This calls into question the accuracy of the absolute values reported in the 1870 census. The total value of southern real estate reported in 1870 was less than 1860, and the decline in very large holdings was considerable, but virtually all historians have considered this to be a measure of loss in value resulting from the war, rather than a false impression created by underreporting of real values. Still it is possible that while southern losses were considerable, the 1870 figures exaggerate the actual extent of losses because holdings were underreported.

But even if respondents had given false reports of their actual real estate holdings in 1870, the errors would be errors of underestimation rather than overestimation, especially underestimation of the value of large holdings. If a planter reported in 1870 that he had the same amount of real estate that he had in 1860, he almost certainly didn't have less, and may have had more. Since our finding was that the merchants and the planter elite increased their share of the wealth in land between 1850 and 1870, the possibility that they might have underreported their actual holdings strengthens the conclusion that they came out of the war in a relatively wealthier position. The increase in the share of land held by the merchants and the planter elite may have been greater than our figures show, and almost certainly was not less.

A second serious problem in the census of population of 1870 is the extent of omissions. The principal deficiency of the 1870 cen-

---

5. U.S. Census Office, *Ninth Census* (Washington, D.C.: Government Printing Office, 1872), III, *Taxation and Wealth*, Introduction; Francis Walker and Charles Seaton (eds.), *Compendium of the Tenth Census* (Washington, D.C.: Government Printing Office, 1883); Caroll D. Wright and William C. Hunt, *The History and Growth of the United States Census* (Washington, D.C.: Government Printing Office, 1900); Robert Gallman, "Trends in the Size Distribution of Wealth in the Nineteenth Century: Some Speculations," in Lee Soltow (ed.), *Six Papers on the Size Distribution of Wealth and Income*, National Bureau of Economic Research Studies in Income and Wealth, XXXIII (New York: Columbia University Press, 1969), Appendix.

sus was that, because of the disruption caused by the war and Reconstruction, the size of the total southern population was underestimated by a considerable amount. Subsequently the census office concluded that the people who had been missed were almost all blacks, and this was confirmed by the more accurate census of 1880.[6] For this reason the 1870 census has been rejected as a source of data by most historians studying tenant farming in this period. But the omission of blacks is not a serious error for a study of planters and merchants, who were all white, needless to say. Nowhere has it been suggested that the 1870 census missed substantial numbers of big landowners and businessmen in the South.

There is no report on individual real estate holdings in the 1880 census; the question was dropped after 1870. We can study the consequences of the war for landholding up to 1870, but changes after 1870 we have missed. An argument could be made that 1880, rather than 1870, is the proper year for a study of postwar southern agriculture; Woodward in fact suggests that the planter class reached its nadir in the mid-seventies, after the depression of 1873. However, evidence from the economic historians indicates that recovery was well on its way by 1880.[7] Although the planters' position may have been eroded after 1870, the erosion was only temporary, and by 1880 the planters appear to have been in a stronger position than ever.

Moreover, the 1870 census has the advantage of forming a continuous series with 1850 and 1860. A new census law was written for the 1880 census, which provided for new questions and procedures; the 1880 census thus is not strictly comparable with the

6. The most authoritative estimate of the undercount of southern blacks in the 1870 census is Roger Ransom and Richard Sutch, "The Impact of the Civil War and of Emancipation on Southern Agriculture," *Explorations in Economic History*, XII (1975), 6–11, who conclude there was a 6.6 percent undercount. This revises the estimate of 9.5 percent given in U.S. Census Office, *Eleventh Census* (Washington, D.C.: Government Printing Office, 1892), xxxv–xliii. See also Francis A. Walker, "Statistics of the Colored Race in the United States," *Publications of the American Statistical Association*, New Series, II (1890), 95–99, 106. Before the census enumeration in 1870, many believed blacks would be underenumerated; see for instance the Radical Demopolis *Southern Republican*, May 18, 1870.

7. C. Vann Woodward, *Reunion and Reaction* (New York: Little, Brown & Co., 1951), 52; Eugene M. Lerner, "Southern Agriculture and Agricultural Income 1860–1880," *Journal of Political Economy*, LXII (1955), 20–40; James L. Sellers, "Economic Incidence of the Civil War in the South," in Ralph Andreano (ed.), *Economic Impact of the American Civil War* (Cambridge: Shenkman Publishing Company, 1967), 100.

three preceding censuses even where they covered the same issues. The censuses of 1850, 1860, and 1870 form a continuous series in which the same questions were asked each year, defined and reported in the same way.[8]

A shortcoming of the data in the census of population is that it gives statistics of value, while the census of agriculture gives statistics of quantity. Since prices fluctuate, and since currency inflation occurred, statistics of value tend to be less reliable than statistics of quantity in measuring change from one decade to another. All things being equal, change in the number of acres under cultivation on a farm can be measured more accurately than change in the value of farm acreage over a decade. On the other hand, statistics on cultivated acreage do not distinguish between fertile black belt acres and sandy, marginal hill lands. Only statistics of value provide a measure of the quality of the soil under cultivation.

A final minor drawback of the statistics used here is that the category "real estate holdings" includes not just plantation land and buildings, which is what we want to measure, but also business and residential real estate in towns. While this would pose a considerable problem in a study of counties with genuine urban areas, our sample counties were predominantly rural, as were almost all southern counties in this period. Thus although there was some town real estate included in the figures on land ownership, it could not have been very much.

Problems also arise from the fact that many county lines in Alabama were changed between 1860 and 1870. Since the census was

8. On linkage methods, see Ian Winchester, "The Linkage of Historical Records by Man and Computer: Techniques and Problems," *Journal of Interdisciplinary History*, I (1970), 107–24; Michael Katz and John Tiller, "Record Linkage for Everyman," *Historical Methods Newsletter*, V (1972), 144–51; Edward A. Wrigley (ed.), *Identifying People in the Past* (London: E. Arnold, 1973). Wrigley is criticized for making "pretentious claims" in "Of Maths and Men," *Times Literary Supplement*, Oct. 12, 1973, p. 1226. My procedure does not require shifting from one source to another, which Thernstrom was required to do in his Boston study, and which has been criticized in Richard J. Hopkins, "Mobility and the New Urban History," *Journal of Urban History*, I (1975), 222–23. Thernstrom anticipated this criticism: *The Other Bostonians: Poverty and Progress in the American Metropolis* (Cambridge: Harvard University Press, 1973), Appendix A. Nor does the procedure here involve the kind of estimation of values that has justifiably earned Fogel and Engerman such devastating criticism: Thomas L. Haskell, "The True and Tragical History of *Time on the Cross*," *New York Review of Books*, October 2, 1975, p. 34.

organized by counties, it is difficult to follow every landholding from one census enumeration to the next. The counties chosen here, however, had very little change in their boundaries. Hale was created out of the other four in the black belt (as well as a sliver of Tuscaloosa County); Perry lost a sliver (two townships on its eastern boundary) during the decade. These lost townships, however, were not plantation districts. It is possible that a few planters who in fact persisted are counted here as not persisting because of these changes in county lines; to the extent that this is the case, the argument here of relatively high planter persistence for 1860–1870 is strengthened rather than weakened. Of the hill counties, Colbert was created out of Franklin in 1866, but the external boundaries of the total five-county area remained the same.[9]

Most criticism of the census as a source of accurate data has aimed at the 1870 census, but apparently the antebellum censuses also contained some rather substantial errors. James B. Sellers in his study of Alabama slavery compared the manuscript reports for agriculture and population in 1850 and 1860. He found that some of the biggest slaveowners "apparently refused to place a valuation on their property." He found no information on value of real estate holdings for 21 percent of the people owning 50 slaves or more in 1850; in 1860 he found that 25 percent of the big slaveowners did not report the value of their real estate holdings.[10] It is remotely possible that a man with 50 slaves owned no real estate, but that seems dubious for a quarter of the big slaveowners. It is also possible that, although Sellers didn't find them, they are listed in the census. But it appears that our list of big planters, based on value of real estate holdings, does not include all the big planters in

9. On changes in county lines, see U.S. Bureau of the Census, *10th Census* (Washington, D.C.: Government Printing Office, 1883), I, *Population*, "Aggregate Population by Counties, 1790–1880," "Remarks" column of Table II, p. 49. For the creation and exact boundaries of Hale County, see *Acts of Alabama 1866–1867*, 477–80; Montgomery *Daily Advertiser*, January 29, 1867; for the changes in Perry County's eastern boundary, see *Acts of Alabama 1868*, 488–90; for the creation of Colbert County out of Franklin County, see *Acts of Alabama 1866–1867*, 351–53.

10. Sellers, *Slavery in Alabama*, 41. A discussion of errors in the 1850 and 1860 census can also be found in Gavin Wright, "Note on the Manuscript Census Samples . . . ," *Agricultural History*, XLVI (1970), 95–99.

the counties studied. However, it is difficult to imagine an argument that this would bias the findings of planter persistence in one direction or the other; unless those who failed to report their landholdings in 1860 were more likely to persist, or less likely, the only conclusion that can be drawn from Sellers's discovery is that the census does not provide complete coverage of the big planters for 1850 and 1860.

Tax lists showing the real estate holdings of big planters have been used to great advantage, particularly by Roger Shugg, but they do not exist for most Alabama counties during this period.[11]

The definition of "family persistence" in this study required linking planters in one list with wives and sons in subsequent lists. The census did not specify family relationships until 1880; thus the relationships "wife" and "son" were inferred from the name, age, and sex of members of the household. If two sons or both a planter and a son appeared in a subsequent list, that was counted as two cases of persistence. Daughters were excluded from this study of planter persistence because a preliminary study of Marengo County found that not a single daughter (out of 99 families) "inherited" substantial landed property in her own name, while sons and wives often did. Since married daughters take their husbands' surnames, they are impossible to trace through the manuscript census. Widows, of course, also remarry, but in the western Alabama black belt many planter widows did not.

Tracing individuals from one census to the next has posed serious problems for social mobility studies. In his precedent-setting *Poverty and Progress*, Stephan Thernstrom found that less than half the workers he was studying remained on the census rolls of Newburyport, Massachusetts, for a decade. Criticized in reviews for ignoring those who left, he wrote in a subsequent article, "There is . . . no feasible method of tracing individuals once they disappear from the universe of the community under consideration." Peter Knights has been most successful at tracing migrants,

11. Shugg, *Origins of Class Struggle*; U.S. Works Progress Administration, *Inventory of the County Archives of Alabama* (Birmingham: Alabama Historical Records Survey, 1940); see also Robert Gilmour, "The Other Emancipation: Studies in the Society and Economy of Alabama Whites During Reconstruction" (Ph.D. dissertation, Johns Hopkins University, 1972), 271.

and he could find only 27 percent of Boston outmigrants in the entire state of Massachusetts in the mid-nineteenth century. Recently hopes have been raised by the soundex indexing of the 1880 and 1900 censuses; however, since the 1880 census did not report real estate holdings of individuals, they are of little use to this study.[12]

The persistence rates of Alabama planters can be compared with rates reported for other groups, but some adjustments must be made in the definitions and calculations. Comparison of the Alabama figures with persistence rates in the Northeast and Midwest suggests that the antebellum planter persistence rate was relatively high. In Wapello County, Iowa, 30 percent of employed males in 1850 were still residents of the same county a decade later; in Trempealeau County, Wisconsin, only 25 percent of employed males in 1860 remained county residents a decade later; in rural Kansas, farm operators had persistence rates for the 1860–1870 decade varying from 26 percent to 42 percent, depending on the area. The highest persistence rate reported anywhere in the rural United States throughout the nineteenth century was for east central Kansas between 1870 and 1880, where 59 percent of farm operators remained residents for a decade.[13]

But these persistence rates are not comparable with the Alabama figures reported here. Each of these studies counted the members

12. Stephan Thernstrom, *Poverty and Progress: Social Mobility in a Nineteenth Century City* (Cambridge: Harvard University Press, 1964), 96–97; Thernstrom, "Urbanization, Migration, and Social Mobility in Late Nineteenth Century America," in Barton J. Bernstein (ed.), *Towards A New Past: Dissenting Essays in American History* (New York: Vintage Books, 1968), 167; Stephan Thernstrom and Peter Knights, "Men in Motion: Some Data and Speculations on Urban Population Mobility in Nineteenth Century America," *Journal of Interdisciplinary History*, I (1970), 27–31; Peter Knights, *The Plain People of Boston, 1830–1860* (New York: Oxford University Press, 1971), 103–18. Thernstrom returns to the problem briefly in *The Other Bostonians*, 38–39. Charles Stephenson, "Tracing Those Who Left: Mobility Studies and the Soundex Indexes to the U.S. Census," *Journal of Urban History*, I (1974), 73–84.

13. Mildred Throne, "A Population Study of an Iowa County in 1850," *Iowa Journal of History*, XXVII (1959), 305–30; Merle E. Curti, *The Making of an American County: A Case Study of Democracy in a Frontier County* (Stanford: Stanford University Press, 1959); J. C. Malin, "The Turnover of Farm Population in Kansas," *Kansas Historical Quarterly*, IV (1935), 339–72. For an analysis of persistence rates of around 90 percent for 1860–1890 in the unusual case of a small town founded as a religious and educational center by Oberlin alumni, see Robert E. Bieder, "Kinship as a Factor in Migration," *Journal of Marriage and the Family*, XXXV (1973), 429–39.

of an occupational group—usually farm operators or employed males—who were *residents* of the same community—usually a county—a decade later. In this Alabama study, persistence was defined not only as continued residence, but also continued membership in the same socioeconomic group, the planter elite. In the previous studies, nonpersistence was defined as geographic mobility; in this Alabama study, nonpersistence included social as well as geographic mobility. The farm operators of east central Kansas in 1870 who had such a high persistence rate may all have fallen in status to become farm laborers, or even unemployed, in 1880, but as long as they were still residents, they were counted as persisting.

While none of the previous studies of rural persistence is comparable to this one, it is possible to revise the Alabama figures to make them comparable to the others. One county was selected and a search made through the census lists of property owners for names of the planters who were not present in the elite at the end of the decade; the cases of persistent residence thus uncovered were combined with the cases of planter persistence. The persistence rate for 1850 planters who were residents of the same county at the end of the decade was thus found to be 61 percent, and the postwar rate was 63 percent—which makes the Alabama planter elite the most persistent rural group known thus far to social science.

But the question in this study was not how many big planters remained in their counties; the question was how many big planters remained big planters. No comparable studies of rural communities exist; we know nothing about how many big farmers remained big farmers in New York State or Ohio or Minnesota in the mid-nineteenth century.[14] The study closest in relevance is Thernstrom's work on career continuity in Boston, which begins in 1880.

14. Gavin Wright shows there were virtually no northern farms as big as southern plantations in 1860: "'Economic Democracy,'" 73. Thernstrom, *Other Bostonians*, 40, 53, indicates that, of the 1870 "high white collar" group, 80 percent were still residents of Boston a decade later. However, this group was quite young. Hopkins's Atlanta data gives occupational differentials in geographic but not social mobility: he found that 58 percent of high white collar employees in 1870 in Atlanta were still residents of the city a decade later. Richard J. Hopkins, "Occupational and Geographic Mobility in Atlanta, 1870–1896," *Journal of Southern History*, XXXIV (1968), 200–13. On the Birmingham working class, see

It is a study of a city, rather than a rural area, and a city which was more than two centuries old, while western Alabama in 1850 had been a frontier area in the recent past. The Boston occupation group with the highest status, which Thernstrom called the "high white collar" stratum, had a persistence rate of 88 percent between 1880 and 1890. But this study also poses obstacles to comparison with the Alabama data, because Thernstrom has 100 percent geographic persistence in his sample—only those who remained in Boston for the decade were included in the study of career continuity. Recalculating the Alabama data on one county to make it comparable to Thernstrom's, one finds that, of the 1850 planters who remained within the county for a decade, 86 percent also remained in the same stratum—as did 93 percent of the 1860 planter elite. The Alabama planter elite, both before and after the war, had a similar persistence rate to Boston lawyers and doctors at the end of the century.

Thus the extent to which the Alabama planters are said to have a high or low persistence rate depends on which statistics are being compared. In terms of geographic persistence, the Alabama planters of both pre- and postwar periods were more persistent than the other rural groups of which studies have been made, although these other studies included lower status groups, which may have been more mobile, and did not measure social class persistence. The studies we have of social class persistence suggest that the Alabama planters, both before and after the war, were highly persistent, as much or more than the eastern urban elites of which we have knowledge. The similarities in the persistence rates of southern and northern elites are more impressive than the differences.

Paul B. Worthman, "Working Class Mobility in Birmingham, Ala., 1880–1914," in Tamara Hareven (ed.), *Anonymous Americans* (Englewood Cliffs: Prentice-Hall, 1971), 172–213. A study of Jacksonville, Florida, found that, of the top 5 percent of wealth holders (real plus personal estate), in 1870, 13 out of 54 had been county residents in the same economic group in 1860: C. A. Haulman, "Changes in the Economic Power Structure of Duval County, Florida, during the Civil War and Reconstruction," *Florida Historical Quarterly*, LII (1973), 175–84.

Index